THE BEST IN TENT CAMPING:

SOUTHERN CALIFORNIA

A Guide for Campers Who Hate RVs, Concrete Slabs, and Loud Portable Stereos

THE BEST IN TENT CAMPING:

SOUTHERN CALIFORNIA

A Guide for Campers Who Hate RVs, Concrete Slabs, and Loud Portable Stereos

Bill Mai

Printed in the United States of America
Published by Menasha Ridge Press
First edition, first printing September 1996
First edition, second printing July 1997

Library of Congress Cataloging-in-Publication Data

Mai, Bill, 1945–
The best in tent camping, southern California : a guide for campers who hate RVs, concrete slabs, and loud portable stereos / Bill Mai.—1st ed.
p. cm.
Includes bibliographical references (p. 192)
ISBN 0-89732-216-9 (pb)
1. Camping—California, Southern—Guidebooks. 2. Camp sites, facilities, etc.—California, Southern—Guidebooks. 3. California—Guidebooks.
I. Title.
GV191.42.C2M25 1996
796.54'09794'9—dc20 96-17945
CIP

Cover design by Grant Tatum
Cover photo by Dennis Coello

Menasha Ridge Press
P.O. Box 43059
Birmingham, Alabama 35243

CONTENTS

Preface xi
Introduction 1

The Coast
Andrew Molera State Park 10
Fremont Peak State Park 13
Kirk Creek/Plaskett Creek 17
Lion's Canyon 21
Malibu Creek State Park 24
Manresa Uplands State Beach 27
Montana De Oro State Park 30
Morro Bay State Park 34
Sycamore Canyon 37
Ventana 40
Zaca Lake 43

The Desert
Arroyo Salado 48
Culp Valley 51
Little Blair Valley 54
Mesquite Springs 58
Mid Hills 61
Saddleback Butte State Park 65
Vallecito Regional Park 68
White Tank 71

The Northern Sierras

Atwell Mill 76
Big Pine Creek 80
Buckeye Flat 84
Cold Springs 87
Dorst 91
East Fork 95
Fairview 98
Four Jeffrey/Sabrina 101
Horse Meadow 104
Lower Peppermint/Camp 6 Fire Safe Area 108
Minaret Falls 112
Moraine 116
Princess 120
Quaking Aspen/Peppermint 124
Rancheria 127
Redwood Meadow 131
Shake Camp 134
Tillie Creek 137
Trapper Springs 141
Twin Lakes 145
Vermilion 148
White Wolf 152
Wishon 156

The Southern Sierras

Dark Canyon .160
Doane Valley .164
Hanna Flat .168
Heart Bar .172
Laguna .175
Marion Mountain .179
Paso Picacho .182
William Heise County Park .185

Appendices

Appendix A: Camping Equipment Checklist .191
Appendix B: Suggested Reading and Reference .192

THE BEST IN TENT CAMPING:

SOUTHERN CALIFORNIA

A Guide for Campers Who Hate RVs, Concrete Slabs, and Loud Portable Stereos

PREFACE

Friends and family get together, and pretty soon somebody starts talking about going camping, fishing the streams, and hiking the high country, and suddenly everybody wants to go. Usually the proposed trip fizzles out the next morning because nobody knows quite where to go, or how to arrange it, and nobody wants to end up camping in a little tent on a slab of concrete surrounded by hard-partying RVers. Nobody knows a sure good campground, so the whole camping adventure dies on the vine.

Well, that's why you buy this book. You'll discover 50 of the most wonderful spots to tent camp in Southern California and learn how to reserve a spot if necessary, what to expect, and how to get there. All 50 campgrounds will be beautiful, clean, safe, and well run.

The 50 best are in the desert, along the coast, and in the mountains. Each of the campgrounds is rated in categories of beauty, site privacy, site spaciousness, quiet, security, and cleanliness/upkeep, so you pick the best from the best. There's not a loser here. Your choice will depend on what you like and what time of year you want to go camping.

I selected my 50 best by going camping, by finding the tent-friendly campgrounds, by talking to rangers, and by buttonholing other campers or locals and asking them their favorite spot. I tried to be objective. I reined in my preference for big country pine and boulder-style campgrounds and gave the nod to some campgrounds located deep in the woods. I spaced out the campgrounds, I picked geographically as well as seasonally, and I stayed away from very small campgrounds because even if a few folks show up, they're full.

When you get out and start camping, you'll find your own hit parade of campgrounds. You'll stumble upon all the tiny gems with three or four sites and explore all the fantastic places in the mountains and desert where you can camp anywhere you want. It's a whole new world.

—Bill Mai

INTRODUCTION

A Word about This Book and Southern California Camping

Drive from a campground below sea level in Death Valley to a campground 10,000 feet up by a glacier in the Sierras in two hours. This diversity is Southern California camping. The Big Sur coast is a wonder of the world. Anza-Borrego State Park is as big as Rhode Island. In the southern mountains, Mt. San Jacinto feels like little Switzerland. Near Julian, you'd swear you were in Vermont. This is a beautiful, beautiful area, and the tent camping is superb.

Geography

For the purposes of this book, Southern California is everything below a line drawn from Santa Cruz across the top of Yosemite National Park to the Nevada border. This area is divided into the Coast, the Desert, the Northern Sierras, and the Southern Sierras.

These four areas represent an amazing diversity in terrain. The Coast includes the 200 miles of sandy beaches north of the Mexican border to above Santa Barbara and the mountains that parallel the shore above the Los Angeles Basin to Santa Cruz. The Desert, in the southeast corner of California, is a vast and fascinating area of three deserts—Mojave, Colorado, and Sonoran—extending to the Colorado River. The Northern Sierras, or Sierra Nevada, the largest mountain mass in the United States, extends north from the Mojave Desert to Sequoia, Kings Canyon, and Yosemite. The Southern Sierras include the San Bernardinos and other minor ranges that extend southeast into Mexico.

Where to go and when

Pleasant camping can be found on the coast year-round. For winter and early spring camping head for the desert. Between Death Valley National Park, East Mojave National Preserve, Joshua Tree National Park, and Anza-Borrego Desert State Park you could camp all winter and never stay in the same spot twice. Camp the Northern and Southern Sierras in the spring, summer, and fall. Never camp the desert in the summer and only camp the mountains in the winter if you are prepared to go snow camping.

The rating system

The 50 best campgrounds are rated in various categories—five stars is best, and one star is acceptable. Use the rating system to select the wonderful campground that combines the elements that best suit you.

Beauty

While all 50 campgrounds in this book are beautiful, some are absolutely sensational. They rate five stars. Mountains, streams, waterfalls, and sunsets all conspiring for a drop-dead campground personality. One- to four-star campgrounds are no dogs, either, but possess a less spectacular beauty that will grow on you.

Site privacy

Some campgrounds are beautifully built. The sites are arranged to take maximum advantage of the contour of the land, and the vegetation gives each one the most privacy possible. Good architecture cuts down on the cringe factor when other campers pull in next door. It makes you feel at home from the moment you step out of your car. What a difference!

Site spaciousness

I want flat land to pitch a tent on. And, I want the flat area far enough from the picnic table so my camping mate can make coffee without waking me and far enough away from the firepit so the embers don't burn little holes in the tent. And, I want a view. A view from each campsite is part of the spacious feeling that qualifies a campground for five stars in this category.

Quiet

Quiet is part of beautiful. There's nothing like the sound of a generator or a boom box to ruin a beautiful campsite. I consider white noise like the roar of a river to raise the quiet rating, since it is a natural noise and drowns out the sounds of other campers.

Security

Most of the campsites in the top 50 have campground hosts that keep a good eye on the property, which makes the campground safer than a good neighborhood. The farther the campground is from an urban center, the more secure it is. Of course, you can leave your valuables with the hosts if you're going to be gone for a day or so, but don't leave little things lying around. A blue jay will take off with a pair of sunglasses, and you never can tell what a visiting bear will decide has food value.

Cleanliness/Upkeep

Most campgrounds in the top 50 are well tended. Sometimes, on big weekends, places can get a little rank—not unlike one's kitchen after a big party. I appreciate the little things like the campground host who came around with a rake after each site was vacated to police the place. That particular campground received five stars in the cleanliness/upkeep department.

Good Planning

A little planning makes a good camping trip great. First, decide where and when you want to go. Then, phone that district's Ranger H.Q. to make sure the campground is open and that it has water. See if the ranger recommends other campgrounds. See if it's going to be busy. If it is, reserve ahead if possible. All National Forest campgrounds must be reserved at least ten days in advance. Remember, if you arrive and don't like the reserved site, the campground host will move you if another site is available.

Next, get your equipment together. Everybody knows what basics to bring tent camping. A tent (of course), the sleeping bags, a cooler, a stove, pots, utensils, a water jug, matches, a can opener, etc. But, it's those little things that you suddenly wish you had that make a happy camper. Number one objective is a good night's sleep.

Bring ear plugs. You need ear plugs to get a good snooze. The first night or two out camping, the unfamiliar flap of the tent drives you crazy if you don't have ear plugs. Also, a snoring mate sleeping a foot away from you is nighttime hell on earth without ear plugs. In addition, ear plugs block out all that night nature stuff which interferes with a righteous camper's zzzzzs.

Don't forget to pack your own pillow. A good pillow gets your shoulders off the deck and lets your hips and behind take the weight. Use your clothes bag as an additional pillow (consider inflatable pillows sold at camping stores). Bring a thin foam mattress or buy the self-inflating pads (phone Basic Design at (707) 575-1220). Buy a spidermat—a device that keeps your pad from slipping on the tent floor and keeps your sleeping bag on top of it. Air mattresses are okay, but susceptible to puncture. Never buy a double air mattress—every time your mate moves you get tossed around. Get a sleeping bag that is good and warm. Nothing is worse than being cold at night, and no sleeping bag is too warm. Just bring a sheet so you can sleep under it at first, then crawl into the bag when it gets nippy. Check the weather. If it's going to be cold, remember to bring socks and sweatpants to sleep in. A sweatshirt with a hood is invaluable, since you lose a lot of heat through your head.

Bring a water bottle to drink from at night. Consequently, a pee jar (a pee pot for ladies) just outside the tent is a great idea. You can stumble outside, use it, and empty it in the toilet in the morning.

Nothing disturbs your zzzzs like grit inside the tent, so bring something to put outside the tent to clean your feet on. In the woods, a square of AstroTurf works fine. At the seashore or in the desert, a tray full of water to dip your feet in works best. Bring a small brush for what grit leaks in.

Remember flashlights. The little mini-mags work okay, and if you take off the lens, you can hang them from a tent loop and actually read. Be careful since the little bulb is damn hot and will burn fabric or fingers. But, what works even better is a head lamp. You can buy them at any outdoor store. Just strap the lamp around your head with an adjustable elastic band. Everywhere you look, there's light. They're great for finding stuff, cleaning up in the dark after dinner, and reading. Remember duct tape. "If you can't fix it, duct tape it" is a camping maxim.

Bring a sponge to clean off the picnic table. A plastic tablecloth is nice, too (bring little pushpins to secure it so it won't blow away). A plastic bowl or a blow-up sink from Basic Designs (around $6 at Sports Mart) is invaluable for washing dishes. Picnic table benches get mighty hard, so bring a cushion. Buy a cheap lawn chair, and get the inexpensive umbrella that attaches to the back of the chair, so you can sit around camp out of the sun. While sitting around, you'll want a fly swatter to wreak revenge on a lazy droning fly or two and mosquito repellent for that irksome gnat in your ear. Bring a little leaf rake to police your camp area. Remember binoculars, a bird book, and a wildflower book, so you can put a name with what you see.

Good water jugs are two-and-a-half gallon plastic jobs sold in supermarkets. On most of them, you can twist the top off and refill them. They travel best with their valves up to avoid any leakage. Take a hot shower. Basic Designs (and other outfits) sells a solar shower bag that really works. After a day in the sun sitting on a hot rock, the water is hot! Or, bring along nonscented diaper wipes for a quick sponge bath. They work.

Don't be afraid to ask fellow campers for help or for stuff you might have forgotten. All campers know what it's like to forget basic stuff and love to help fellow campers. There's always a mechanic on vacation camping next site over when your car won't start or somebody with extra white gas for your stove. Think hearty about your fellow campers. Wave and say, "hi."

The campfire is an important camp event. Stores around the campground sell bundles of wood, and often, the campground host and hostess sell wood. Also, there maybe windfalls around the campground from which you can take wood (ask the campground host). You need a good camp saw for that. An absolute essential is a can of charcoal starter fluid. This guarantees a fire even in a driving rain. Naturally, don't forget marshmallows, graham crackers, and chocolate for roasting.

Fix your car up before you go. Nothing can be a bigger bummer than a mechanical breakdown on your way. Have a mechanic check your water hoses and the air pressure in your tires before you load up. Remember, your car will be loaded down with stuff, and this will put a strain on your tires and cooling system. Bring an extra fan belt. Nothing can shut down the car like a snapped fan belt that you have to special order from Japan. Even if you don't know a fan belt from third base, bring one. Somebody will come along who knows how to install it. Make sure your spare tire is correctly inflated. Mishap

#999 is when you put on your spare, let the car down, and find out the spare is flat.

If you fish, be sure to get a license and display it. Fishing without a license is a misdeamenor, punishable by a maximum fine of $1000 and/or six months in jail. On your way into the campground, stop at a local store and find out what the folks are using for bait. Buy it. This will save you a lot of experimentation and probably provide you with a good meal.

Remember the bears! We have few mosquitoes here in Southern California, but a lot of black bears. Never leave your cooler out. Put it in the trunk or disguise it with a blanket if you have a hatchback or a van. Don't eat in your tent. Take all cosmetics, soap, etc. and put them in the car. Disguise them, too. A bear will rip off a car door to get a tube of chapstick. Bring a small bottle of Clorox to wipe down your picnic table at night. Bears don't like Clorox (but, don't put too much faith in this!). If a bear raids your camp looking for food, shoo him away like you would a naughty dog. Don't worry. Even the boldest bears don't go into tents unless they smell food.

Think about dispersed camping. With a fire permit, a shovel, and a bucket of water, you can camp just about anywhere in the National Forests (consult Ranger District H.Q.), and, of course, in Anza-Borrego Desert State Park. The fire permit costs nothing, and there are miles and miles of fire roads and lumber roads you can explore to find the dispersed campground of your dreams.

Settling in

When you come into a campground be aware of a certain psychological barrier. This is a new place. Suddenly, you've driven all this way, and the campground doesn't look that hot. You feel disappointed. You feel like the "new kid at school." The other campers look up from their game of gin rummy and hope you won't camp next to them as you drive around the campground loops and look helplessly at the open sites. Nothing looks good enough.

Park your car. Pull into the first available site that could possibly do. Then, walk around the campground. You have half an hour to decide before you pick your site and pay. Once you get out and walk, you'll break through that "new kid at school" dilemma and soon feel like you're a part of the place. It's odd. Suddenly, you don't mind camping next to the gin rummy players. You realize that this is your campground as well as theirs. By the next morning, the whole place will feel like home, and the gin rummy players will seem like the best of neighbors. You won't understand why you didn't immediately recognize this campground as the best of all campgrounds.

When you plan a camping trip, try to stay in one campground for at least three days. Stay one day, and you end up spending most of your time packing and unpacking and getting familiar with the campground. Stay three days and you'll relax and have fun.

Go tent camping. Live in paradise for a few days. Camping makes you want to sin like the damned, sleep like the righteous, and hike like the last of the great American walkers. Balm for the weary soul!

SOUTHERN CALIFORNIA

THE COAST

ANDREW MOLERA STATE PARK

Big Sur, CA

Go to Andrew Molera State Park and walk the 1-mile trail to the ocean. The beach is awesome—4 miles of Big Sur's longest beach. Find sea fig, sand verbena, silverwood, and beach primrose on the side of the dunes. On the bluffs, look for seaside painted cups, sea lettuce, beach sagewort, and coast eriogonum. On my last trip to Andrew Molera, I brought a plant identification book and actually identified a few of these named above.

I had better luck with the birds. I saw black long-necked cormorants off Molera Point, willits, and a great blue heron. Look for the mass of tiny sanderlings flowing in behind a wave to feed before the breakers come again. They are looking for small sand crabs.

Last March when I visited Andrew Molera, I hiked out on the Headlands Trail and saw a pod of gray whales heading south. Also, keep an eye out for otters. They are actually members of the weasel family with slim bodies, high hips, broad heads, and short furry tails. Weighing in at about 80 pounds, the otter has feet that function like hands, so they can use rocks as hammers to smash shells. They have lovely, light whiskers and live together in groups called rafts in the kelp beds a mile or so from shore. This is where the mothers teach their babies to swim down and get food from the ocean floor below. They also teach them to hide among the bulbs of the

CAMPGROUND RATINGS

Beauty:	★★★★★
Site privacy:	★★★★
Site spaciousness:	★★★★
Quiet:	★★★★
Security:	★★★★
Cleanliness/upkeep:	★★★★

Andrew Molera has it all—Big Sur, a river, the sea, mountains full of big trees, and tent camping only in a grassy meadow.

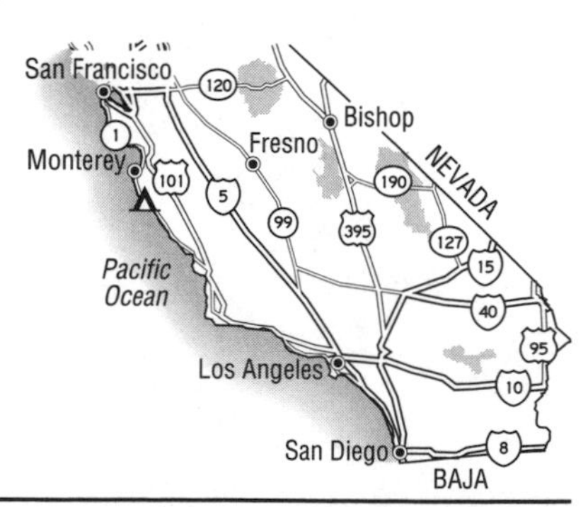

bull kelp, so the great white shark can't find them and eat them.

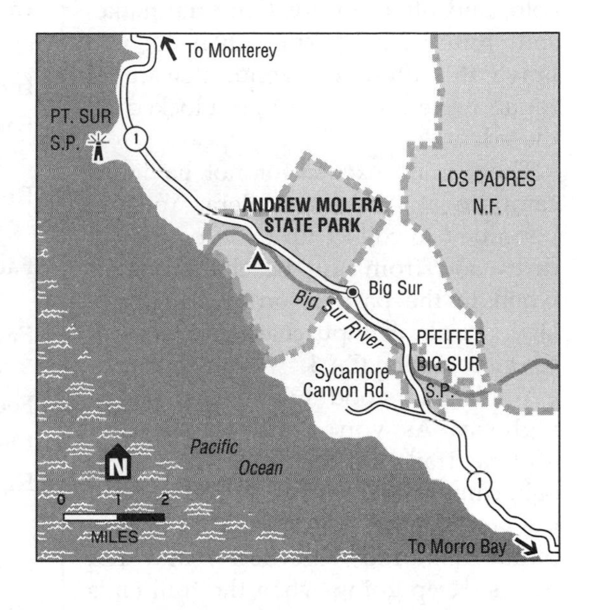

Once thought extinct, the otters are still an endangered species. The last count was 2,239 otters (including pups) living along the California coast—ranging from Vandenberg Air Force Base in Santa Barbara County to the San Francisco Bay.

Storms where the pups get separated from their mothers are a big problem for the pups since they can't survive alone. Lucky pups who get washed ashore and found by nice folks are taken to the Monterey Bay Aquarium for rehabilitation. Here, they are paired with a surrogate mother and are taught to swim, hunt food, and groom their fur. The surrogates are not other otters, but scientists in diving gear!

From the bluffs, the ocean reflects incredible colors. The purer the water, the deeper the color—this prismatic show all depends on how the sunlight is scattered by the water molecules. The old lava beds of Point Sur show the rainbow shades, and the kelp beds turn spots of blue to deep green. The light blue and turquoise along the cliffs are caused by the surf forcing air into the water. Plumes of red, brown, and green are the streams pouring Santa Lucia silt into the ocean.

The camping in Andrew Molera is pure tent camping. The sites are in a beautiful, grassy meadow a short walk from the parking lot (the last time I was there I had a cooler heavy with ice, beer, and soda and wished I'd brought one of those airport dollies you use to carry heavy suitcases). There are vault toilets and piped water spigots set around the meadow. The campsites are not numbered, and the Ranger told me there is no limit to the camping capacity. The crowd was young and very friendly. And the price ($3) is right as rain. There is a three-day limit, and then you have to stay away for seven days before returning.

The Big Sur River meanders through Andrew Molera offering good sandy banks for sunbathing and shallow water for wading. But the ocean here is rough, cold, and often windy. Only the makeshift huts built by sunbathers let you brave the afternoon wind. Beware of rogue waves, and don't get blocked by the tides.

There is no excuse for not having a campfire at Andrew Molera. You are permitted to collect up to 50 pounds of driftwood from the beach. All other wood in the park is protected. Really lazy people can purchase firewood at the stores along CA 1.

You'll find good hiking east of the highway. As you climb on the East Molera Trail, see madrone, coast live oak, canyon oak, and then, redwood at the crest of the ridge. Look for Indian paintbrush, red elderberry, and red maids. Keep going when the trail ends and reach the South Fork Little Sur River down the other side of the ridge.

To get there from San Francisco, drive south on CA 1 to Carmel, then drive 21 miles south on CA 1 to Andrew Molera State Park on the right.

KEY INFORMATION

Andrew Molera State Park
c/o Pfeiffer Big Sur State Park #1
Big Sur, CA 93920

Operated by: Department of Parks and Recreation, State of California—The Resources Agency, P.O. Box 942896, Sacramento, CA 94296-0001

Information: (408) 667-2315

Open: All year

Individual sites: Unlimited

Each site has: Limited picnic tables, fireplaces

Registration: Ranger will come collect fee

Facilities: Piped water and vault toilets

Parking: In parking lot; walk to campground

Fee: $3

Elevation: Near sea level

Restrictions:

Pets—Allowed on leash ($1)

Fires—In fireplaces

Vehicles—Not allowed in campgrounds

Other—3-day stay limit (must vacate for 7 days to return)

FREMONT PEAK STATE PARK

San Juan Bautista

Fremont Peak State Park is deliriously beautiful in April and May when the spring grasses are green and feathery, and the flowers are blooming. It's a great place to go when the coast is socked in with fog. Climb the peak and look out over the richest farmland and the richest marine area in the world. Imagine your life without fishwiches and brussels sprouts, because you're looking at where they all come from.

The drive up to the park from San Juan Bautista is alternately lovely, chilling, and lovely again. At first, you take a winding, old country road out of the valley and up into oaks with hanging mistletoe. There are rounded California hills resembling loaves of bread, and then you burst into *Road Warrior* country. On the left is the Hollister Hills State Vehicular Recreation Area. This is where the boys and girls drive their off-road vehicles. It's a land of tire-ripped hills, brush torched from flaming exhausts, and spectral arms of burned manzanita clawing at the sky. Scary. However, persevere and you arrive at the mountaintop and enter Fremont Peak State Park with its oaks, pines, and incredible views. Thank God.

The camping here is primitive and best suited for tents. All the sites are roomy, grassy, and shaded by oaks. The water is good, and each site has an incredible view of the Monterey Bay, which is why John C.

CAMPGROUND RATINGS

Beauty:	★★★★★
Site privacy:	★★★
Site spaciousness:	★★★★
Quiet:	★★★★
Security:	★★★
Cleanliness/upkeep:	★★★

Come to Fremont Peak State Park for spring camping and to see San Juan Bautista for California's yesterdays. You won't regret it.

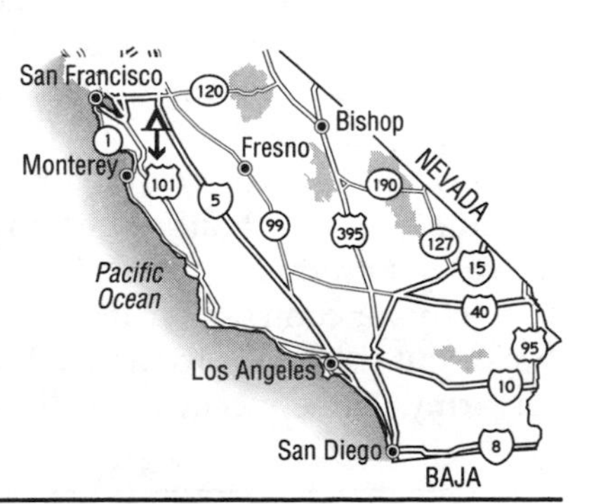

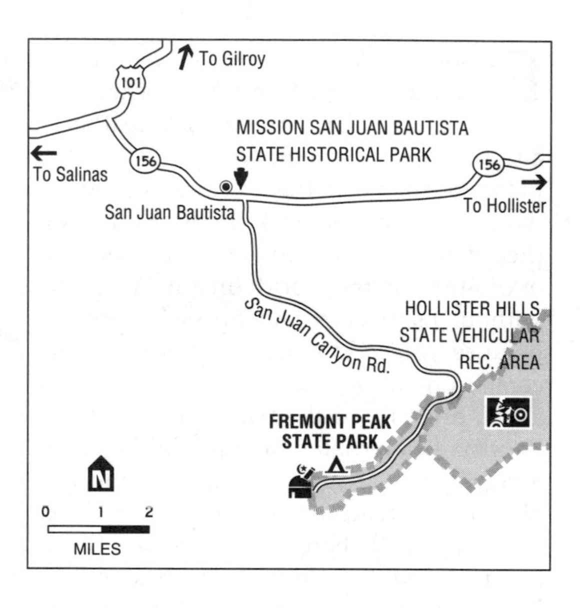

Fremont built a fort there on a fateful day in 1846. This is the story.

Fremont Peak State Park is actually *not* situated on Fremont Peak but on Gavilan Peak. This is where John C. Fremont almost kicked off the Mexican War of 1846. California, then a territory of Mexico, was seething. The Mexican government wanted to get rid of the American settlers, and the settlers were forming ragtag armies to take over the territory. To add to it, former Mission Native Americans were arming and trying to retake their former lands. Into the middle of this rode John C. Fremont, a Brevet Captain of Topographical Engineers of the United States, to map the California Trail.

The Mexican governor, Jose Castro, ordered Fremont and his group of Delaware Native Americans and hard-bitten frontiersman to leave the territory. Fremont refused. Cheekily, he marched his men up Gavilan Peak to the area by the Fremont Peak State Campground and built a rough log fort within plain sight of General Castro's headquarters in San Juan Bautista. Fremont raised the American flag up a stripped sapling. His men cheered.

General Castro was livid. He posted a proclamation: "Fellow Citizens: A band of robbers commanded by a captain of the United States Army, J. C. Fremont, have without respect to the laws and authorities of the department, daringly introduced themselves into the country and disobeyed the orders both of your commander-in-chief and of the prefect of the district . . . " Castro broke out the liquor to induce local Native Americans and Mexicans to join his army. Three pieces of artillery materialized. Then, Mexican cavalrymen from Monterey rode north toward San Juan.

Fremont set an ambush for the cavalrymen. At the last minute, the Mexican officers inexplicably ordered their troop back to Monterey. Back on the peak, the westerly wind kicked up and blew the crude flagpole down. Taking this as a sign, Fremont abandoned his fort and grudgingly retreated.

General Castro called the Americans "cowards and poor guests," and the incident was over, but it kicked off the subsequent turn-over of Mexican California to the United States. Both Fremont and Castro would play a giant role in this.

Near the campground is the Fremont Park Observatory with a 30-inch reflecting telescope. They have special programs in the spring and fall. Even if they have programs in the summer, avoid them. Gavilan Peak breeds a nasty, little, biting, black fly in the summer months. Write or phone The Fremont Park Observatory Association, P.O. Box 787, San Juan Bautista, CA 95045, (408) 623-2465, for the program schedule.

A good hike to the peak begins in the parking lot. You'll see a road and a trail. The trail, signed with a hiker's symbol, leads to the observatory. Take the road for a short distance, then join the signed Peak Trail, which circles the mountain. The trail climbs to a saddle before meeting a short summit trail.

On the high ridges, see Coulter pine and madrone. The northern slopes are full of manzanita, toyon, and scrub oak, and the southern slopes spill over with

To get there from L.A., drive 330 miles north on U.S. 101 to Salinas, then continue north on U.S. 101 a few miles and turn east on CA 156. Turn right (south) on San Juan Canyon Road and drive 11 miles to the campground.

KEY INFORMATION

Fremont Peak State Park
P.O. Box 1110
San Juan Bautista, CA 95045

Operated by: Department of Parks and Recreation, State of California—The Resources Agency, P.O. Box 942896, Sacramento, CA 94296-0001

Information: (408) 623-4255 or (408) 623-4881 at the San Juan Bautista State Historic Park

Open: All year (avoid summer)

Individual sites: 25

Each site has: Picnic table, fire ring

Registration: At entrance

Facilities: Pit toilets, piped water

Parking: At site

Fee: $7, $5 (extra vehicle)

Elevation: 2,750 feet

Restrictions:

Pets—Allowed ($1 per dog)

Fires—In fire rings (no firewood available at campgrounds)

Vehicles—18-foot trailers, 26-foot RVs

grasses and wildflowers. Don't forget your binoculars when you climb Gavilan Peak (meaning Hawk Mountain).

Visit San Juan Bautista where General Castro prepared to attack Fremont. In those days, San Juan was the district headquarters of the northern half of Alta, California. All roads met at San Juan, including the El Camino Real, the King's Highway. The 1906 earthquake destroyed half the town, and soon cows grazed on the Plaza, lending truth to what Will Durant once said. "Civilization exists by geological consent, subject to change without notice." San Juan slept until it was resurrected by the Old Mission benefactors and the California Department of Parks and Recreation. Now, it is a beautiful little town that has survived the ravages of the 20th century by missing out on the railroad (it went through Hollister) and U.S. 101 (it misses San Juan by 3 miles).

I can't count the number of times I have driven U.S. 101 and passed by San Juan Bautista. However, after one visit, I'm a believer. The Mexican food on the main drag is superb. Parking is easy. The docents at the Mission and the park rangers at the Historic Park are wonderfully relaxed and friendly. The Old Mission and the Plaza have been lovingly restored. Don't miss San Juan or the the camping at Fremont Peak State Park—it's beautiful.

KIRK CREEK CAMPGROUND / PLASKETT CREEK CAMPGROUND

Lucia

Kirk Creek and Plaskett Creek campgrounds are like fraternal twins. They occupy the most isolated stretch of CA 1, north of San Simeon and south of Big Sur. About 5 miles apart, on the best stretch of Los Padres National Forest coastline, these campgrounds offer the most relaxed camping on the entire Southern California coast.

Kirk Creek lies on a bluff overlooking the ocean. Set in gorse, it gets quite a lot of wind. Of course, the view is shockingly immediate—as if you are suspended over the ocean itself. The sites are separated and private until you stand up; the brush surrounding the sites is about chest high on the average bear. This does give you some relief from the oceanic blasts when Triton has a tantrum. Thank God for the fence along the edge of the precipice that keeps somnambulists from wandering over the edge of the cliff and plunging hundreds of Cary Grant–movie-like feet to the jagged rocks and hungry surf below. However, just south, there are goat trails leading down to a rocky point with a sandy cove at low tide. You can navigate these trails during the daylight hours.

Plaskett Creek Campground is oriented more toward small RVs, since the site areas seem larger and more level. Plaskett is farther from the beach, behind a line of Monterey pines, and not as subject to the ocean's gusty blasts. The area is nice and grassy, and it feels like a rural county

CAMPGROUND RATINGS

Beauty:	★★★★★
Site privacy:	★★★★★
Site spaciousness:	★★★★★
Quiet:	★★★★★
Security:	★★★
Cleanliness/upkeep:	★★★★★

Come for the huge cliffs of jade. Stay for great camping and hiking in the mountains.

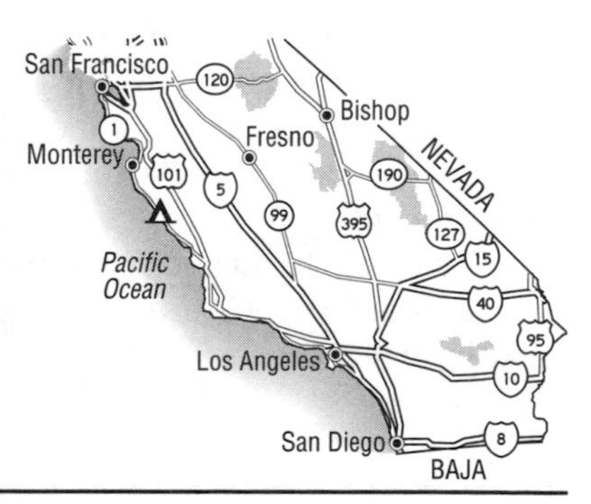

fairground. The sites are roomier, but not as private—without the impenetrable gorse cover of Kirk.

I love both campgrounds. A Ranger Station is nearby, so the sites feel remote but safe. Many CA 1 tourists speed through this area because they don't want to stay in the middle of nowhere. Being at Kirk or Plaskett will make you feel as if you're between the devil and the deep blue sea, and many folks would rather get the next range of mountains out of the way before they sleep.

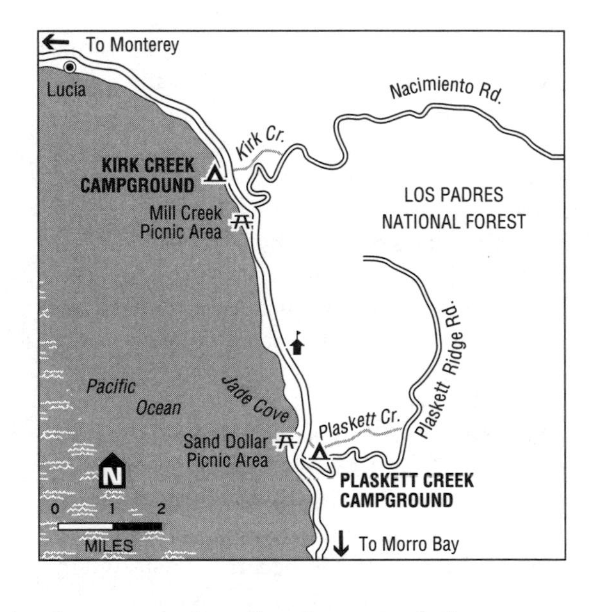

There is mountain hiking in the mountains directly east of the campground (information and maps are available at the Ranger Station). Though the hiking is good and the weather is cooler, the big draw here is the beach. Go to Jade Cove. You'll agree that Jade Cove is aptly named when you see the huge cliffs made entirely of jade. What a magical experience! Walk down from the picnic area, over the cattle gate to the beach, and, right away, as the stairs hit the sand, you'll see the jade on the left. Then, walk south on the beach and see entire cliffs of jade. I came here once as a child and was overwhelmed by the magic of the green rock, the huge whips of kelp, the surf and white spume, and the shockingly cold water. We had left the Delaware coast weeks before, determined to "dip" in the Pacific. We "dipped," and it was icy cold.

Child or adult, no one can help but react viscerally to the primordial beauty of this coastline. We are all drawn by our hearts to the sea. Why? We are mostly water, and our blood has the same saline content as the sea. We were carried in water in the womb, which was like the sea. Another explanation goes farther back than that.

There was a dark age of humanity known as the Pliocene Gap that occurred from four to seven million years ago. Herbivorous apes went into it, and carnivorous ape-men came out of it. There are no fossils to explain the transformation, but one au courant explanation is that our ancestors passed through a water-living stage.

This would explain our layer of subcutaneous fat unique to humans (as opposed to other primates), as well as the partial webbing between our fingers and toes. Our spines are more flexible than apes, allowing us to swim like otters, and we have a sense of balance equal to that of sea lions. We are streamlined (having very little hair) and can swim well, whereas great apes can't swim at all. We can hold our breath for as long as three-and-a-half minutes and possess a diving reflex like other marine animals that closes down our airways, constricts the small air passages to the lungs, and slows our heart to half speed. Human babies automatically hold their breath when placed under water and quickly learn to swim. By contrast, apes panic when their faces hit water and quickly drown.

Theorists believe that the sea-ape got a taste for fish and shellfish and, developing tools, became more ambitious and returned to land with an expanded taste

To get there from San Francisco, drive south on CA 1 through Monterey to Lucia. Then drive 4 miles farther south on CA 1 to Kirk Creek Campground on the right. Plaskett Creek Campground is 5.5 miles still farther south from Kirk Creek Campground. After you pass the Ranger Station, Plaskett Creek will be on your left.

KEY INFORMATION

Kirk Creek Campground / Plaskett Creek Campground
Los Padres National Forest
6144 Calle Real
Goleta, CA 93117

Operated by: U.S. Department of the Interior

Information: (805) 683-6711 or (408) 385-5434, Monterey District

Open: All year

Individual sites: Kirk 33; Plaskett 43

Each site has: Picnic table, fireplace

Registration: At entrance (first come, first served)

Facilities: Piped water, flush toilets

Parking: At site

Fee: $12

Elevation: Near sea level

Restrictions:

Pets—Allowed on leashes

Fires—In fireplaces

Vehicles—Small RVs

for meat. From then on, fossils show our ancestors to be a hunting ape that behaved more like a territorial wolf pack than a wandering monkey troop.

Think about this as you sit on your blanket on the beach, wade through the tidal pools, or dive into the waves and hold your breath under water. We had to come from somewhere, and the Garden of Eden might have been a gorgeous cove along this incredible coast.

To the south, don't fail to go pebble hunting on the San Simeon coast. Find reddish brown and green chert pebbles. Native Americans fashioned arrowheads and spear points from chert. Look for jade (jadite), as well. The best hunting is on Moonstone Beach Drive. Turn off CA 1 in Cambria at Windsor Boulevard. Jog seaward a bit, then go northwest about 0.4 mile on Moonstone Beach Drive to the large, paved state beach parking area. Go down to the beach and walk northwest to where the waterline is near the sea cliff. Also, try the beach at Pico Creek, 2.5 miles north of San Simeon Beach Campground. Look for the beach access sign near the north end of the cluster of motels south of Pico Creek.

In July and August, be sure to get to Kirk or Plaskett by Thursday. They do fill up, and no reservations are accepted. If you are in a self-contained vehicle and find that the campgrounds are full, you may park in turn-outs along CA 1 for the night. Tent campers should stop at the Ranger Station between the two campgrounds and get directions up Nacimento Road or Plaskett Ridge Road into the wilderness where you will find dispersed camping areas.

LION'S CANYON CAMPGROUND

Los Padres National Forest

Lion's Canyon Campground is the nearest get-away-from-it-all destination to Los Angeles. Other campgrounds closer to L.A. are only islands in the urban sea, while Lion's Canyon Campground is on the edge of the wilderness. And, it is only a quick hour and a half from Santa Monica.

This entire area was once grizzly country. Jeff Howard, one of the first Anglo residents, loved to hunt grizzly. He said he could always scare one up on short notice. However, the history of the poor grizzly bear (Ursus arctos) in California is a disasterous story. California is the only state in the union that has an extinct animal as its symbol. The last grizzly in Southern California was killed in Trabuco Canyon in 1908. The last one in the state was killed in 1922.) Old grizzly weighed about 900 pounds and used his long claws and muscle to rip up roots, bulbs, and tubers, as well as to tear up logs to get ants and termites. He roamed the lowlands and the valleys, and that's where he ran into the aforementioned Jeff Howard.

Howard was also famous for killing a Basque sheepherder in a gunfight in 1877. Locked in the Ventura jail, he promptly escaped and rode back to his place near Lion's Canyon Campground to hunt more grizzly. The good townspeople were outraged, so Howard lit out for Arizona. The sheriff put a $500 reward on his head, and Howard was arrested in Prescott, Arizona,

CAMPGROUND RATINGS

Beauty:	★★★★
Site privacy:	★★
Site spaciousness:	★★★
Quiet:	★★★
Security:	★★
Cleanliness/upkeep:	★★

Lion's Canyon Campground offers good stream swimming, trout fishing, and hiking in the Sespe wilderness.

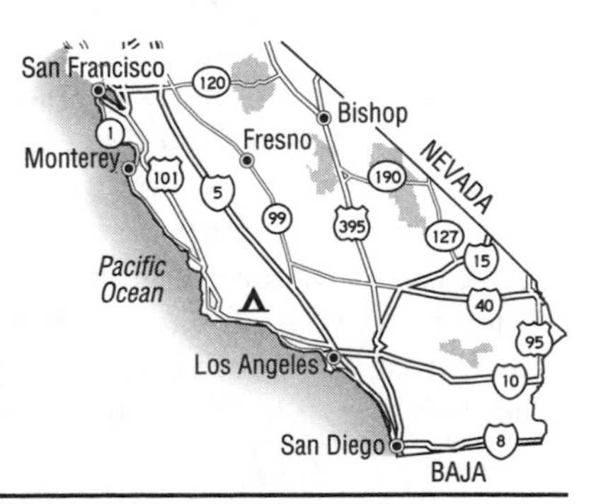

and returned to jail in Ventura. This time, he filed through his leg irons, tore open the window bars of the new town jail, and escaped.

Howard's pal, the editor of the local newspaper, would report on his health from time to time, which infuriated the locals, but Howard was gone, never to be seen again. Reportedly, he died in bed in 1910 somewhere in Arizona.

The campground is in the narrow Lion's Canyon squeezed between high rounded hills by a branch of the Sespe Creek. The swimming hole near the middle of the camp is a good one. The water feels like silk, and schools of trout nose upstream waiting for something delectable to float by. Lion's Canyon drops off into some wild country, so the hiking is superb.

There's a Shangri-la atmosphere about the place, especially in the fall and spring. Up high enough, Lion's Canyon and the nearby Rose Valley often escape the spring fog blahs that blanket the coast. I think spring and fall are the prime times to visit; it's too hot in the summer for me. Most of the other campers are hikers or hiking fishermen, and those folks usually go to sleep early, which makes for a quiet campground. Although the campground purportedly has piped water, both times I have visited there wasn't any—so bring water. The campsites have very little cover—again favoring a fall or spring rather than a summertime visit when it gets crowded.

Classic Lower Chaparral, Lion's Canyon has greasewood and ceanothus growing on the south-facing slopes. Greasewood is a shrub standing anywhere from two to fifteen feet high with small needle-like leaves. Its flowers are small, white, and in showy clusters. All the California lilacs (or ceanothus) have a smooth, olive green bark. Rub the pale blue flowers for a moment or two in water, and they will develop a cleansing lather. That's why this plant is sometimes called "soap bush."

On the north-facing slopes, find scrub oaks, coffeeberry, and holly-leaved cherry. Scrub oaks are hard to miss because of their evergreen leaves and acorn fruit. Holly-leaved cherry is an evergreen shrub with white flowers that forms a purple-black fruit. Bees like it, and Native Americans fermented the fruits into an intoxicating drink. Coffeeberry is another shrub with small greenish flowers that forms a soft green, black, or red fruit shaped like a commercial coffee bean. Native Americans used the berries to correct the effects of an acorn diet, and the bark was used as a laxative. In the vine department, look for wild peas, honeysuckle, and wild cucumbers.

A couple miles away (you would have passed the turnoff on your way in) is the Rose Valley Falls Campground. The falls is a scenic highlight in this section of Los Padres National Forest—especially in the winter and spring when there is enough water in Rose Valley Creek to make a splash. It's only a short hike from the campground to the falls, and a trail continues around to the top of the falls.

A good night walk is back up the road from Lion's Canyon Campground. You can't get lost, and the view is spectacular.

If you want to camp this area when Lion's Canyon Campground is closed, go a few miles south to Wheeler Gorge Campground. You'll find reservable family camping with some decent trout fishing thrown in.

KEY INFORMATION

Lion's Canyon Campground, Los Padres National Forest
6144 Calle Real
Goleta, CA 93117

Operated by: U.S. Department of the Interior

Information: (805) 683-6711

Open: April to December

Individual sites: 30

Each site has: Picnic tables, fireplaces

Registration: At entrance

Facilities: Vault toilets, piped water (don't count on it)

Parking: At site

Fee: $7

Elevation: 3,000 feet

Restrictions:

Pets—On leash

Fires—In fireplaces

Vehicles—RVs and trailers under 16 feet

To get there from L.A., drive west on U.S. 101 to CA 33. Go north to Ojai. From Ojai, drive 15 miles north on CA 33. Turn right (east) onto Sespe River Road and drive 7 miles to the campground.

MALIBU CREEK STATE PARK

Malibu

Situated on a big hunk of the most coveted real estate in Southern California and surrounded by the rapidly encroaching megalopolis of the L.A. area, Malibu Creek State Park Campground is a precious gem. It is beautiful! Once owned by Bob Hope, Ronald Reagan, and 20th Century-Fox, the park now covers over 7,000 acres. This is a great place to tent camp in fall, winter, and spring. Protected by a mountain range from the fog blahs that hit the beaches in Southern California in the spring, Malibu Creek State Park lies between two major tourist thoroughfares—CA 1 and U.S. 101. It's just a hop down the hill to Malibu and all the wonderful beaches. You're also near Santa Barbara on U.S. 101 and Universal City to the east.

You'll find safe mountain biking and hiking, so this is a great place to bring children camping. It's also a good first night's camp if you are flying into LAX and a good escape from L.A. if you happen to live there. I've camped there several times over Saturday night with my wife, eaten at the nearby Saddle Peak Lodge (excellent food), then ducked back to Malibu Creek State Park to our humble tent for a weekend combining the high life and the great outdoors.

High season at the campground begins with spring break and goes through the end of September. Since Malibu Creek is a first come, first served campground, be

CAMPGROUND RATINGS

Beauty:	★★★★★
Site privacy:	★
Site spaciousness:	★★
Quiet:	★★★
Security:	★★★★★
Cleanliness/upkeep:	★★★★

Malibu Creek State Park is a good base camp from which to explore Los Angeles. It's also good for kids with its easy hiking and bicycling.

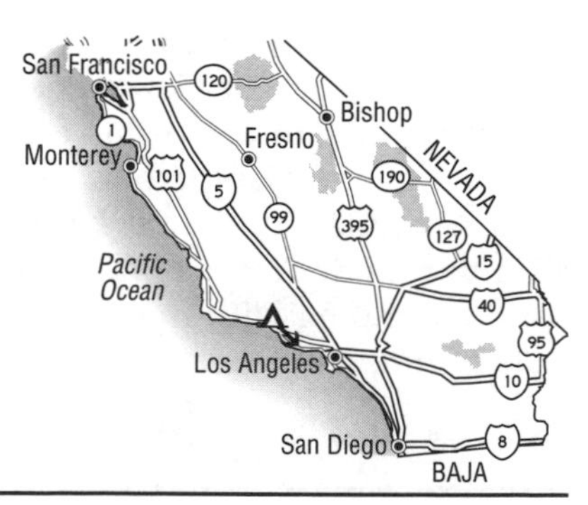

sure to come early on weekends during the summer. The ranger recommended arriving by noon on Friday to reserve a spot for a summer weekend. The campground is very clean, well patrolled, and well maintained, but the sites themselves are unremarkable. It's the incredible vista and the "neighborhood" that make this a fun camping experience.

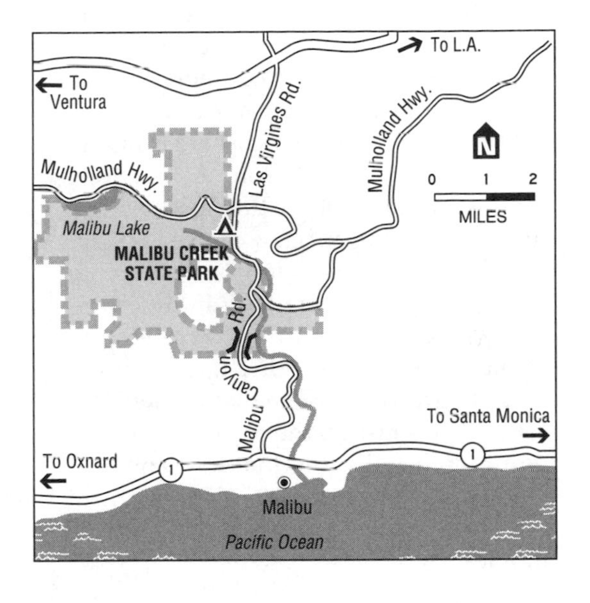

A good introductory walk is along Malibu Creek to Century Lake, then back again. From the camground, walk down to a wide fire road. Cross the stream, and you'll see that the road splits into a high road and a low road. Either one will do. Pass the Visitor Center and find the Gorge Trail. Follow it upstream to where the creek turns dramatically around volcanic rock cliffs into the Rock Pool. Remember the *Tarzan* movies and the "Swiss Family Robinson" TV series? Parts from both were filmed here.

Back on the high road you'll come to the crest of a hill and look down on Century Lake. Look around carefully and spot the distinctive hills that doubled for Korean terrain in the television series "M*A*S*H." When I first hiked the park, part of the set was still lying around, and you could feel the ghosts of Hawkeye, Radar, and all those choppers.

Another good hike is up to the Backbone Trail. From there, you could conceivably hike all the way to Will Rogers State Park in Los Angeles. Don't try it, though, unless you are a walking fool. Farther on is a swampy pond always good for bird-watching, and then Ronald Reagan's ranch with some good hiking. (Obtain a good map of the park from the ranger at the gate for $1.)

Note that wood fires are not allowed (charcoal is okay) because of the fire hazard. This area is near the scene of the 1993 fires that burned parts of Malibu and even threatened Santa Monica. Fires in the Lower Chaparral are as common as cats and so much a part of the cycle of nature that Native Americans would set controlled fires to help Mother Nature along. They were interested in burning the brush fuel underneath the bigger trees that they used for food before the brush grew enough to burn the larger trees. Fire, also, allowed more access and helped expose the game animals.

My favorite time of year here is fall to spring—their off season. I find the mountains too hot in the summer for hiking or biking (pack a canteen if you decide to visit then). However, camping at Malibu Creek State Park in the summer would afford one a good base camp to hit the beach and other L.A. summer tourist attractions. Note that the Renaissance Fair is just up the road at the Paramount Ranch (Santa Monica Mountains National Recreation Area) along with an old-time western town used in the movies.

To get there from Santa Monica, drive north up CA 1 through Malibu, turn right on Malibu Canyon Road and drive 5 miles to the park entrance on the left. From the San Fernando Valley, drive east on U.S. 101 to the Las Virgenes exit and drive 6 miles west on Las Virgenes Road to the park entrance.

KEY INFORMATION

Malibu Canyon State Park
Angeles District, Malibu Sector
1925 Las Virgenes Road
Calabasas, CA 91302

Operated by: Department of Parks and Recreation, State of California—The Resources Agency, P.O. Box 942896, Sacramento, CA 94296-0001

Information: (800) 533-7275 or (818) 880-0350

Open: All year

Individual sites: 62 tent sites; 4 RV sites

Each site has: Picnic table, fireplace (no wood fires), no hookups

Registration: By campground entrance

Facilities: Flush toilets, hot solar showers (all accessible to disabled patrons)

Parking: By site

Fee: $14

Elevation: 500 feet

Restrictions:

Pets—On leash

Fires—Charcoal only

Vehicles—RV maximum length 18 feet

Other—Be careful with fire

MANRESA UPLANDS STATE BEACH

La Selva Beach

CAMPGROUND RATINGS

Beauty: ★★★★★
Site privacy: ★★★
Site spaciousness: ★★★★
Quiet: ★★★★
Security: ★★★★
Cleanliness/upkeep: ★★★★★

Manresa Uplands State Beach offers the best tent camping on the Southern California beach. Think Victorian-style camping, bring equipment, and reserve ahead.

Manresa Uplands State Beach offers the best in beach tent camping in Southern California. In fact, RVs are not even allowed. Cars must be parked in a designated lot a few hundred yards away from the sites. It's wonderful. There's a 20-minute parking area near the campsites where you can unload your equipment, carry it to your campsite, and then move your car to the lot. In a land where RV campers outnumber tent campers three to one, this is tenting bliss.

The campground lies on a bluff overlooking Monterey Bay. Eucalyptus and Monterey pine shade the well-spaced sites. A trail leads down to an endless sandy beach, good for swimming, sunbathing, and walking. This is a popular campground, as well it should be. Reserve early and plan on spending some time here. It wouldn't be a bad idea to buy one of those big two-room tents, which go on sale in early summer ($200 maximum). You want inside space to stand up and move around and aluminum chairs for sitting around outside under a shade screen. Bring a good ground cloth to pitch the tent on. Think Victorian-style summer camping—luxury equipment and comforts such as thick summer novels.

Look out over Monterey Bay and imagine the wilderness below inhabited by kingdoms of marine creatures. Under the surface of the bay are forests of giant kelp.

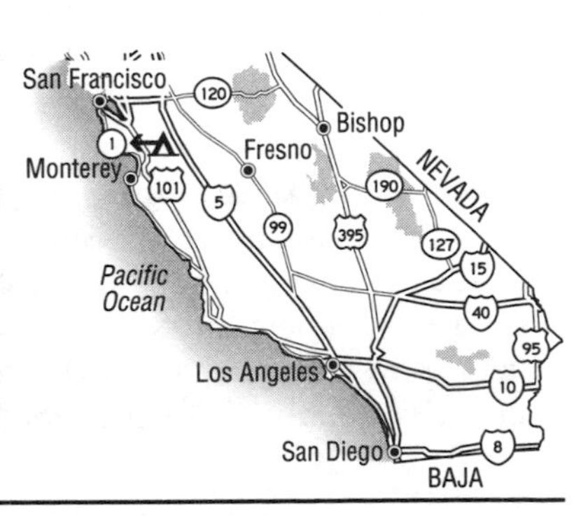

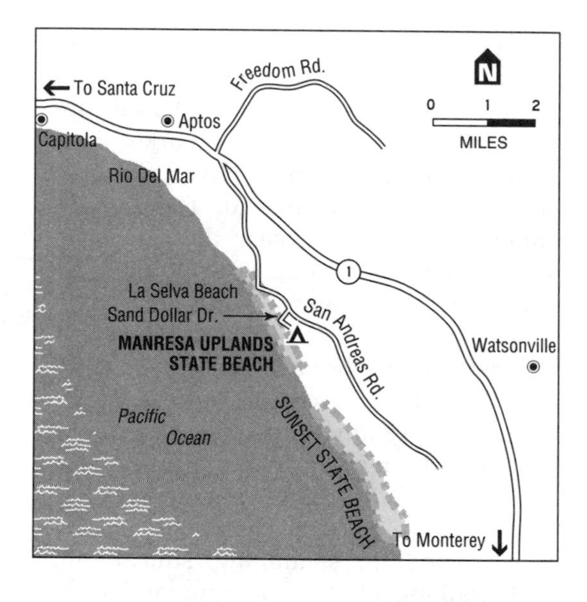

The kelp's tough stem, or stipe, climbs more than 100 feet from the ocean floor, supporting flat golden brown fronds held afloat by small, gas-filled bulbs. In late summer or early winter, look for bull kelp piled up on the shore. You'll recognize it by the air bladders at the base of each blade. (Native Americans ate the bull kelp and made musical instruments from the hollow stipes and bladders—a trumpet can be made with a section of stipe and half a bladder!) The bull kelp rots on shore and shelters millions of sand hoppers that become breakfast, lunch, and dinner for the sandpipers.

Half a mile off the beach, a large submarine canyon slashes across the sea bed. It's big enough for the Grand Canyon to fit inside easily. There are reefs, rocks, and underwater granite, volcanic cliffs that mirror the canyonlands in the Southwest. Rich nutrients, accumulated for centuries, are caught in the upwelling of deep ocean waters and thrown up toward the surface to support a marine community so rich that it contains every marine habitat known to man except coral reefs and mangrove swamps. The submerged rocks are carpeted with sponges and sea anemones. The rainbow of underwater Monterey Bay comprises reds, pinks, blues, and purples. A ceiling of kelp leaves covers the ocean's surface, allowing beams of sunlight to highlight the amber leaves. Some say it's like a magnificent cathedral with stained glass windows.

Go to Monterey for scuba lessons—Monterey Bay is a mecca for scuba divers from around the world. The first divers here were Native Americans called *Ohlone* (abalone people) who shared the shellfish with the sea otter.

Then came the Japanese who dove for abalone, and the sandy Monterey roads were lined with great piles of discarded red abalone shells. When Jacques Cousteau invented the scuba gear (self-contained underwater breathing apparatus) during World War II, the abalone were already thinning out, and the industry cried out even then for strict regulation.

According to an anonymous traveler in 1850, the road from Monterey north to the campground was "a mere trail through thick chaparral, crossing some deep ravines . . . with grizzlies living in the brush, particularly bold and savage." Most people traveled by boat. The Pajaro Valley, away from the sand dunes, was rich, marshy land—more like a lake in winter. It was full of birds. They say you could clap your hands, wait a three-count, fire your shotgun up into the air, and kill a hundred birds without aiming. Today, this is some of the richest and most heavily chemically treated farmland in the world. Note the fields behind the campground stubbornly holding out against creeping urban development.

Look at the artichoke fields, and imagine the city of brown meadow mice living in them (about 3,000 mice per acre). They eat the artichoke leaves and stems while dodging hawks, owls, crows, and gulls. I've read that gulls hate crows so bad that they will attack a lucky crow with a captured mouse just to make him drop it—out of pure spite and malice.

Visit Santa Cruz. Even after the damaging earthquake, downtown is very charming. Pedestrian friendly, it has bookstores, sidewalk restaurants, brew pubs, surfer museums, outdoor markets, and a horde of handsome students from the university on the hill. Very user-friendly, Santa Cruz wants your tourist dollar and gives you good value for it.

KEY INFORMATION

Manresa Uplands State Beach Campground
205 Manresa Beach Road
La Selva Beach, CA 95076

Operated by: Department of Parks and Recreation, State of California—The Resources Agency, P.O. Box 942896, Sacramento, CA 94296-0001

Information: (408) 761-1795

Open: All year

Individual sites: 63

Each site has: Picnic table, fire ring

Registration: At entrance

Facilities: Flush toilets, coin-operated showers

Parking: At parking lot

Fee: $16

Elevation: Near sea level

Restrictions:

Pets—Allowed ($1 fee)

Fires—In fire rings

Vehicles—None in camping area

Other—No tent pitching in green areas; no sleeping in vehicles in parking lot

To get there from San Francisco, drive 78 miles south on CA 1 to Santa Cruz. Then drive south on CA 1 to the San Andreas Road Exit. Drive south to Sand Dollar Drive and follow signs to the park entrance.

MONTANA DE ORO STATE PARK

Los Osos

After a week, smog city Los Angeles seems full of snarling attack dogs and housewives with Mercedes car keys jammed in their fists ready to carve your liver out over a parking space at the shopping mall. But, drive north of Santa Barbara where the air is clear and you'll see smiling women hiking alone on cliffs at sunset, papas with babies in backpacks, ball-chasing lab retrievers, and unattended bicycles—especially at Montana de Oro State Park. Its azure, rocky coves feel like Greece; the sandwiched cliffs jutting out over the ocean remind you of Cornwall; and the long sand dunes resemble Provincetown on the Cape. Spectacular and huge, this is one of California's largest state parks with 7 miles of coast.

The northernmost part of Montana de Oro State Park begins at the Morro Rock and goes south along a huge sandspit, some 85 feet high. This is prime hiking, picnicking, sunbathing, and swimming land. You can get lost in little, private, sandy hollows in the dunes. If you look to one side, you can see the sea, and, on the other, Morro Bay, the largest, least disturbed saltwater marsh on the California coastline. Bring a big backpack to cram with blanket, water, food, and drinks, because the sandspit is an all-day affair.

Farther south, the sandspit gives way to more dunes that fall off to cliffs, flat sheet rock, and small cove beaches below. You

CAMPGROUND RATINGS

Beauty:	★★★★★
Site privacy:	★★
Site spaciousness:	★★★
Quiet:	★★
Security:	★★★★★
Cleanliness/upkeep:	★★★★★

Montana De Oro State Park offers year-round camping with 7 miles of virgin California coast. You'll find good spring hiking and prime family tent camping.

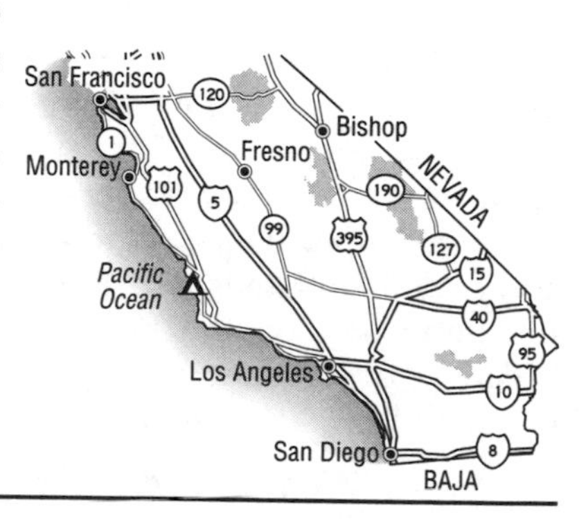

should park on Pecho Valley Road above at turnouts and hike over the dune and down. Again, bring supplies, because once you get down there, you won't want to leave.

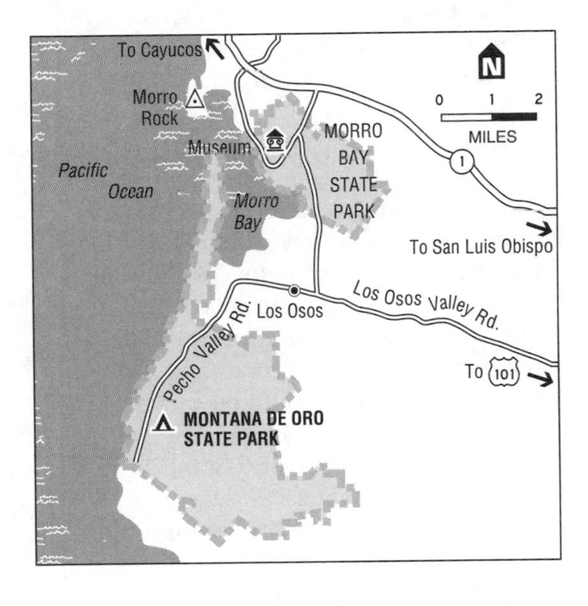

Finally, from Park Headquarters south is an ancient wave-cut terrace with sharp, upended cliffs of Monterey Shale that fall abruptly to the sea. Here and there, you'll spot accessible coves with more sun-bathing and wading (at *low tide only*). Don't miss Corallina Cove about a mile south of the Ranch House Visitor Center. At low tide, you can spot many of the plants and animals that live in the tidal pools. Obtain a free pamphlet and tidal schedule at the Visitor Center before you go.

East, off the coast, the park takes in about 8,000 acres of prime hiking, including Valencia Peak at 1,347 feet. From here, you can see the whole sweep of coast from Vandenberg Air Force Base (64 miles) in the south to Piedras Blancas (80 miles) in the north. I think Montana de Oro provides the best spring hiking in California. By summer, it becomes too hot, and unless the day is foggy, you must hike early and head for the beach when it warms up.

Visit the Morro Bay State Park Museum near Morro Bay State Park. Rent a kayak or canoe from the marina near the museum ($10/hour) and cruise around the estuary.

Explore the sandspit south of the Morro Rock. From the Montana de Oro Campground, drive north 3.6 miles to Monarch Road on the left. Park along the road and walk past where it dead ends, then bear right. You'll see the trail that goes west to the sandspit. A trail to the right goes to the estuary.

The campground is in the canyon just behind Spooner Cove where big sailing ships were brought in to unload supplies and take on hides and tallow. Here, the canyon is narrow and runs along Islay Creek, which Spooner dammed up to run a water wheel for power. The two campsite loops are in line, so all traffic goes by the neck of the canyon. It gets busy, so the best camping is in the back loop. As a trade-off, you'll have a longer walk to the beach from the back.

Camping in the canyon is close, but the atmosphere is friendly. The Ranger Station is right by the H.Q. and the Information Center, which is staffed by very friendly docents from the local community. The Montana de Oro Campground makes you feel warm and safe. In the summer, count on lots of children. This means bicycles, skate boards, in-line skates, and the trill of youthful voices. Montana de Oro is a prime family tent camping vacation spot. If you can't handle that, pack up and head for the walk-in environmental campsites in the park.

There is tap water. However, it is heavily chlorinated and useful for washing only, so bring drinking water. Also bring one of those plastic bag showers to hang in a tree and sluice the sand and salt off. It wouldn't be a bad idea to bring a bucket to set by the tent to dip sandy feet in before entering the tent. And a brush and dust pan is a must to keep sand out of your sleeping bag.

Montano de Oro was Chumash Indian territory until the Spanish Mission

To get there from L.A., drive north on CA 101 to the outskirts of San Luis Obispo. Turn left on Los Osos Valley Road and drive west to Los Osos where the road becomes Pecho Valley Road. Continue south 5 miles to Montana de Oro State Park.

KEY INFORMATION

Montana de Oro State Park
c/o San Luis Obispo Coast Area
Department of Parks and Recreation
20–A Higuera Street
San Luis Obispo, CA 93401

Operated by: Department of Parks and Recreation, State of California—The Resources Agency, P.O. Box 942896, Sacramento, CA 94296-0001

Information: (805) 528-0513

Open: All year

Individual sites: 50

Each site has: Picnic table, fireplace

Registration: At Old Spooner Ranch H.Q.

Facilities: Heavily chlorinated tap water, pit toilets

Parking: At site

Fee: $9

Elevation: Near sea level

Restrictions:

Pets—Allowed

Fires—In fireplaces

Vehicles—RVs up to 24 feet

Period, which was "Taps" for the unfortunate Chumash who were missionized, then abandoned when the missions were secularized. By then, few Chumash were left, and they did not remember their former way of life. Then came the Pechos, a Spanish family, who dealt in cattle and sold the hides and tallow (for candles). After the Pechos came the ranching Spooners and then Alexander Hazard, who planted hundreds of eucalyptus trees in hopes of selling them to the railroad for ties.

Hazard's lumber dreams hit the same rocks as did the hopes of other eucalyptus timber barons of Southern California. The trees grew fast, but the tree grain spindled so as not to be good for anything—even firewood. It was thought that the wrong variety of eucalyptus had been imported from Australia, but that wasn't the problem. Botanists have determined that eucalyptus planted in California has no natural pests, so it grows so fast it spindles. In Australia, its growth is slowed enough by insects that the trunk doesn't spindle and grows straight enough to be utilized. The lesson here is that nothing is as simple as it seems.

The Morro Bay region is still in a state of grace. There are weeks of wonderful things to do. The natural scenery is as pristine as it can get in 1996, and the people who live there are friendly toward tourists. The restaurants are fun and affordable. The fishing is incredible. It's a wonderful year-round place to go.

MORRO BAY STATE PARK

Morro Bay

This campground is on Morro Bay, the last natural estuary in California. The bay is insanely beautiful. A snow white dune field on the horizon encloses the bay, and the luscious mud flats exposed by low tide are filled with feeding birds. You'll see scaups, grebes, goldeneyes, and buffleheads, as well as the more prosaic gulls and scoters—mostly in the winter month, from November to March. Bring field glasses and a bird book. On Los Osos Creek, 50 yards from the campground, a small marina rents canoes, rowboats, and the like to explore the bay. It is safe sailing and makes a wonderful adventure for kids.

Outside the dunes, the ocean thuds against the sand like the beat of a huge heart. During the winter months, the Monterey pines and eucalyptus around the campground are alive with monarch butterflies. As a flock, the monarchs make long-distance migratory round-trips between Canada and the Sierra Madre of Central Mexico. Gliding on the wind, at altitudes of 10,000 feet, the monarchs find their way by using sun orientation—an ability used by migratory birds, whales, and salmon.

The last time I camped at Morro in January, I went looking for the monarchs in the eucalyptus around 8 or 9 A.M. At first, I didn't see them. Then, they appeared! Butterflies in clusters so thick I

CAMPGROUND RATINGS

Beauty:	★★★
Site privacy:	★★
Site spaciousness:	★★★
Quiet:	★★
Security:	★★★★
Cleanliness/upkeep:	★★★★

At Morro Bay State Park, you'll find great off-season camping situated on wonderful Morro Bay. Be sure to make reservations for the summer or for holiday weekends.

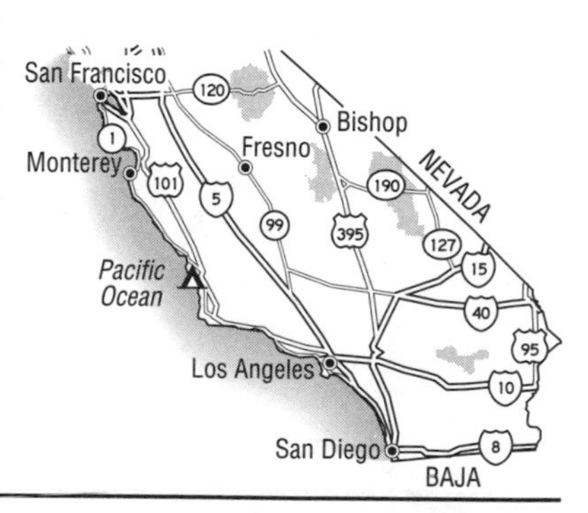

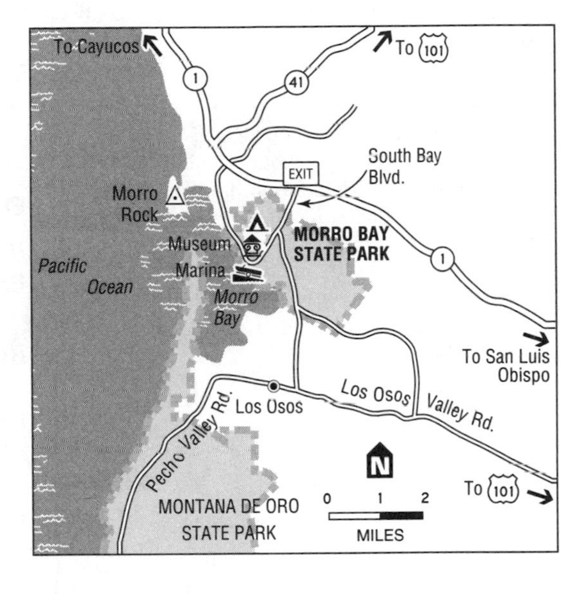

could barely make out the eucalyptus leaves. As the day warmed up, the monarchs disengaged and fluttered above me. In a short time, the sky was full of swirling butterflies. They feed off the eucalyptus bloom—their diet is 90% water and 10% nectar. In the afternoon, as the day cooled, the monarchs returned to the trees and formed dense clusters to stay warm during the night.

When the monarchs migrate from the cooler north and the mountains to the warm central coast, the male flies in spirals around the female of his choice and gives off an attractive scent. The female monarch may accept his overtures by following him to a protected place. There, the male struts in front of her, opening and closing his wings. If all goes well, the pair mate.

Afterward, the female looks for a milkweed plant where she will lay her eggs. The larvae eat their way out of their casings and feast on the milkweed so heartily that their weight increases 2,700 times until they metamorph into mature monarchs and fly away.

The campground is heavily used in the summer and on holidays. Fall, winter, and spring are the best times to visit (and to see the monarchs). The area is friendly and safe. By the marina, you'll find a good outdoor cafe for lunch or coffee. On the headland, visit the museum staffed by extremely helpful volunteers who are knowledgeable about the area.

The campsites feel close and safe under huge trees. A golf course runs along one side. There are flush toilets and coin-operated showers. Since Morro Bay is pretty far from any major urban center, campers have that bonhomie of folks accustomed to being on the road.

The town of Morro Bay is just around the shore with a battery of alluring fish restaurants on the waterfront. We opted for a fresh fish purchase from the fish market to be grilled on the campsite barbecue. (Wood is for sale at the camp office.) Locals tell me the cafe on the pier in Cayucas, a little town just up the coast, is a prime spot for good, fresh food.

To get there from L.A., take U.S. 101 north to San Luis Obisbo (about 200 miles). Take CA 1 north 13 miles to South Bay Boulevard, then .7 mile to the park entrance. Or, from the town of Morro Bay, go to the south end of Main Street. Watch carefully for the entrance to the park, since it is not very well signed.

KEY INFORMATION

Morro Bay State Park
c/o San Luis Obispo Coast Area
Department of Parks and Recreation
20–A Higuera Street
San Luis Obispo, CA 93401
(805) 772-2560

Operated by: Department of Parks and Recreation, P.O. Box 942896, Sacramento, CA 94296-0001

Information: (805) 772-2560; for reservations, phone (800) 444-7275

Open: All year

Individual sites: 115

Each site has: Picnic table, barbecue, food-storage cabinet

Registration: At office by entrance

Facilities: Piped water, flush toilets, canoes and rowboats for rent nearby

Parking: At individual sites

Fee: $12–14 ($1 per pet)

Elevation: 50 feet

Restrictions:

Pets—On leash

Fires—In barbecues

Vehicles—RVs or trailers

SYCAMORE CANYON CAMPGROUND

Point Mugu State Park

A school of dolphins pushing bait fish into the shore, working them around the rocky points—dolphin skin wet black against the blue water—that was my first impression of Sycamore Canyon Campground. The beach is gorgeous, a white sand jewel of a place to picnic, sun, and swim on an unspoiled stretch of coastline.

Later, I discovered that the Chumash Native Americans once lived in the canyon and believed that dolphins were their brothers. At one time, the Chumash lived on over-populated islands to the west. Legend has it that their mother god told them to cross over the sea to the mainland by walking on a rainbow. The caveat was that they couldn't look down. Of course, some did and fell into the sea. But, the mother god took pity on them and turned them into dolphins.

The Chumash fished from 25-foot canoes lashed with sinew and caulked with asphalt from seeps. They gathered clams, oysters, and abalone along the shores and made soapstone bows inlaid with mother of pearl from the shells. They hunted and gathered food in the upper reaches of the canyon and lived a life of ease, culture, and bounty. However, the Spanish put a quick end to that, and now we can camp where they lived at the mouth of the canyon where it is cool in the summer and warm in the winter.

CAMPGROUND RATINGS

Beauty:	★★★★★
Site privacy:	★★
Site spaciousness:	★★★
Quiet:	★★★
Security:	★★★★★
Cleanliness/upkeep:	★★★★★

Sycamore Canyon Campground offers beautiful vistas of the sea, the sky, and the canyon. Just outside Los Angeles, this campground is a jewel.

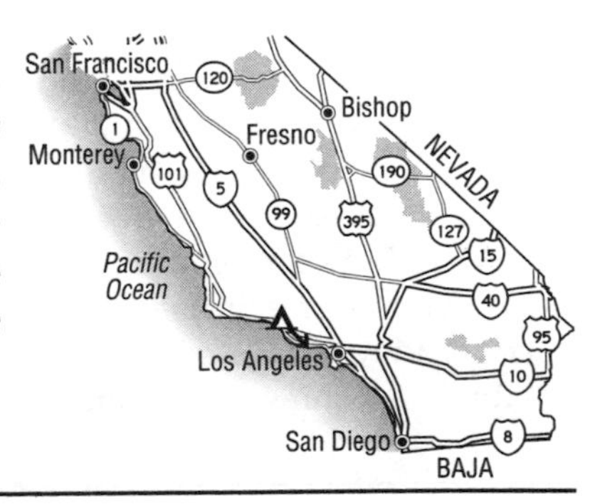

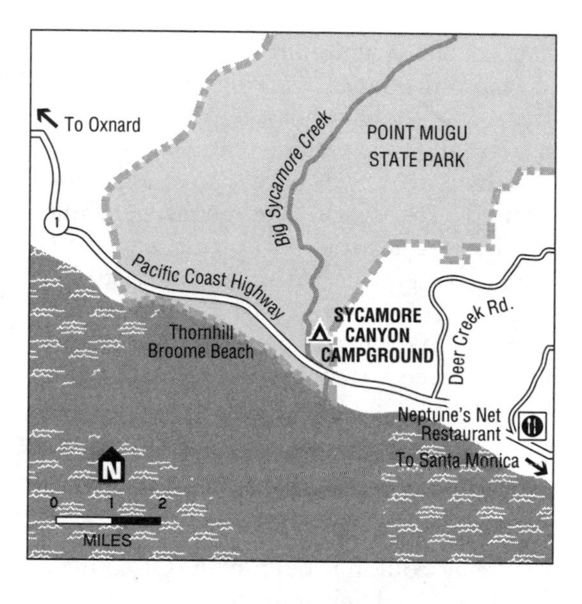

Like Malibu Creek State Park, Sycamore Canyon Campground is heavily used, both for overnight camping and for day use. Buses of school kids come for the morning. Mountain bikers access the fire roads up in the canyon. And many hikers come for the wildflowers. Still, the pristine beaches, hills, and savannah meadows, as well as the glorious canyon next to the Greater Los Angeles Metropolitan Area, makes Sycamore Canyon a must-visit campground. Try to visit in off-season, but watch the weather in order to schedule the best hiking days. Or, reserve ahead and hit the beach in the summer. The canyon is cool enough in summer for biking. Prime surf fishing is available off Thornhill Broome State Beach just up the road. You can buy bait just south at Neptune's Net.

This is an excellent area for viewing monarch butterflies. They clump in the sycamore in the canyon and eat milkweed up in the meadows. Why don't sea gulls just descend on the easily spotted, brightly decorated monarchs and have a big chow-down? Because milkweed is poisonous. Rasputin used it to knock off other members of the Russian court. Milkweed is toxic enough so that when birds pick up a milkweed-eating monarch, they feel sick and learn to leave them alone. The monarch's bright colors serve to alert the birds to eat at their own risk.

Clearly, in Sycamore Canyon you'll find many sycamores. You'll also find coast live oak and areas of chaparral and coastal shrub. Look for blue elderberry, wild rose, California bay, purple sage, and, of course, poison oak. Make a habit of washing your hands and other exposed areas with dish detergent after a hike, and don't swim in any stream or stream-fed pond after even a gentle rain. The oil from the poison oak is in the water and will make you very unhappy.

Like Malibu Creek State Park, there is a Ranger Headquarters at Sycamore Canyon. The park feels safe, well regulated, and well patrolled, which is comforting so close to dense urban areas. If you tire of the Sycamore Canyon's small beach, remember there are miles of beaches just a short drive away. The aforementioned Neptune's Net, just south of the campground, is a good place to eat fish and chips or buy crab or lobster to grill. On some weekends, the outdoor patio restaurant can be overrun with biker gangs. Upon close examination, of course, the bikers look and act like very well-behaved middle-class Americans (and probably are!). They fit right in with the younger surfers and us middle-aged campers.

You must *plan* a visit to Sycamore Canyon Campground. Watch the weather and avoid the June blahs. Beware of weather predictions calling for "early-morning and late-afternoon fog along the coastline." And don't forget to make reservations. Don't expect the actual campground itself to be too scenic. Look to the sea, the sky, and the canyon for incredible vistas.

To get there from L.A., drive 32 miles north up CA 1 or drive 16 miles south of Oxnard.

KEY INFORMATION

Sycamore Canyon Campground, Point Mugu State Park
Santa Monica Mountain District
2860 A Camino Dos Rios
Newbury Park, CA 91320

Operated by: Department of Parks and Recreation, State of California—The Resources Agency, P.O. Box 2390, Sacramento, CA 95811

Information: (818) 880-0350; reserve through DESTINET at (800) 444-PARK ($6.75 DESTINET fee)

Open: All year

Individual sites: 54

Each site has: Picnic tables, fire grills

Registration: At entrance

Facilities: Piped water, flush toilets

Parking: At site

Fee: $14

Elevation: Sea level

Restrictions:

Pets—Allowed ($1 fee)

Fires—Allowed (no wood gathering)

Vehicles—RVs up to 31 feet

Other—None

VENTANA CAMPGROUND

Big Sur

CAMPGROUND RATINGS

Beauty:	★★★★★
Site privacy:	★★★★★
Site spaciousness:	★★★★★
Quiet:	★★★★★
Security:	★★★★★
Cleanliness/upkeep:	★★★★★

At Ventana Campground you'll find luxury tent camping nestled in the towering trees on Big Sur.

Henry Miller, the famous author, washed up in beautiful Big Sur after a long life of roaming the world and was suitably impressed. He describes Big Sur's majesty as "almost painful to behold. That prehistoric look. The look of always. Nature smiling at herself in the mirror of eternity." The Spanish named the country *el país grande del sur* or big country to the south—*Big Sur.*

Big Sur is about 80 miles of rugged Santa Lucia Mountains slashed by canyons and gorges that fall hundreds of feet into a wild emerald sea full of otters, sea lions, and whales. There are beach cliffs of jade, streams clear as glass, and the world's largest trees, the coastal redwoods. It rains like hell in January and February, and summers hit about 70°F with morning fogs that burn off by noon.

The first white settler in Big Sur was George Davis (1853). He had a spat with his wife in Monterey and moved down on the Big Sur River, which runs though Pfeiffer Big Sur State Park and Andrew Molera State Park. After eight years, he cooled off and moved home. Then came a trickle of others—Michael and Barbara Pfeiffer on the side-wheeler *Nevada* and William and Anselma Post who packed in their stoves and beds on mule-driven wagons.

Most of this incredible highway was built by convicts from San Quentin and Folsom who lived at work camps at Little

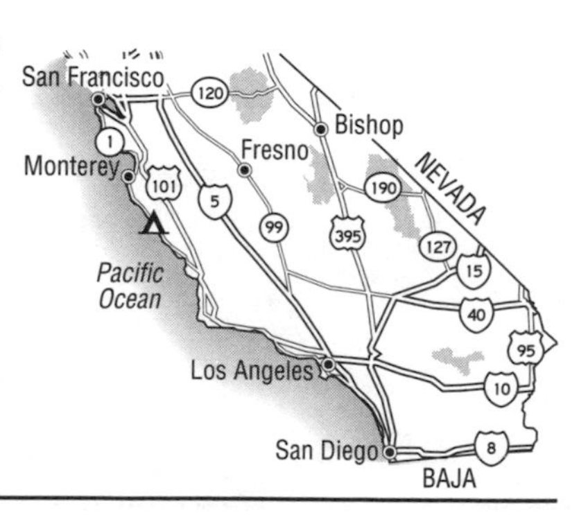

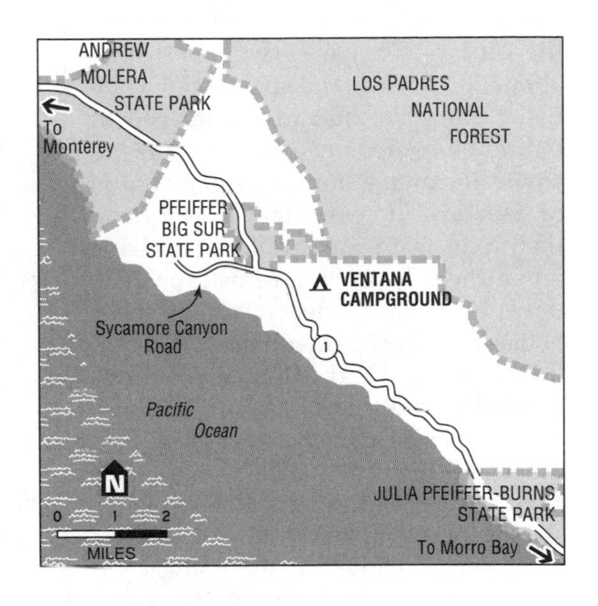

Sur River, Anderson Creek (later the site of guru Henry Miller's cult of sex anarchists!), and Salem Creek. They picked up a princely $2.50/day for pick and shovel labor. Although the work was grueling, the men loved the chance to be outside and work with their hands. And the Department of Corrections claimed that it prepared the men "for return to free society—both physically and psychologically." It took nine years for the convicts and the underpaid Chinese laborers to finally finish the Carmel San Simeon Highway.

The tourist business started in about 1902 when Florence Pfeiffer grew plenty tired of the stream of guests lounging around Pfeiffer Ranch with her husband, John. She finally cracked when one guest hit a mule with a stick. From then on, her husband's friends were required to pay $3/day for room and board, or they would be asked to leave. Now, the tourist business is booming. The traffic on CA 1 is often constant, and the campgrounds are jammed, especially in the summer.

Only lovely Ventana Campground seems to have any available sites. Ventana is located in the redwoods below Ventana Inn on a 40-acre piece of land once owned by the Posts. The campground is now owned by the Inn and run by Scott Parker, a local landscape architect. All the sites are situated on the mountainside, so as to give each site maximum privacy, view, and space. The forest floor is clean and soft—great for tent camping. And, indeed, Ventana caters to tent campers. It is clean and well regulated—a perfect place to enjoy Big Sur.

You can hike behind the Ventana Inn on fire roads, but the best hiking is down in Pfeiffer Big Sur State Park near Ventana Campground. The State Park has 821 acres and 6 hiking trails ranging from a 20-minute stroll to a 4-mile, 2-hour hike. The stream that runs through the park, Big Sur River, is perfect for wading during most times of year.

While hiking, keep an eye out for wild pigs. Apparently, hunters introduced the wild boar back at the turn of the century for sport. The boar weigh about 300 pounds and sport some nasty tusks. They are nocturnal and feed at twilight on bulbs and roots. One hungry sow can rip up a hundred square yards of meadow in one night. They drop their piglets in the spring, and that's when their disposition turns especially ugly. It's best to steer clear of these babies and their porker mamas.

Just north of the Ventana Campground turnoff is Sycamore Canyon Road, which leads to Pfeiffer Beach. This beach is usually not signed—the locals have a time-honored tradition of chainsawing off the signpost leading to their local beach. However, the natives are not churlish about sharing the sand and incredible view once we find our way.

In fact, I found the natives to be surprisingly good-natured and friendly. There was a big movement to close CA 1 off to tourists at one time. Then, nature did it for them in 1983 with a huge mudslide between Julia Pfeiffer Burns State Park and Partington Ridge. It closed the road for more than a year and took 150 men and women working 7 days a week with 30 bulldozers and 7,700 pounds of explosives to clear the road. The closure hit the area hard causing layoffs and cutbacks, and most locals realized that no matter how beautiful Big Sur is, it's the tourists who put hay in the barn.

KEY INFORMATION

Ventana Campground
P.O. Box 206
Big Sur, CA 93920

Operated by: Ventana Big Sur

Information: (408) 667-2688

Open: All year

Individual sites: 75

Each site has: Picnic table, fire ring

Registration: At entrance. For reservations, send $20 two weeks in advance, noting site number desired, to Ventana Campground, P.O. Box 206, Big Sur, CA 93920. Include a cover letter confirming dates of stay and a stamped, self-addressed envelope for a return confirmation letter

Facilities: Piped water, hot coin-operated showers

Parking: At site

Fee: $22 (1 vehicle, 2 people); $5 per extra person; $5 per extra vehicle

Elevation: 400 feet

Restrictions:

Pets—On leash ($3 fee for dogs)

Fires—In fire rings (firewood available)

Vehicles—No RVs over 22 feet

Other—Personal checks not accepted

To get there from Carmel, drive 30 miles south on CA 1. Ventana Campground is on the left just past Pfeiffer Big Sur State Park.

ZACA LAKE CAMPGROUND

Los Olivos

The Chumash Native Americans believed that the Rainbow of Life rose in Ojai and arced over the San Rafael Mountains to Zaca Lake. It must be true. Lie on a raft in the middle of tiny Zaca Lake, stare at the blue sky ringed by piney shale mountains, and you'll know why the Chumash elders came here to die. They believed that under the lake, through a hole in the bottom, was another world, a mirror of Zaca Lake, the afterlife.

Privately owned, Zaca Lake has been a resort of some kind since the early 1900s. At the head of the lake is a lodge with a gourmet kitchen and a dining room with a pronounced tilt down toward the quacking ducks on the veranda outside. A rogue bowling ball would take out half the lodge.

Log cabins (think of Bogart in *Sierra Madre*) rent for hefty change, but under the oaks, you'll find the campground. It's far enough from the cabin crowd, around a steep bluff, to be quiet and secluded. About 20 loosely organized sites are equipped with rickety picnic tables. Open fires are verboten, but there are barbecues down by the lake. Portable hibachis are allowed—so I was told by the relaxed staff, all of whom reflect the general tenor of Zaca Lake's current owner, the non-profit Human Potential Foundation. It's wise to phone ahead, since a week or two out of every year the entire lake is rented out

CAMPGROUND RATINGS

Beauty:	★★★★★
Site privacy:	★★★
Site spaciousness:	★★★★
Quiet:	★★★★
Security:	★★★★★
Cleanliness/upkeep:	★★★

This campground near Santa Barbara is one of a kind. It's best to avoid holiday weekends, although you will not be turned away.

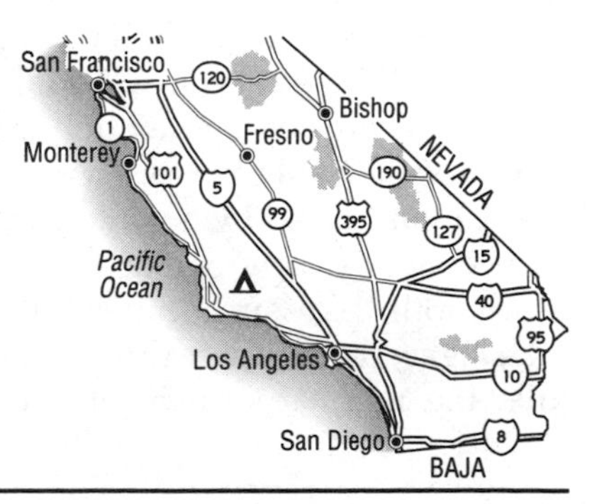

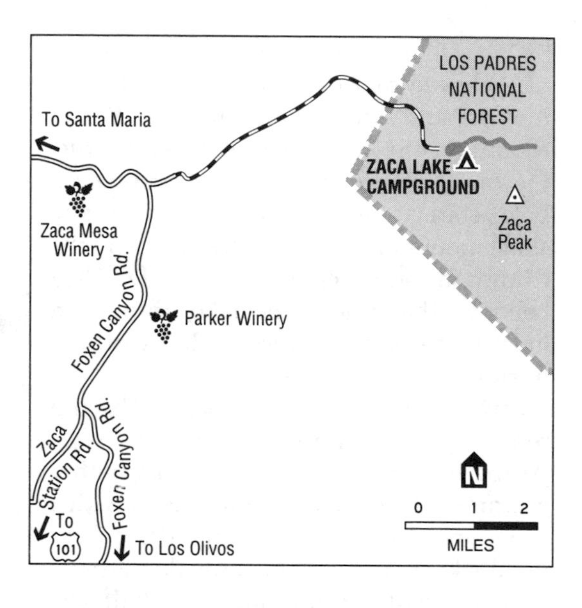

to a large group. Otherwise, campers are never turned away but are accommodated in fields below the campgrounds.

The drive up from Los Angeles is excuse enough to visit Zaca Lake. Take CA 1 up through Malibu to U.S. 101 past Santa Barbara. You will see the Pacific on the left and the rolling California hills (covered with flowers all spring, but baked golden by July) on the right. Follow U.S. 101 until Route 154 to arrive in Los Olivios, the prettiest town in southern California. Then backtrack on Route 154 a couple hundred yards, head north up Foxen Canyon Road, and go right when you meet Zaca Station Road. You're in wine country for sure. Don't miss the Fess Parker Winery on the right (remember Davey Crockett?) with wine tasting from 10 A.M.–6 P.M., to-go chilled chardonnay highly recommended by the author, and picnic tables. A mile or so farther is the Zaca Lake Resort turnoff on the right.

The partly paved access road crosses Zaca Creek seven times in fords so gentle that even a Geo Prism need not fear. In 6 miles, you'll wind up at the lodge, and there's the lake. You'll see why the Chumash maintained a village there for centuries and left only when the Spanish soldiers drove them out to work for the Santa Barbara Mission.

Zaca Lake is fed by hot and cold springs, and one theory asserts that it was carved out by a pyrogenic (steam) explosion like the one that blew out the Mammoth Lakes area. Indeed, in the winter, the sulfur coming up feeds the lake algae, so the water turns a hallucinogenic medley of rainbow colors. This kills the non-native fish, of course. Only the hardy carp gasp their way through to spring. More prosaic geologists maintain that a landslide dammed up the lake centuries ago.

The hiking here is great. The mountains are vertical shale—the floors of ancient seas scrunched up by the moving continents. The trails hook up with the huge Los Padres National Forest trail system. A more modest hike can be found ascending Zaca Mountain. (Always take a lot of water and tell the friendly folks at the lodge where you are hiking.)

Swimming in the lake is great fun. Plan to visit in the spring or fall unless you want to take a winter tour of the wineries, see old-world Danish Solvang, or try your luck at the Chumash Bingo Casino on the Santa Ynes Chumash Reservation.

For bicyclists, the area is heaven—miles and miles of winding country roads with no traffic. Mountain bikers need only to access a fire road into the Los Padres National Forest, and they're gone forever.

To get there from Santa Barbara (95 miles north of Los Angeles), drive 45 miles north on U.S. 101. Turn right on CA 154. Drive 2.4 miles, then go left on Foxen Canyon Road for 3.3 miles. Bear right at the intersection and go 1.9 miles, then turn right at the Zaca Lake turnoff. Go 6.3 miles to the lodge.

KEY INFORMATION

Zaca Lake P.O. Box 187
Los Olivos, CA 93441

Operated by: Human Potential Foundation

Information: (805) 688-4891

Open: All year (call ahead to be sure)

Individual sites: 100

Each site has: 40 sites have picnic tables

Registration: At lodge by entrance

Facilities: Piped water, chemical toilets, float raft, canoes and rowboats for rent

Parking: At individual sites

Fee: $6 per vehicle, $5 per person

Elevation: 2,500 feet

Restrictions:

Pets—On leash; no swimming in lake ($3 per pet)

Fires—In portable barbecues

Vehicles— RVs or trailers

Other—No fishing

SOUTHERN CALIFORNIA

THE DESERT

ARROYO SALADO PRIMITIVE CAMPGROUND

Anza-Borrego Desert State Park

Arroyo Salado is badlands camping. It is in malpais (bad country) in the huge Anza-Borrego Desert State Park (ABDSP), which has everything—palm-studded canyons, cactus gardens, mountain pinyon forests, hot springs, waterfalls, bighorn sheep, Native American pictographs and petroglyphs, historic emigrant trails, stage stops, and ghost towns. A good way to come into Arroyo Salado is on CA 86, off I-10, via Indio and Coachella through the date palm orchards. Stop and have a date shake at one of the stands. Then, carry on along the shore past Salton City Beach and turn east on S-22. Notice Travertine Point on the right and the wave terraces cut into the mountainsides—in recent geological times, the Salton basin was a huge lake. Near the wave terraces are traces of the Native Americans who lived by the lake.

Now, you're in the malpais. This area is characterized by abrupt gullies with banks of sun-hardened clay, gravel-strewn sand, and strange shapes of clay. Red and yellow are the prevailing colors, with mud-hued grays and drabs for a background. After the winter rains, all the flowers bloom—flame-tipped ocotillo, verbena, desert sunflower, lavender, brittlebush, creosote bush, primrose, teddy bear cholla, and beavertail cactus. The entrance to the Arroyo Salado primitive camping area is 11.8 miles on the left (or, from the other direction, 19 miles from the Park H.Q. in Borrego Springs).

CAMPGROUND RATINGS

Beauty:	★★★★★
Site privacy:	★★★★★
Site spaciousness:	★★★★★
Quiet:	★★★★★
Security:	★
Cleanliness/upkeep:	★★★★

Arroyo Salado Primitive Campground is situated in malpais with lizards, flowers, and the rainbow colors of the dunes. For the hard-core tent camper seeking a unique experience. Not appropriate for young children.

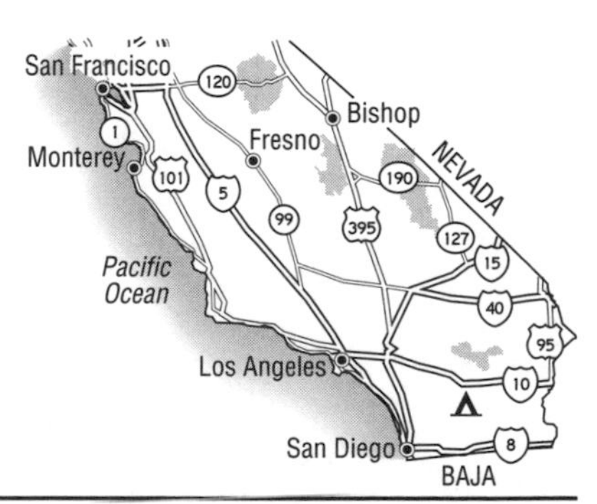

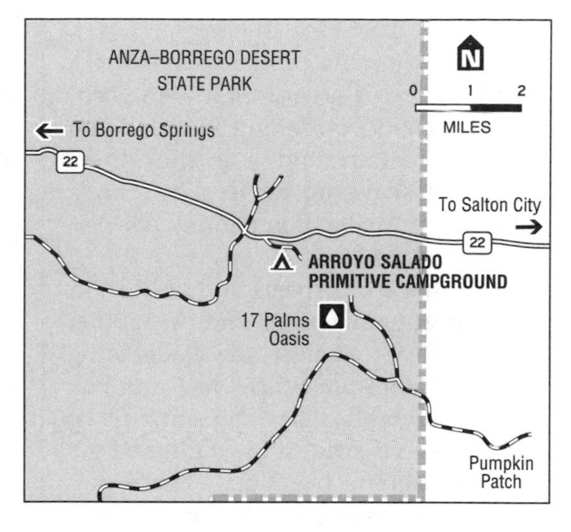

The campground is marked by a small wooden stake with "Arroyo Salado" carved on it. As with all the signs in ABDSP, they are small and unannounced, so you have to be on your toes to see them. Often, there is a turn-around past the entrance to make reapproaching a little easier.

A sandy road goes down the wash with various turn-outs where you can park your car and camp. Carry your tent up over the hummocks, and, suddenly, you'll be alone in untracked malpais. Everywhere is a good place to pitch a tent. The desert floor is clean and sandy. Sit down and listen to the wind and look for lizards flitting over the rocks and dunes. Wait, and the desert comes to you.

The sandy road continues down to 17 Palms Oasis, Una Palma, and Five Palms. None of these places has the number of palms their names advertise, but there is a spring at 17 Palms, as well as a visitor's register consisting of a wooden keg full of notes lodged in the palm fronds of two adjoining palm trees. This desert post office was begun by early-day travelers and prospectors. These considerate travelers also left a fresh water supply for those who followed. The saline water here is drinkable, although highly laxative. In the early 1900s, the famous British traveler J. Smeaton Chase came this way and noted that "rice boiled in it was thoroughly disgusting in color and taste; no amount of sugar could render it more than just bearable. The tea had a dirty gray curdle and a flavor like bilge, and when I tried cocoa as an alternative the mixture promptly went black."

Past 17 Palms, the road continues south and connects with a network of roads traversing the Borrego Badlands. Don't attempt to go farther unless you have a four-wheel-drive in good shape and a lot of water. Note that you can camp anywhere you want in ABDSP as long as you don't park your car more than ten feet off established dirt roads. Of course, you must carry out your garbage. Bring a gardening trowel and dig a narrow deep cat hole for bodily waste. No fires are allowed, unless you bring in wood and burn it in a metal container—a portable barbecue would be fine.

It's not a bad idea to carry a shovel. Either buy a collapsible shovel from a surplus store or saw off part of the handle from an old gardening shovel. If you ever get stuck in sand, your shovel will be your best friend. Remember, carry a lot of water; one gallon per day per person should do it.

Bring some old sheets and light rope. You can sit on one sheet and rig another with the rope to make some shade. Bring a cheap aluminum beach chair and buy the little umbrella that clamps to it. Sleep under a sheet early in the night and get in your sleeping bag later when it gets cold. A sheet is good, too, to use in front of the tent for taking shoes on and off and keeping sand out. I always bring a small brush as well to clean out the tent when sand inevitably creeps inside.

Go to Borrego Springs for supplies and picnic under shade trees on the traffic circle where they sell grapefruit and oranges. Just up the road on Palm Canyon Drive is the ABDSP H.Q. and Visitor Center where you can buy maps and books and see the exhibits. There is an easy 3-mile round-trip nature trail up Borrego Palm Canyon leaving from the Palm Canyon Campground one mile from the Visitor Center. Finally, go out and go camping. There are over 600,000 acres of open country in the park.

KEY INFORMATION

Arroyo Salado Primitive Campground
Anza-Borrego Desert State Park
P.O. Box 299
Borrego Springs, CA 92004-0299

Operated by: Department of Parks and Recreation, P.O. Box 942896, Sacramento, CA 94296-0001

Information: (619) 767-4684 or (619) 767-5311

Open: All year (avoid summer)

Individual sites: Open area

Each site has: No facilities

Registration: Not required

Facilities: None

Parking: Some pullouts; otherwise, less than 10 feet off established dirt roads.

Fee: None

Elevation: 800 feet

Restrictions:

Pets—Dogs on 6-foot leash; at night, in tent or vehicle

Fires—In portable barbecues

Vehicles—Suited for pickup campers

Other—Don't camp near water holes, since wildlife depends on them for water

To get there from L.A., take I-10 east to CA 86. Head south to the junction with S-22 near Salton City. Turn right and travel 11.8 miles. On the left is the entrance to the primitive campground.

Or, take I-10 east to I-15 south to Temecula. Take CA 79 to the junction with S-2 past Warner Springs. Take S-2 to S-22 to Borrego Springs and the ABDSP Visitor Center. Drive 19 miles east of the Visitor Center on S-22 to the campground.

CULP VALLEY PRIMITIVE CAMPGROUND

Anza-Borrego Desert State Park

Culp Valley Primitive Campground is perched high in the San Ysidro Mountains overlooking the Borrego Valley. It's a good choice for late spring when it is too hot in the valley below and the wildflowers are still in bloom higher up. In winter or early spring, Culp Valley may be too cold and windy for comfortable camping.

The mountains of Culp Valley are composed of old granite, and the exposed peaks and hills have eroded into huge piles of granite boulders scattered around the meadows. The trees found in this area are California juniper, sumac, scrub oak, mountain mahogany, and silk-tassel bush. The meadows were covered with tiny flowers when I was there in March. Spring was happening slower in the mountains at 3,400 feet than it was down in the Borrego Valley where the flowers were in full bloom.

As you pull into the campground, there is a dirt road to the left—the California Riding and Hiking Trail. You'll find good pullout spots a few hundred yards up the trail with places to pitch a tent that have full views of the Borrego Valley below. More places to camp are in the regular campground ahead. You'll have no problem parking, but the challenge is finding a flat area to pitch a tent. I parked, carried my tent about 50 yards up into the meadow, and pitched it on a nice grassy area filled with wildflowers. It wasn't quite flat,

CAMPGROUND RATINGS

Beauty:	★★★★★
Site privacy:	★★★★★
Site spaciousness:	★★★★★
Quiet:	★★★★★
Security:	★
Cleanliness/upkeep:	★★★★

Culp Valley Primitive Campground provides cool camping when ABDSP heats up. Good for birding and great hiking through bighorn sheep country with incredible views. With no facilities, Culp Valley is for the hard-core tent camper who doesn't mind carrying gear away from the car. Not recommended for children.

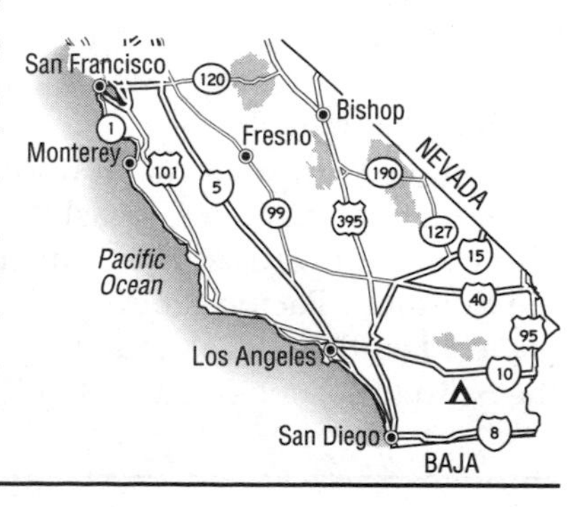

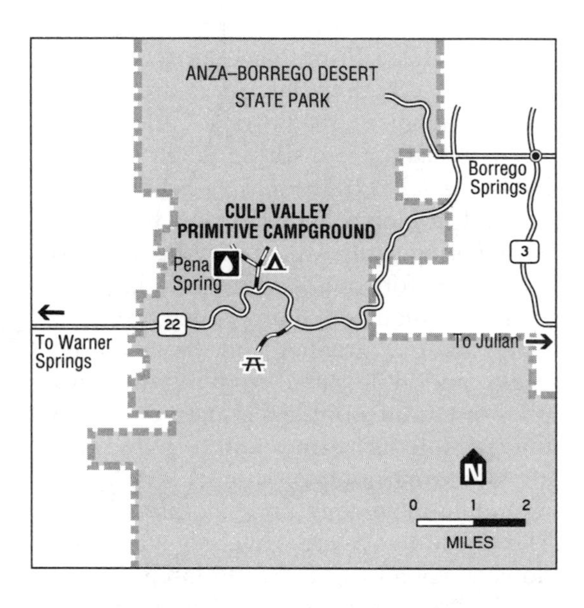

but as long as my head was up and my feet down, I had no problem sleeping. Watch for gopher holes and ant hills as well.

Pena Spring is .75 mile west of the campground. Follow the west fork of the Culp Valley Campground access road 0.3 mile to the parking area. Then, walk down the old road until it dead-ends. A few yards to the west is the spring. Bring binoculars, as Pena Spring is a great birding spot, especially when water is hard to find, and the birds must travel to Pena Spring to get it.

From the campground, a 0.6-mile trail leads to an overlook of the Borrego Valley. I walked up at dusk and caught the whole floor below me, as well as the blue of the Salton Sea on the horizon. In Old Pegleg Smith's days, there was no Salton Sea—just the floor of an ancient sea and a few salt companies that worked the dry alkali basin. Land speculators had dreamed of irrigating the Imperial Valley south of the Salton Sea and starting a land rush. In 1901, their dreams came true. Sluice gates opened on the Colorado River and diverted water through canals and ditches into the valley. It was a modern engineering miracle.

Then, in 1905, the Colorado River broke through the main canal and ran wild, inundating towns, smashing bridges, and flowing into the Salton Basin. Thousands of Native American and Mexican laborers fought the flood, and the Southern Pacific Railroad drove freight trains filled with rock into the breach. Finally, the Colorado River subsided, leaving a permanent saline lake, the Salton Sea, one of our nation's first environmental disasters.

Another good hike is down the California Hiking and Riding Trail about 8 miles into the valley below. I thought I saw a bighorn sheep about halfway down, but, by the time I got out my binoculars, it was gone. The trail dead-ends at the Park Visitor Center, where I phoned a Borrego Springs taxi for the return trip.

I desperately wanted a close-up view of a bighorn. I once read an account by a hiker in which he described the bighorns' eyes. "Their eyes are a clear, golden amber with a long oval, velvety black pupil." Keen sighted, the bighorn can pick out the stealthy movements of a mountain lion from miles away. They can bound and run like the wind. Their specially adapted hooves have bottoms that cling to smooth surfaces and edges that cut into snow or ice and gain a purchase on the smallest projections of the rocks. The bighorn is truly a remarkable animal.

Three-quarters of a mile down the road from the Culp Valley Campground is the Culp Valley Road (dirt) on the right, which leads to the Culp Valley Picnic Area. Follow the dirt road about .5 mile west, then make a left turn through big boulders to the picnic area. This is a really nice spot, and I've rarely met anyone else there. I understand the picnic area is built on the old homesite of an early cattle rancher.

To get there from L.A., take I-10 east to I-15. Go south to Temecula. Take CA 79 east to the junction with S-2 just past Warner Springs. Turn left on S-2. Go left again on S-22. The Culp Valley Salado Primitive Campground is on the left, 9.3 miles from your CA 79 turnoff.

KEY INFORMATION

Culp Valley Primitive Campground, Anza-Borrego Desert State Park
P.O. Box 299
Borrego Springs, CA 92004-0299

Operated by: Department of Parks and Recreation, P.O. Box 942896,

Sacramento, CA 94296-0001

Information: (619) 767-4684 or (619) 767-5311

Open: All year (avoid summer heat)

Individual sites: Open area

Each site has: No facilities

Registration: Not required

Facilities: None; bring plenty of water

Parking: Some pullouts; otherwise, don't park more than 10 feet off established dirt roads.

Fee: None

Elevation: 3,400 feet

Restrictions:

Pets—Dogs on 6-foot leash; at night, must keep in tent or vehicle

Fires—In portable barbecues

Vehicles—Suited for pickup campers

Other—Don't camp near water holes, since wildlife depends on them for water

LITTLE BLAIR VALLEY PRIMITIVE CAMPGROUND

Anza-Borrego Desert State Park

In the middle of March, I camped in Little Blair Valley on the edge of a meadow big enough for General Robert E. Lee to bivouac with his entire army of North Virginia with space left over for General Sherman and the boys. The moon was so full that the tiny flowers sparkled from between the startlingly green grass. What a night!

I was alone until morning when a guy with a Yale sweatshirt drove by with his wife in an econo rental car. They were lost and looking for the Native American pictographs. We consulted his map, then they were off in a cloud of dust. The rest of the morning it was just me and the sun moving across the rocks and the valley.

The S-2 turnoff to Little Blair Valley is 4 miles south of Scissors Crossing, about 31 miles from ABDSP H.Q. in Borrego Springs. On the left, you'll see the tiny stake sign embossed with "Little Blair." The road, usually passable by all passenger cars, goes a mile or so over a ridge into the valley. Here, you'll encounter another stake sign indicating the S-2 highway back in the direction from which you just came. To the left is a wonderful area for camping. The road leads up to the rocks, but the slope is a bit pronounced for tent pitching there. I backed off down the hill a little and camped in the soft meadow grass.

The road to the right of the S-2 marker curls around the edge of the valley passing

CAMPGROUND RATINGS

Beauty:	★★★★★
Site privacy:	★★★★★
Site spaciousness:	★★★★★
Quiet:	★★★★★
Security:	★★
Cleanliness/upkeep:	★★★★★

Little Blair Valley is primitive tent camping in a valley full of wildflowers and Native American pictographs and mortreros. Plan a trip in the spring and bring water.

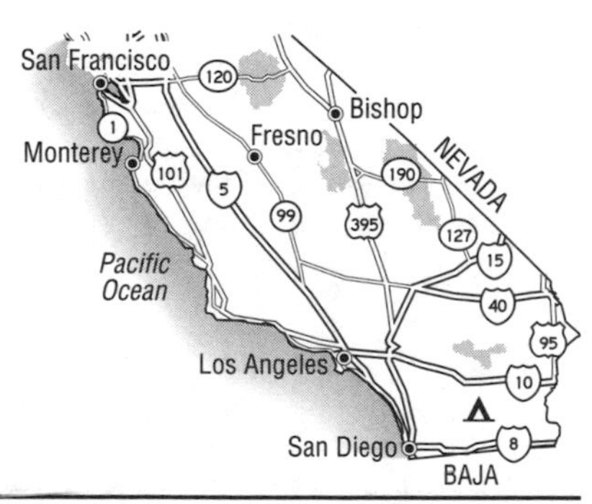

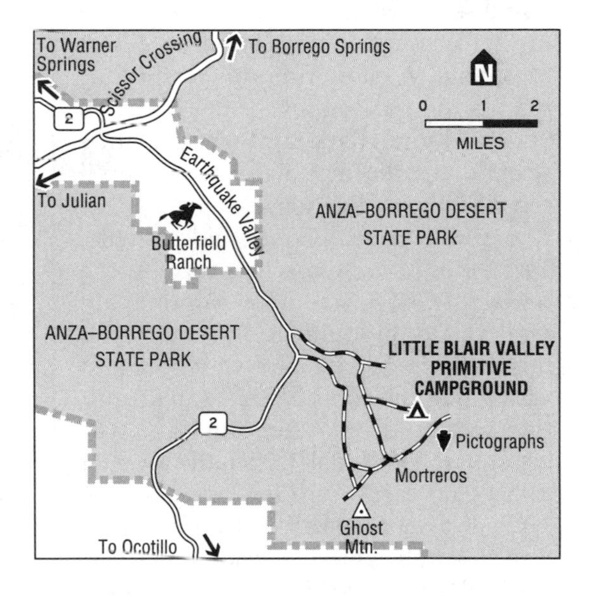

several turnouts with many promising spots for parking and camping. Before you pick one, think about how the sun will travel and when you want to be in the shade or in the sun.

From here, three short, good hikes are within easy range. Drive up to the head of Little Blair Valley and you'll see another stake signing the Mortreros. There is a parking area and a short .75-mile trail leading to large rocks filled with Native American grinding holes. Here, the women pulverized coarse seeds and pods, such as mesquite beans, and made a pulp to be dried in the sun and used later for bread. Also, fine seeds and delicate plant parts were rubbed or lightly ground on smooth, polished patches of rock known as slicks. The trail continues another mile or so east through a ruggedly beautiful canyon.

Back in the Mortreros parking lot, you can follow the sign 0.1 mile to the Pictograph Trail. Usually passable, the 1.5-mile dirt road leads to the Pictograph parking lot. From there, climb a ridge and go down the other side to a huge boulder painted in geometric red and yellow designs. Notice the different vegetation—juniper, white sage, and pinyon pine.

Go past the pictographs and see more Native American mortreros at the base of the ridge to the right. Continue down the wash and into Smuggler Canyon. When the canyon makes a sharp turn to the right, you'll see the Vallecito Valley and the Vallecito Stage Station from the edge of a steep drop.

Smuggler Canyon got its name from the Chinese laborers who came by boat from China via the Sea of Cortez to Mexicali. They were then smuggled up to the canyon to avoid law enforcement and angry locals. Once past the frontier, they worked in mines and on farms and railroads. A strenuous hike is down Smuggler Canyon to where it hits S-2 a few hundred yards east of Vallecito Stage Station. Arrange a pickup, since the return is heavy going.

Retracing your route, drive 2 miles past the Mortreros pullout into the Blair Valley (not Little Blair Valley), and you'll see a signed turn to the left going to the Marshall South Home on Ghost Mountain. A short ride down this dirt road is the parking lot for the Marshall South Home. Park and hike 1 mile straight up the mountain; here, you'll see the ruins of the house.

In 1932, Marshall South and his wife, Tanya, built a house on top of the beautiful Ghost Mountain—a mountain they called "Yaquitepec." They saved rainwater in cisterns and ate yucca and agave like the local Native Americans. Everything from the outside was brought in by Model-T from the town of Julian and carried up the mountain by mule or man. Marshall and Tanya raised three normal children and supported themselves by writing articles for *Desert Magazine.* Finally, in a phrase that sends a chill down the spine of every married man, Tanya "tired of the eccentricities of her husband" and moved to San Diego where she remarried. But, what a wonderful dream!

From the parking lot, you can drive back to S-2 through Blair Valley passing

To get there from L.A., take I-10 east to I-15. Go south to Temecula. Take CA 79 east past Warner Springs to Julian. From Julian on CA 79 drive 12 miles east to S-2. Go right 4 miles on S-2 and find the stake marker "Little Blair" on the left. Follow the dirt road about a mile to Little Blair Valley.

KEY INFORMATION

Little Blair Valley Primitive Campground
Anza-Borrego Desert State Park
P.O. Box 299
Borrego Springs, CA 92004-0299

Operated by: Department of Parks and Recreation, P.O. Box 942896,

Sacramento, CA 94296-0001

Information: (619) 767-4684 or (619) 767-5311

Open: All year (avoid summer heat)

Individual sites: Open area

Each site has: No facilities

Registration: Not required

Facilities: None

Parking: Some pullouts; otherwise, don't park more than 10 feet off established dirt roads

Fee: None

Elevation: 2,500 feet

Restrictions:

Pets—Dogs on leash no longer than 6 feet; must be under immediate control of a person and kept in tent or vehicle at night

Fires—In portable barbecues

Vehicles—Suited pickup campers

Other—Don't camp near water holes, since wildlife depends on them for water; all vegetation (even dead wood) is protected several pullouts and some good camping sites. Blair Valley is accessed and trafficked by RVers and tent campers alike. However, it is not a bad idea to check with the ABDSP H.Q. on the condition of the roads, especially after a rain. I have found the H.Q. to be very conservative, but remember your shovel just in case.

There is a good restaurant up the road at Butterfield Ranch where I had an excellent enchilada. They were about to open a store where you can buy ice, beer, and other absolute necessities. Also, a few miles southeast of S-2, there is another store at the turnoff to Agua Caliente County Park. Both Butterfield Ranch and Agua Caliente County Park have swimming pools and welcome swimmers for a reasonable fee. At Agua Caliente County Park there is also a mineral bath should you want to take a cure.

MESQUITE SPRINGS CAMPGROUND

Death Valley National Park

On your way to Mesquite Springs, stop at the legendary Mad Greek's Restaurant in Baker for the lunch of your life. The souvlaki is unforgettable. However, if you can't bear Greek, there is a park with shaded picnic tables in town. Remember, your last chance to fuel up is 51 miles from the campground in Furnace Creek.

Despite its morbid name, Death Valley is a pretty lively place. For thousands of years Native Americans lived on the shores of successive lakes that filled the basin. When the last lake dried up, nomadic Shoshone camped in the valley near the springs in the winter and in the mountains in the heat of the summer. For the last thousand years, they lived on the ample game, mesquite beans, and pinyon nuts.

It took an overly eager forty-niner to dub the bountiful valley "Death Valley." He was one of a group of impatient argonauts who ignored their experienced wagon master and took a Native American trail in hopes of shaving miles off the trip. The group wound up bogged down in the sand around Furnace Creek. When rescued, the forty-niner theatrically exclaimed, "Goodbye, Death Valley" as he turned his back on his own folly.

Seeing Death Valley for the first time is like seeing the earth without clothes. Immense land forms, volcanic craters, and rainbowed landscapes of salt flats and snow-capped mountains cover the area.

CAMPGROUND RATINGS

Beauty:	★★★★★
Site privacy:	★
Site spaciousness:	★★★★
Quiet:	★★★★
Security:	★★★★★
Cleanliness/upkeep:	★★★★★

This campground in Death Valley National Park is one of two campgrounds in the park that are not overrun by large snowbird RVs in the winter. Don't come here in the summer; Death Valley is one of the hottest places on earth.

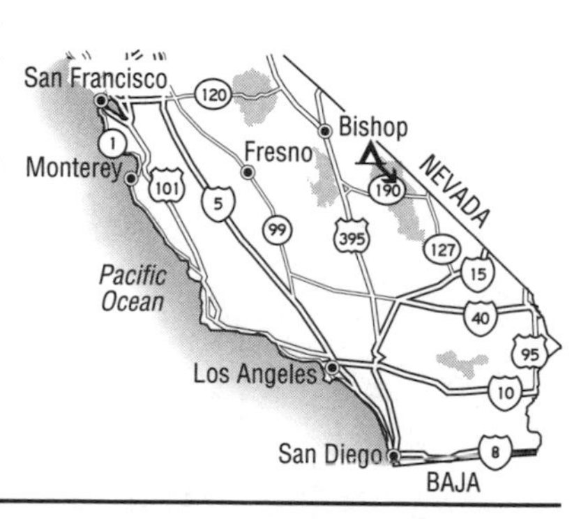

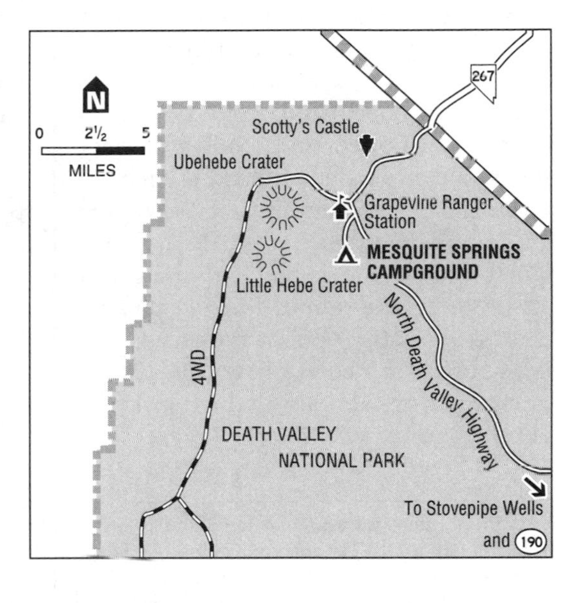

There are original water springs, Ice Age fish, ghost towns, lost mines, plants found nowhere else in the world, and even a Spanish-Moorish castle—Scotty's Castle, built in the middle of nowhere.

Below Scotty's Castle is the Mesquite Springs Campground set in the Grapevine Canyon wash. It has spring water spigots, flush toilets, and well-maintained tent/RV sites with fireplaces and tables. You'll find soft, sandy spots where you can pitch a tent and a beautiful view of the entire valley with snow-covered Telescope Peak rising 11,000 feet in the south.

Far enough from Stovepipe Wells and the golf course at Furnace Creek, Mesquite Springs Campground is not heavily camped except during Easter holiday. Still, it's not a bad idea to phone the Ranger Station near the campground at (619) 786-2331 to check on availability. It's a hefty drive back to Furnace Creek and the Texas Spring campground, which is your alternative. Remember too, that the only supplies in Death Valley are sold in Furnace Creek and Stovepipe Wells.

A visit to Scotty's Castle is a half-day affair. After the guided tour, the bookstore, and a stroll around the grounds, find the tree-shaded picnic tables for lunch. Nearby is Ubehebe Crater and Little Hebe, which constitute another half-day excursion.

In Death Valley, distance shrinks. The locals think nothing of driving 60 miles for a cup of coffee. In that spirit, the ghost town of Rhyolite and Beatty with its gambling casinos (64 miles away) are just around the corner, as are the mining towns of Tonopah and Goldfield.

Hiking around Mesquite Springs Campground is fun. It's almost impossible to get lost because of the terrain. Still, always take a lot of water with you, even if you are just going out for a stroll. The last time we camped there it was a full moon, and we could see the entire valley far below us gleaming in the light. From the trees near the spring, an owl swooped down and rose again with a little creature in its claws. What a magical night!

This is a good campground for children. The campground roads are easily navigable and safe, so bring their bicycles. There is swimming at Stovepipe Wells and Furnace Creek. (Remember, Death Valley is long-haul driving country.) The fee is a nominal $2 per person. The water in the pool at Furnace Creek is as pure as can be. It's new water being generated inside an extinct volcano about 10 miles away.

To get there from L.A., drive 65 miles east on I-10 to I-15. Go north 135 miles to Baker. From Baker, drive 86 miles north on CA 127 through Shoshone to Death Valley Junction. From there drive 29 miles on CA 190 to Furnace Creek. Head north 51 miles to Mesquite Springs Campground on the left just before the Ranger Station.

KEY INFORMATION

Mesquite Spring Campground
Death Valley National Park
Death Valley, CA 92328

Operated by: Department of the Interior

Information: (619) 786-2331

Open: All year

Individual sites: 30

Each site has: Picnic tables, fireplaces

Registration: At entrance

Facilities: Piped water, flush toilets, sanitary disposal station

Parking: At individual sites

Fee: $6 per vehicle

Elevation: 2,500 feet

Restrictions:

Pets—Allowed on leash

Fires—In fireplaces

Vehicles—RVs or trailers

MID HILLS CAMPGROUND

Mojave National Preserve

The East Mojave isn't half as wild and woolly today as it was in 1826 when Jedediah Smith came through with a pack of angry Mojave Native Americans on his trail. Ambushed crossing the Colorado River, Smith lost half his trading party to Mojave war clubs before he forted up in a thicket of cottonwoods. With only five Kentucky rifles, Smith and his mountain men discouraged the Mojaves enough with pinpoint rifle fire to escape and run for their lives across the East Mojave Desert.

It was August 18th and hotter than Hades. Tormented by thirst, the men "found some relief from chewing slips of the Cabbage Pear" (Smith's diary). Men dropped from exhaustion and could not go on until water could be found and brought back to them. "It seemed a more fitting abode for fiends than any living thing that belongs to our world" (James Ohio Pattie). Traveling by night, the men spent the days by springs that Smith vaguely remembered from his trip the year before. They followed the Old Mojave Trail—a trading route used by the Mojave for hundreds of years—and passed near present-day Mid Hills Campground on their terrified flight across the desert wastes toward the Cajon Pass.

Nowadays, Mid Hills Campground is about the most pleasant place to spend some time in these parts. Set in rolling country among juniper and pinyon pine,

CAMPGROUND RATINGS

Beauty:	★★★
Site privacy:	★★★★★
Site spaciousness:	★★★★
Quiet:	★★★★★
Security:	★★
Cleanliness/upkeep:	★★★

Come to Mid Hills Campground for the spring bloom—avoid a summer visit. The back roads are good for mountain biking. This untracked area is spectacular!

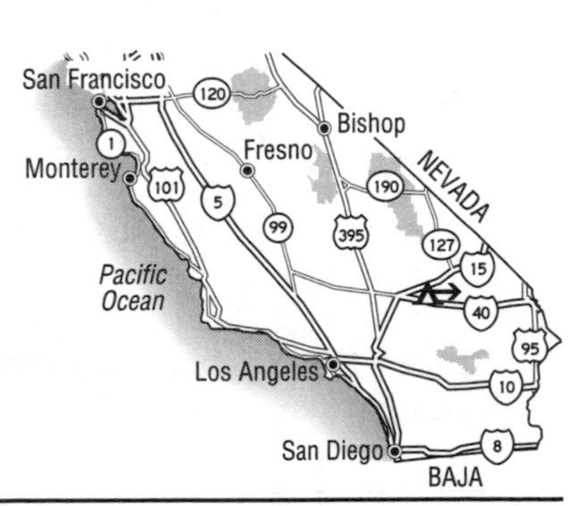

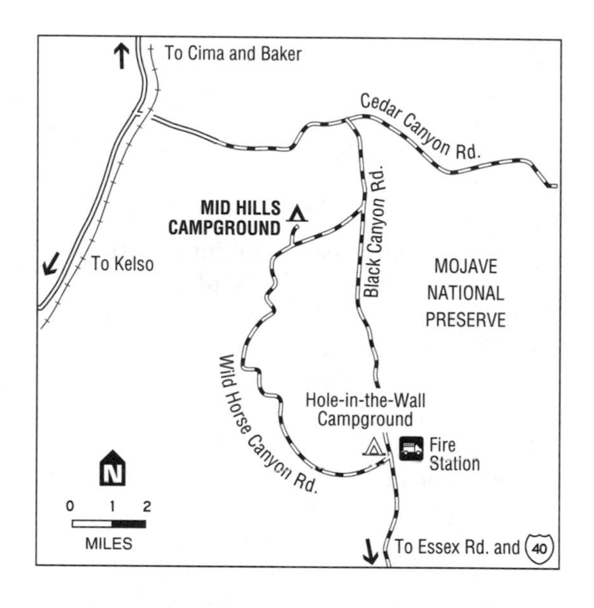

Mid Hills is high enough to get snow sometimes in May. I liked site #14 for its views of the mountains through the trees and the many places to pitch a tent. Still, other sites situated on the edge of a drop with a view of the vast Cima Dome with the Kelso Dunes to the south are enticing as well.

Between the Providence and New York mountains, Mid Hills is the trailhead for the 8-mile hike from Mid Hills to Hole-in-the-Wall Campground—a great hike. Start at Mid Hills for a mostly downhill trek to Hole-in-the-Wall Campground and arrange a return ride. A mile or so into the hike, there is a small cold-water seep coming from beneath a dead juniper, and I can imagine Jedediah Smith and his boys lying around there in the blazing sun waiting for the Mojave to fall on them with their famous war clubs.

The trail features incredible views, and the land changes quickly from the pine-juniper forest to desert, blasted rock, and incredibly bright, delicate desert flowers. (My last visit was in mid-April—phone the H.Q. to keep track of the bloom.) At the end of the hike, coming up a blind canyon, there are rings set in the rock that help get you over the steep places to Hole-in-the-Wall Campground.

Hole-in-the-Wall Campground is the only organized alternative to Mid Hills. When both campgrounds are full, campers may tent in "previously disturbed areas." This option gives you a couple thousand beautiful campsites from which to choose. In fact, just around the corner from Hole-in-the-Wall Campground, you'll find a whole series of turnoffs on the incredibly scenic Wild Horse Canyon Backcountry Byway, as this road has been declared. Be sure to drive it even if you don't camp by it—you'll see everything from cholla and wildflowers on volcanic slopes and rocky mesa to sage to the pinyon-juniper woodland of Mid Hills Campground.

Water, gasoline, firewood, charcoal, and wind are considerations when visiting the Mojave National Preserve. Water is paramount. Count on at least a gallon per day per person. Phone the park before you leave to see which campground has water. When we visited, Hole-in-the-Wall had water, but Mid Hills didn't. Plan ahead.

Gasoline is also scarce. Fill up when you can. It is illegal to burn anything found in the preserve—even dead wood—so bring your own wood or charcoal. Wind is another consideration. Mid Hills is protected by trees and hills, but Hole-in-the-Wall is out in the open. The first night tenting in the wind is usually rough. By night two, however, if the wind is still blowing, count on sleep since one habituates quickly to the walls of the tent slapping around like a luffing sail in a storm. Good earplugs help and are de rigueur anyway for snoring tent mates.

Between the Mitchell Caverns (tours available weekdays at 1:30 P.M., weekends at 10 A.M. and 3 P.M.), Kelso Dunes, Cinder Cones National Natural Landmark, Cima Dome, Fort Piute, Whiskey Pete's casino-hotel-restaurant-truck stop

To get there from L.A., take I-10 east to I-15 north to I-40. Go east on I-40 near Essex, then take the Essex Road exit and drive 16 miles north to Black Canyon Road. Then drive 19 miles north following the signs to the campground.

KEY INFORMATION

Mid Hills Campground
c/o Mojave Desert Information Center
Mojave National Preserve
P.O. Box 241
Baker, CA 92309

Operated by: U.S. National Park Service

Information: (619) 733-4040 or the California Desert Information Center at (619) 255-8760

Open: All year (forget summer)

Individual sites: 20

Each site has: Fireplaces, picnic tables

Registration: At entrance

Facilities: Vault toilets, piped water (sometimes)

Parking: At site

Fee: None at publication date

Elevation: 5,500 feet

Restrictions:

Pets—On leash

Fires—In fireplaces

Vehicles—No restrictions

Other—Bring own firewood/charcoal

just across the border in Nevada, and the Mad Greek's Restaurant in Baker you could easily spend a week camping around the Mojave National Preserve and still have reason to come back for more.

On the way into the Mojave National Preserve, stop at the California Desert Information Center in Barstow (831 Barstow Road; open 9 A.M.–5 P.M. daily; (619) 733-4363) for maps, guidebooks, and information. All we had was the AAA San Bernardino County map, and though it served us well, I wished we had obtained a more detailed map. Since the area has only recently been bumped up to a National Preserve, count on changes. The campgrounds are being modernized, and the rules are being revised. Be sure to phone ahead with any questions.

Mojave National Preserve is a seasonal area for camping. Don't come in the summer unless you want to chew "slips of Cabbage Pear" (barrel cactus) like Jedediah Smith's boys. Spring is the time to come. Not only are the riots of flowers in bloom, but also the desert is scoured clean by winter leaving a crust over the sand to keep the dust down.

SADDLEBACK BUTTE STATE PARK

Lancaster

CAMPGROUND RATINGS

Beauty: ★★★
Site privacy: ★★★
Site spaciousness: ★★★
Quiet: ★★
Security: ★★★★★
Cleanliness/upkeep: ★★★★

Saddleback Butte State Park is good for a quick desert-camping hit. See the desert flowers and the museum. It's a fine first desert trip for children from Los Angeles.

Saddleback Butte State Park is little known, well run, and very convenient to the Los Angeles area. It lies just over the hill on the Antelope Freeway, an oasis in the creeping suburbia of Antelope Valley. I like the park because of its proximity to Los Angeles. It's perfect for a quick desert camping hit if you don't have time to drive to Joshua Tree National Park or Anza-Borrego Desert State Park.

The San Gabriel Mountains on the south block out the smog. From February through May, you'll see wildflowers among the many Joshua trees. In fact, the park was once called Joshua Tree State Park, but everyone confused it with Joshua Tree National Park, so they renamed it after Saddleback Butte, a mountain a few hundred yards to the east of the campground.

Look for horned larks and alligator lizards, as well as the golden eagle, desert tortoise, and the usual compendium of desert creatures. Examine the Joshua tree, which John C. Fremont dubbed the "most repulsive tree in the vegetable kingdom" in 1844. Later, J. Smeaton Chase likened the poor tree to "a misshapen pirate with belt, boots, hands, and teeth stuck full of daggers . . . " Lighten up a bit, dudes. I think the *Yucca brevifolia,* as the Joshua tree is known botanically, is as beautiful as it can be and as strong as it has to be to survive in a harsh environment.

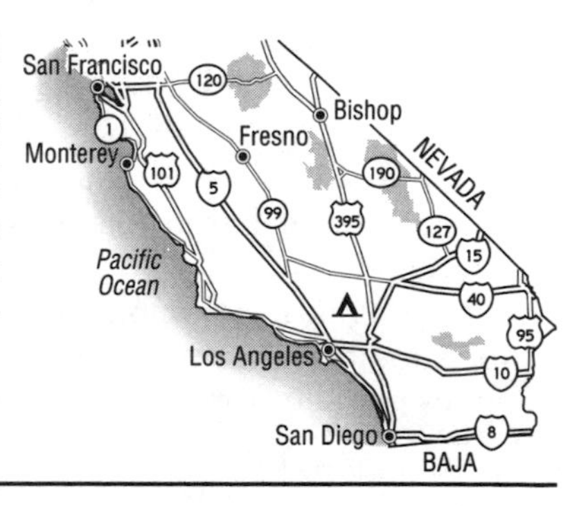

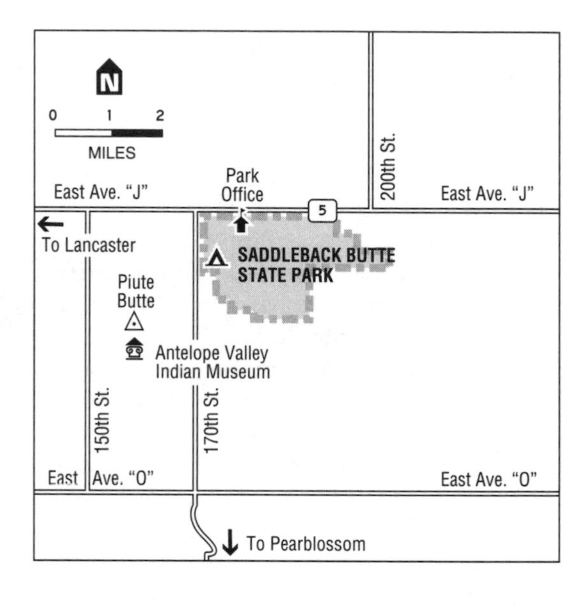

The Joshua tree is a natural supermarket. Woodrats gnaw off the lower leaves to make nests. Weevils lay eggs in the tree's terminal bud, which causes the multiple branching effect. Yucca moths are the sole pollinator, and in turn, lay their eggs in the flower. Butcher birds (the loggerhead shrike) hang their prey out to dry on the sharp leaves, and woodpeckers dig holes in the limbs looking for insects. In the past, Native Americans ate the the flowers raw or roasted and then the seed pods. They made sandals and carrying nets from the fiber in the leaves, and the roots were used to make dyes and medicines. In all, the Joshua tree is a useful plant. It's most beautiful in spring covered and surrounded by flowers or in winter, when the sunlight hits its tufted branches covered with snow.

The area around Saddleback Butte State Park was once antelope country. Imagine the Piute Native Americans on top of the 3,600-foot butte scouting for herds of pronghorn antelope on the distant horizon. Then came the iron horse, the railroad, in the 1870s. Not only were there hordes of trigger-happy sportsmen on the train blazing away at anything that moved, but also the pronghorn antelope had their own fatal flaw. For some reason, they couldn't cross railroad tracks. Something in the pronghorn make-up wouldn't let them. So, unable to follow their normal grazing patterns, they starved to death.

The pronghorn are among the fastest animals in the world. Three feet high at the shoulder, the pronghorn can run 65 miles per hour in short bursts and 35 miles per hour for 4 miles. There are a few left in sagebrush country on the

Modoc Plateau, but it's an uphill fight. Nobody wants a pronghorn antelope who can jump an eight-foot storm fence and eat the ornamentals surrounding the condo swimming pool.

The trail up Saddleback Butte starts in the campground and moves due east up an easy grade passing through creosote and Joshua trees. It winds around the alluvial fan and climbs up the saddle-shaped hunk of granite. From the top, you can see the other buttes in the area. All of them, including Saddleback Butte, are the tops of granite mountains silted up by the alluvial plain, which is Antelope Valley. To the north is Edwards Air Force Base, and farther west is Lancaster and the Antelope Valley California Poppy Reserve where poppies blanket entire hillsides in brilliant orange. This area is worth a visit. Remember to phone ahead at (805) 724-1180 to find out when the poppies are in bloom. From the Antelope Valley Freeway in Lancaster, take the Avenue I exit and drive 15 miles west to the reserve.

The Antelope Valley Indian Museum is also worth a stop. It is a folk museum of various Native American tribes and houses a unique southwestern collection. It is open weekends from 11 A.M. to 4 P.M., September 15th to June 15th. To get to the museum, take 170th Street 3 miles south from the Park to Avenue M. Go west for 1 mile to the museum sign. You won't regret it.

Saddleback Butte State Park is first come, first served; however, the park is only really busy one or two weekends during peak flower time in the spring. Don't camp here in the summer. October and November are pleasant times to visit. Check the weather report and wind conditions before you leave; it can really blow here. In anticipation, there are windscreens by every campsite.

KEY INFORMATION

Saddleback Butte State Park
17102 East Avenue J East
Lancaster, CA 93535

Operated by: Department of Parks and Recreation, State of California—The Resources Agency, P.O. Box 942896, Sacramento, CA 94296-0001

Information: (805) 942-0662

Open: All year

Individual sites: 50

Each site has: Stove, picnic table, windscreens

Registration: By entrance

Facilities: Flush toilets, piped water

Parking: At site

Fee: $10

Elevation: 2,700 feet

Restrictions:

Pets—On leash ($1 per pet)

Fires—In stove

Vehicles—RVs and trailers up to 30 feet

To get there from L.A., drive north on I-5 to I-14 north to Lancaster. Turn east on Avenue J (County Highway N5) and drive 17 miles to the park entrance.

VALLECITO REGIONAL PARK

Near Anza-Borrego Desert State Park

Native Americans lived on the site of Vallecito Regional Park for thousands of years. Then came the Spanish conquistadors, Kit Carson and General Kearny, the forty-niners and the Conastoga wagons, and then, the stagecoaches. Vallecito oasis is on the main southern route west coming from St. Louis down through Texas to avoid mountains and weather. The last water is near Yuma on the Colorado River, and then there's nothing but a hundred miles of trackless, dry wasteland.

One anonymous forty-niner quoted on a park billboard describes Vallecito this way: "Imagine the weary traveler, ragged and dirty, surrounded by barren, burning sands, with no green thing upon which to rest his eye. See him toiling to ascend the sandy rise. He reaches the top and in the distance he sees the green countenance of Vallecito. Gratitude to God fills his heart when he reaches the spot where he can lie down in green pastures and refresh himself."

After ripping through the desert in an air-conditioned car, you won't get quite the same sensation, but Vallecito is truly a magical spot. Surrounded by mountains of heat-blasted rock, Vallecito is soft, green, and filled with wildlife. Behind the campground is a privately owned preserve, a mesquite forest alive with bees and birds.

The campground is simple. Under the trees, with the restored stage station and

CAMPGROUND RATINGS

Beauty:	★★★
Site privacy:	★★
Site spaciousness:	★★★
Quiet:	★★★
Security:	★★★★★
Cleanliness/upkeep:	★★★★★

Vallecito Regional Park is good for children, winter camping, and Old West lore.

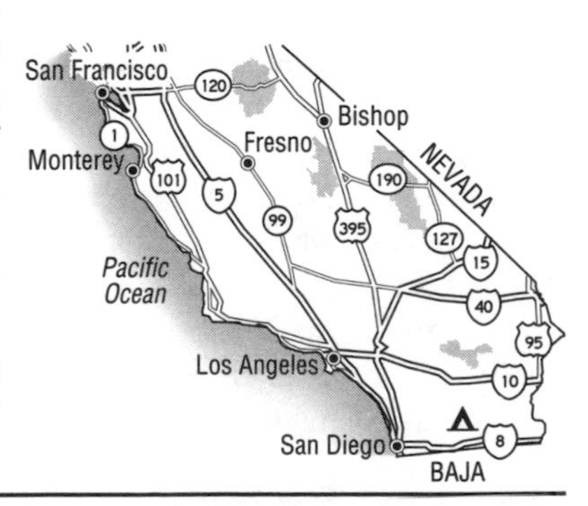

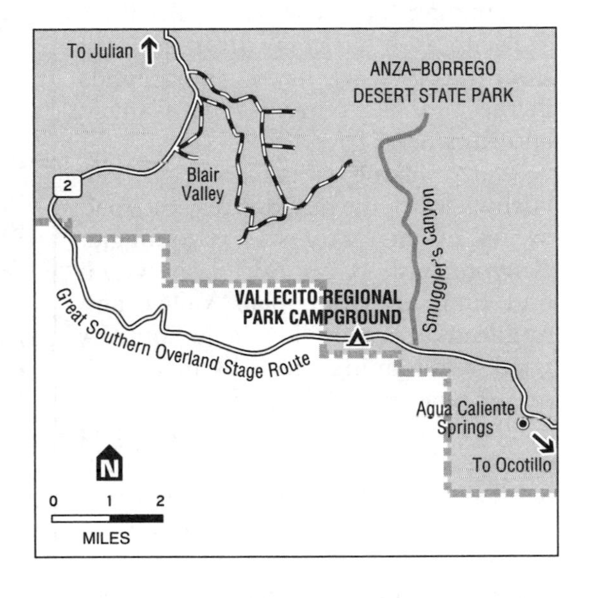

cemetery on the only high ground, the 22 tent-only spots are well away from the RV and trailer area. The rest rooms are simple and clean. The ranger, Bill Draper, is on top of everything. This is a beautiful, well-run camp! A perfect place to come with children for a first-time camping trip or to frame nights spent in Anza-Borrego Desert State Park primitive campsites.

There is a children's playground for little ones. Rabbits hop across the campground along with road runners, lizards, and quail. Bring binoculars and a bird book, as well as charcoal and grillables. If you forget, you can buy supplies at the two stores nearby—Butterfield Ranch and Agua Caliente. Both places also have swimming pools available for a small fee.

The reconstructed stage station is fascinating and full of history involving hauntings, lost gold, and murder. One man rode his white horse into the station one night and shot his brother dead at the bar. Another story tells of a young woman who came off the stagecoach and expired in the station. An elaborate wedding dress was found in her baggage. She was buried in it, and sometimes her apparition is seen wafting through the rooms of the stage station at dusk. Some days, hundreds of Conastoga wagons camped around the station as the oxen and emigrants gathered strength for the final push over the mountains.

The stagecoaches ran 24 hours a day. At night a man on horseback rode ahead carrying a lantern to light the way. A six-horse team pulled the stage. There were quick stops to change horses and only one meal per day for the passengers. The 2,800-mile trip from St. Louis to San Francisco took 24 days. Imagine over 100 miles per day in an unsprung stage! No wonder people alit in San Francisco battered and bruised and swore never to ride another stage.

The two times I've slept in the park, the place was deserted. However, the ranger warned me that on Easter or other big weekends, the park fills up. It makes sense to reserve if you are planning on camping then. The rest of the time, Vallecito is a welcome drop-in relief from the other organized campgrounds in the area like Borrego Palm Canyon and Tamarisk Grove.

Nearby hiking is available. You can bushwhack in the desert across the road or trek up the sandy wash of Smuggler Canyon. A short car ride away, you'll find Emigrant Trail, Blair Valley, and trailheads at Bow Willow in the south. A good gem-hunting trip is located south on S-2 almost to Ocotillo. On the left is Shell Canyon Road. Drive as far as you can, then hike. The canyon is filled with fossil shells and onyx. Go east on S-80 4 miles past Ocotillo and turn left on Painted Gorge Road. Again, be careful of the sand. There is agate and jasper immediately on the left and fossils in the hills to the right farther up the mountain. This is a good hike even if you aren't interested in gems.

To get there from L.A., take I-10 east to I-15. Go south to Temecula. Take CA 79 east to Julian and CA 78 down Banner Grade to Scissors Crossing. Then take S-2 about 18 miles to the park.

KEY INFORMATION

Vallecito Regional Park
Department of Parks and Recreation
5201 Ruffin Road, Suite P
San Diego, CA 92123-1699

Operated by: County of San Diego

Information: (619) 694-3049; for reservations, (619) 565-3600

Open: October to June

Individual sites: 22 for RVs, trailers, and tents; 22 for tents only

Each site has: Picnic table, barbecue, fireplace

Registration: By entrance

Facilities: Piped water, flush toilets, playground

Parking: At individual sites

Fee: $8

Elevation: 1,500 feet

Restrictions:

Pets—On 6-foot leash; must be attended at all times ($1 fee)

Fires—In established barbecue stoves or fire rings

Vehicles—RVs or trailers

Other—No generators

WHITE TANK CAMPGROUND

Joshua Tree National Park

First, we wanted to know why the arborescent tree yucca (*Yucca brevifolia*) is called the Joshua tree. I have it on good authority that a group of Mormons were laboring across the trackless wastes under a blazing sun when they entered a *Yucca brevifolia* forest. Out of nowhere a cloud blocked the sun. Did God send the cloud to stop the sun like the prophet Joshua had commanded? Apparently, for in their ecstasy, the pioneers proclaimed the strange plants Joshua trees. Indeed, the tufted branches do resemble an old, robed prophet with his hands in the air imploring the heavens for something.

Next, we taxed our bones trekking up the strenuous trail to the top of Ryan Mountain where my wife, who had stopped speaking to me on the rigorous ascent, saw the snows on Mount San Jacinto and the Little San Bernardinos and the Lost Horse Valley spread below her. Relenting graciously, she offered me some words and allowed that the carrot was worth the climb.

Then came White Tank Campground where we found a cozy campsite set in an alcove among a jumble of rocks. The pitch was soft and sandy, and boulders blocked the wind. We packed a lunch basket with white wine and fresh strawberries and set out to find White Tank. The following were our instructions: "Take the Arch Rock Trail. When you come to the sign that designates "Arch," stop and look around. To

CAMPGROUND RATINGS

Beauty:	★★★★★
Site privacy:	★★★
Site spaciousness:	★★★
Quiet:	★★★★
Security:	★★★★
Cleanliness/upkeep:	★★★★

Don't get caught alive here in the summer! Otherwise, White Tank has incredibly beautiful, dramatic winter and spring camping.

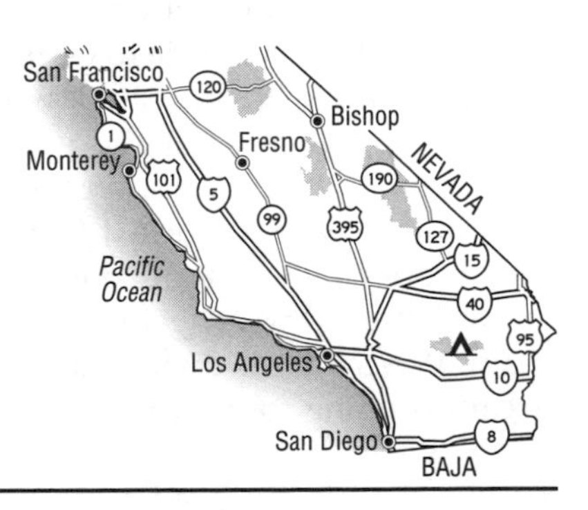

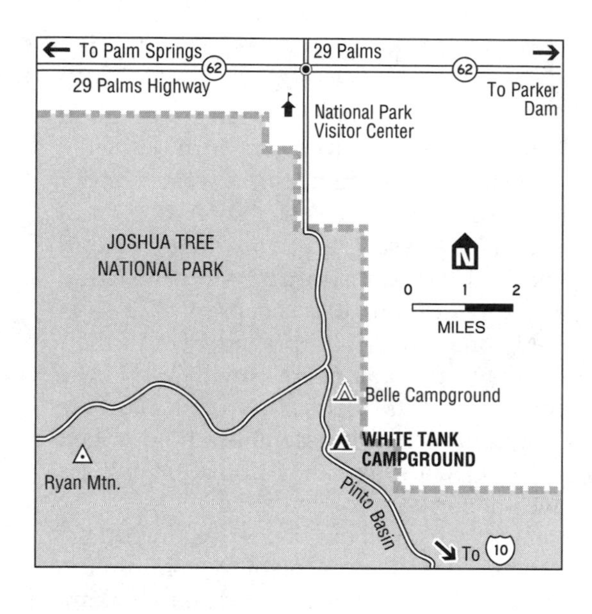

the south, 20 feet away, see the slabs of sandwiched rock. Climb over those keeping the Arch Rock on the left, and you'll come down into sandy sheltered White Tank, a prime place for a picnic." We did, and with only minimal difficulty. We learned to slide on our bottoms where the rocks were steep. The "White Tank quartz monzonite," as the boulders around here are described, sticks tight to blue jeans and sneakers and makes a hairy climb pretty easy.

White Tank lived up to its billing. It was warm in the sun and cool under the huge rocks, and the sand was as white and clean as a Bahama beach. What a lunch!

Afterward, with a load of Dutch courage, we back-tracked to the "Arch" sign. Somewhere out there was Grand Tank, which actually features a body of water with colonies of fairy and tadpole shrimp. How did they get here? The friendly ranger down at the Park H.Q. in 29 Palms told me that ancestors of the shrimp hitched a ride to Grand Tank on the feet of migrating ducks!

To find Grand Tank, head downhill from the "Arch" sign and follow a trail that goes across a wash and up a hill. It can be seen plainly from the sign. After a bit, the trail splits. We went left. "Follow the strong trail!" I urged my companions who suggested I engrave that on my tombstone. I was mocked even more when we headed up under some boulders to a dead end. Backing up, we climbed west again, up over some rocks and found the "strong trail" again. We saw birds diving into what we discovered was Grand Tank and the stream running south from it.

Vindicated at last, I identified white-winged doves and house finches circling the water. Grand Tank is about 15 feet deep. I looked in vain for the much-vaunted hitch-hiking shrimp. As the day went on, I led my group of doubting Thomases south along the stream and, searching for the "strong trail" to the right, down below the impenetrable jumble of rocks safely back to the campground.

That night was a full moon. With field glasses we examined the moon to see if the figure on the lunar surface was indeed a rabbit all curled up with long ears as the Chinese believe or, in fact, a man as has been widely advertised most of my life. Swayed perhaps by the next day being Easter Sunday, I conceded that it could be a rabbit on the moon after all.

A mile and a half back toward the Park H.Q. in 29 Palms is Belle Campground, which is just as charming as White Tank and as accessible to the California Riding and Hiking Trail that crosses Cottonwood Springs Road between the two campgrounds. The trail is good for early-morning and evening walks when the light gives the flat desert richness and texture. Along with Ryan Campground in Lost Horse Valley, Belle and White Tank make the best tent camping in Joshua Tree. The other Joshua Tree campgrounds are overrun by RVs and rock climbers in fall and spring, which is the only time you want to be caught alive in this part of the world.

To get there from L.A., take I-10 east to CA 62 past Banning over the San Gorgonio Pass. Go north and east to 29 Palms. Drive 8 miles south on the Utah Trail to the intersection with Cottonwood Springs Road. Then go left (south) 1.5 miles to the campground.

KEY INFORMATION

Joshua Tree National Park
74485 National Park Drive
29 Palms, CA 92277

Operated by: U.S. Department of the Interior

Information: (619) 367-7511

Open: Closed in summer

Individual sites: 17

Each site has: Picnic table, fireplace

Registration: Not required

Facilities: Pit toilets, *no piped water*

Parking: At site

Fee: None

Elevation: 3,800 feet

Restrictions:

Pets—On leash

Fires—In fireplaces (bring your own firewood or charcoal)

Vehicles—RVs up to 27 feet

Other—All vegetation in park protected

It's not a bad idea to check the weather report before you come to Joshua Tree. The wind comes as Santa Anas in the fall and from the coast in the winter bringing rain. When it really blows, you must decide whether to tie your tent to the car or actually get into the car. Sometimes it will blow for days—sometimes hours.

In either case, you can go for lunch or dinner at the wonderfully idiosyncratic 29 Palms Inn adjacent to the Park H.Q. on the Oasis of Mara, which was 29 Palm's original raison d'être. The food is great. Walk around and look at the ducks on the pond and the beautiful truck garden fenced by palm fronds, which provides greens and vegetables for the restaurant. Some of the guest cabins were miners' cabins from the old days. This place has a rustic, western ambience. It's a great place to have a beer and let the wind blow itself away.

SOUTHERN CALIFORNIA

THE NORTHERN SIERRAS

ATWELL MILL CAMPGROUND

Mineral King, Sequoia National Park

Drive through torrid Visalia on any July afternoon and you'll know why the Yokut and Monache Native Americans fought over the summer camps by Atwell Mills where it is pleasant during the day and cool at night. They built little round thatched houses and carpeted the floor with oak leaves and ferns. The women gathered most of the food, and the men spent most of their time in the sweat house telling lies. Summer was a time of plenty for them with pine nuts, fish, manzanita cider, wild tobacco, and an occasional deer. The deer were stalked by one man alone in a deer disguise using arrows poisoned with rattle-snake venom. The Native Americans here led a great life, but it went like the wind when the white man appeared on the scene hot after the riches of Mineral King.

The road up to Atwell Mill follows the old Native American trail. It's steep, but near Atwell Mill the ground levels out. This is one of the few areas around flat enough to camp and work on. A.J. Atwell of Visalia thought so as well and built a small sawmill in the meadow below the campground. You can still see the remains of the steam engine near the stumps of the giant sequoias that it helped reduce to shingles, grape stakes, and fence posts.

Steam engines tore their way through the American West. Anywhere there was fuel for the boiler, the engine could do the work of hundreds of men. The Native Americans

CAMPGROUND RATINGS

Beauty:	★★★★★
Site privacy:	★★★★★
Site spaciousness:	★★★★★
Quiet:	★★★★
Security:	★★★★★
Cleanliness/upkeep:	★★★★★

Native Americans loved Atwell Mill, and so will you. This campground is one of the two best backcountry campgrounds in Sequoia and Kings Canyon National Parks.

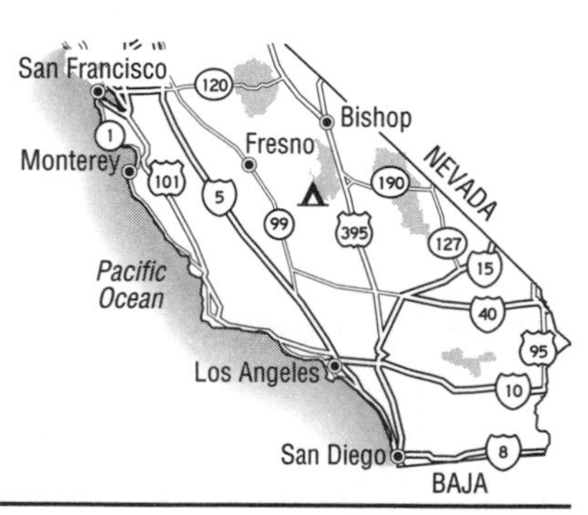

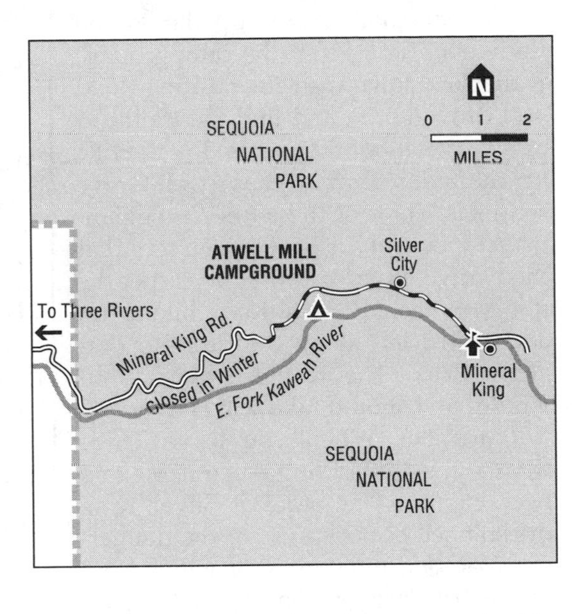

thought it was a devil, and, for them, I think it was.

Folks knew the how of the steam engine devil for a thousand years before they could make iron plate durable enough for steam boilers. It took a boom economy in England in 1600 to accomplish this. People suddenly bought more kitchen utensils. One particular black-smith experimented with burning coke in order to make a better frying pan and discovered the process that brought us the high-grade iron that makes the boiler that feeds the steam engine that runs the saw that chewed up the big trees at Atwell Mill and spelled the end of the Native American way of life.

Still, there's a magic to Atwell Mill. It's in the huge stumps left over from a hundred years ago and in the scars the loggers left as they cut down the trees. It's in the young sequoias reaching up for the sun by the stumps under the shade of cedars, pines, and white firs. This is classic big-tree mountain camping.

All winter, the campsites are cleansed by 20 feet of snow. In the summer, the air smells clean and rich with the odor of redwood and pine. Walk up the little ridge above the campground and watch the sun set on the mountains across the Kaweah River. Or better yet, head down the Atwell Hockett Trail between campsites #16 and #17. The trail passes the supine steam engine on the right and heads over the hill. Exactly 129 steps from the metal sign banning firearms and dogs, go to the right about 30 yards down to the famous Native American bathtubs. The rock outcropping there is a great place to have lunch or a sundowner. There, manzanita opens up the forest to give you a great view of the mountains and sky.

Back on the main trail, carry on past little Deadwood Creek to East Fork Kaweah River gorge with its giant sequoias and mist kicked up by the falls. Rough trails head up either side of the gorge for more private picnicking and sunning spots. Or, keep walking up the trail toward Hockett Meadows many long miles away until your dogs give out.

Another good hike is up the Atwell Redwood Trail. From the campground, walk back down the Mineral King Road you drove up on and find the trailhead at a curve about 500 yards down. Hike up the mountain into the Atwell Grove sequoias. Three of these trees are gigantic. At their feet are the bracken fern that the Native Americans used to carpet the floors of their houses. Keep hiking up and to the left along the ridge to Paradise Peak. The round-trip is about 9 miles and should take you all day.

Remember. When you leave Three Rivers you are bidding adieu to ice and beer country. The store at Silver King doesn't sell beer because of the dangerous road out, and their ice machine went on the fritz last year. So, ice up. Remember, block ice lasts about three days to cube ice's one day. Think about buying an extra cheap Styrofoam cooler at Three Rivers and filling it with block ice. Tape the cooler closed, and the ice will last until you need it to replenish the other cooler.

To get there from L.A., take I-5 north over the Tejon Pass to CA 99. Drive north on CA 99 past Bakersfield. Take CA 65 north to Exeter. Go east (right) on CA 198 to Three Rivers. Three miles past Three Rivers turn right on the Mineral King Road. It's about 20 miles to Atwell Mill. Plan on the 20-mile trip taking 1½ hours.

KEY INFORMATION

Atwell Mill Campground
Superintendent Michael J. Tollefson
Sequoia and Kings Canyon National Parks
Three Rivers, CA 93271

Operated by: Department of the Interior, National Park Service

Information: (209) 565-3341

Open: May to September (depending on road and weather conditions)

Individual sites: 21 tent sites

Each site has: Picnic table, fireplace

Registration: At entrance

Facilities: Piped water, pit toilets

Parking: At site

Fee: $5 (reservations not accepted)

Elevation: 6,650 feet

Restrictions:

Pets—Allowed on leash (no pets on trails)

Fires—Allowed in fireplaces

Vehicles—No RVs or trailers

Other—Don't leave food out—use bear boxes

Look for the sign where the Mineral King Road takes off from CA 198. It should tell you if Atwell Mills and Cold Springs have campsites available. Since this sign is mechanical and not always up to date, phone the Ranger Station up in Mineral King to make sure at (209) 565-3341. It *is* a three-hour round-trip, so you don't want to arrive and not find a campsite. On the Mineral King Road turn your lights on. It helps on-coming traffic see you a split second earlier, which means a lot on this hairy road. Bring bug repellent in August to deter biting pests. And, remember to use the bear boxes!

BIG PINE CREEK CAMPGROUND

Big Pine Creek, Inyo National Forest

Eat breakfast in the town of Big Pine at the Country Kitchen where owners Jim and Liz serve up the morning special of one egg and a couple sausages in tandem with the tour de force—biscuits and gravy! I love biscuits and gravy, and so do all the cowpokes from miles around. This is real food, and you don't need teeth to chew it, either. I don't know what the gravy is made from, nor do I particularly want to know, but that gravy in the right belly at the right time could inspire sonnets, fight wars, and punch cows. It's the fuel that won the West.

Camp at Big Pine Creek Campground, hike the surrounding trails, and sleep like the righteous. Definitely on my hit parade, this campground is impossibly beautiful. Jump out of your tent in the morning to see the ice and snow on the Palisades, the southernmost active glacier in North America. The canyon walls are steep and gray and trimmed in light green. On the canyon floor Jeffrey pines shadow Big Pine Creek and the hopeful fisherman.

A couple hundred yards away is Glacier Lodge where you can buy ice, beer, and sundries. On Sunday, there is a barbecue on the front steps of the lodge if you're tired of camp cooking. Or, drive the easy 9 miles back to the town of Big Pine and eat at Rossi's Steak and Spaghetti. The Rossi family has been around for generations, and mementos of their lives adorn the

CAMPGROUND RATINGS

Beauty:	★★★★★
Site privacy:	★★★★★
Site spaciousness:	★★★★★
Quiet:	★★★
Security:	★★★★★
Cleanliness/upkeep:	★★★★★

Big Pine Creek Campground might just be my favorite campground. Come for good fishing, superb hiking, and leisurely camping.

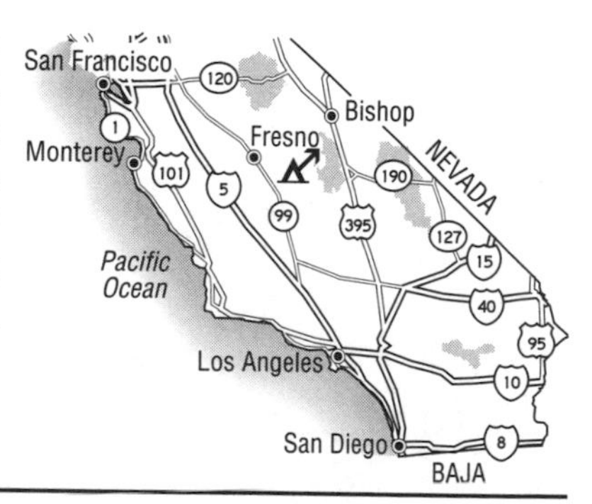

walls of the restaurant. Meat from the local ranches is served at your table. cowpokes come in for a brewski on Sunday afternoons in the adjoining bar where the beams are branded with the irons of local spreads. Folks come in and dance in the back room. Everybody knows everybody else, and pretty soon you do, too.

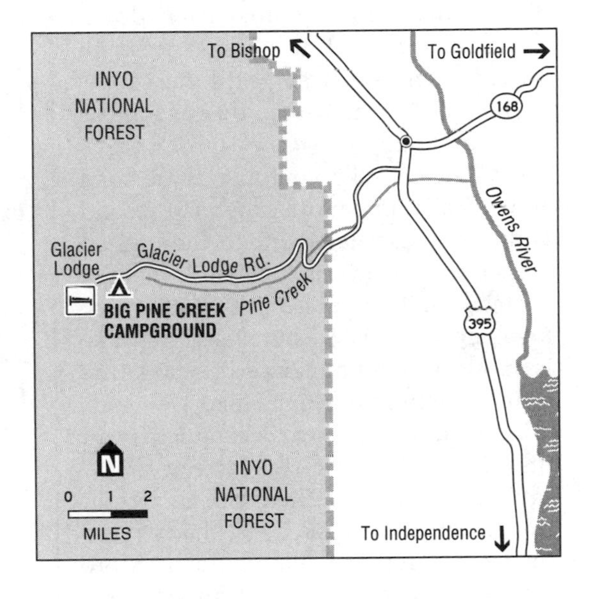

Drive back up to Big Pine Campground. Notice the large lateral moraines (ridges of dirt, gravel, and rock deposited by the glaciers). Notice how the glaciers carved out the U-shaped upper valley back in the ice ages. What happened is that cooler temperatures and heavy precipitation meant that winter snows didn't melt completely in the summer, so the snow fields grew larger and deeper until their weight turned old snow into glacial ice. Gravity tugged, and inevitably the glaciers became rivers of ice moving slowly downhill. They cut out steep cirques, stair-step lake basins, and, of course, U-shaped valleys.

As the glaciers lumbered down, they picked up boulders and rocks along the way. This rubble was deposited when the glacier melted. Ridges of the debris were formed along the edges and at the end point of the glacier. These big glaciers are all gone now. The glacier we see above Big Pine Campground, the Palisade Glacier, is a remnant from a mini ice age about 4,000 years ago.

Above the campground, the north and south forks of Big Pine Creek tumble down from the glaciers and flow together under the bridge in front of Glacier Lodge. The divided north and south canyons rise steeply from the lodge to the Sierra Crest. You can see Middle Palisade, Disappointment Peak, Clyde Peak, and Palisade Crest from here.

A fun, short walk leads up to First Falls. Go across the bridge in front of the lodge and to the left up the road around the locked gate. Walk between the creek and private cabins on the right. Cross the bridge at the base of the falls and take the stone stairway to the right. Climb up through the woods to the old road (closed by an avalanche) and another wooden bridge. This is called Trail Camp. There are picnic tables and rest rooms. You can hike back down along the old road. It crosses the south fork and winds its way past some cabins to the lodge. Round-trip, this walk lasts about an hour.

For a longer hike, continue up the road above Trail Camp into a canyon to Second Falls. You can take either the signed Upper Trail or stay on the road leading to a steep trail on the right. Both come together above the Second Falls. This hike is about one-and-a-half additional hours round-trip from the First Falls.

Keep climbing above Second Falls and find Lon Chaney's (the screen actor) cabin built in 1925. The creek goes right by the cabin. This is a good shady place to lie around and have lunch. More ambitious hikers can head for Brainard Lake, Willow Lake, and the Finger Lakes toward Sierra Crest or 1st Lake through 7th Lake in the other direction. On all hikes, remember, you're up there at 7,700 feet and above. It's very dry. Drink water before you're thirsty.

Big Pine Creek Campground is very comfortable and easily suitable for a

To get there from L.A., take I-5 north to CA 14. Go north to U.S. 395 near Inyokern. Continue north on U.S. 395 for 108 miles to the town of Big Pine. From Big Pine, go west on Glacier Lodge Road and drive 9 miles to the Lodge and Big Pine Creek Campground.

KEY INFORMATION

Big Pine Creek Campground, Inyo National Forest
White Mountain Ranger District
873 North Main Street
Bishop, CA 93514

Operated by: U.S. Department of Agriculture, Forest Service

Information: (619) 873-2500

Open: May to mid-October

Individual sites: 30

Each site has: Picnic table, fireplace

Registration: At entrance

Facilities: Piped water, pit toilets

Parking: At site

Fee: $9; for reservations phone (800) 280-CAMP ($7.50 fee)

Elevation: 7,700 feet

Restrictions:

Pets—Allowed on leash

Fires—In fireplace

Vehicles—No limit

week's stay. The pit toilets are clean. The sites are mostly private and separated from one another by trees. The campground host and hostess were very conscientious. The host ran around on his motorbike and policed empty campsites for cigarette butts, while the hostess and her killer Scottie dog ran the show from the trailer. If you arrive and find Pine Creek Campground loaded, just head back down the road to Upper Sage Flat (21 sites) or Sage Flat (28 sites). Both campgrounds are on the creek and almost as beautiful as Big Pine Creek Campground.

You must book National Forest Campgrounds at least ten days in advance. The reservation number, (800) 280-CAMP, is often busy. Rangers advised me that the best time to phone is between 4–6 P.M. Pacific time, since the office is in the East where it's 7–9 P.M., an off-peak time for them.

BUCKEYE FLAT CAMPGROUND

Sequoia National Park

Buckeye Flat is a good sleeping campground. The sun comes up over the mountains behind you, and it's good snoozing until about 10 A.M. The rushing cataract of the Middle Fork of the Kaweah River supplies comforting white noise. And, with only tent camping allowed, there is no morning TV or hum of a generator from a nearby RV.

Then, you crawl out of the mummy bag into a beautiful world. Morning mists swirl about the high peaks and green slopes. Peer down at the Kaweah River and see a gorge out of the movie *Last of the Mohicans*. Walk the narrow campground access road, and even that is beautiful. Paralleling the gorge, it was built by the Civilian Conservation Corps in the 1930s when men could still work with rock.

In May, when the buckeyes or horse chestnuts around the campground bloom, they seem tipped with pom-poms. By late August, the leaves fall, and the trees show the pear-like seed pods hanging from their bare branches. The Native Americans used the chestnut meat in much the same way they did acorns—by repeatedly leaching and drying the meal until edible. It was also used as a fish poison. Apparently, a mash of horse chestnuts thrown into a small stream would stupify the fish, so they would float to the surface and be taken by nets.

CAMPGROUND RATINGS

Beauty:	★★★★★
Site privacy:	★★★
Site spaciousness:	★★★
Quiet:	★★★★★
Security:	★★★★★
Cleanliness/upkeep:	★★★★★

Buckeye Flat Campground, like a scene out of Last of the Mohicans, *is by a magical gorge. Use the bear boxes!*

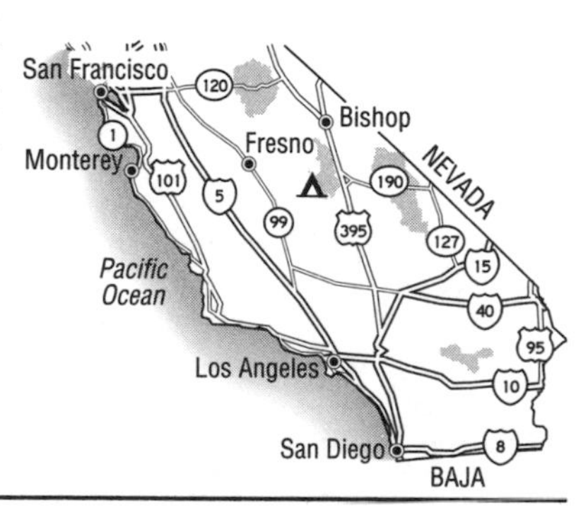

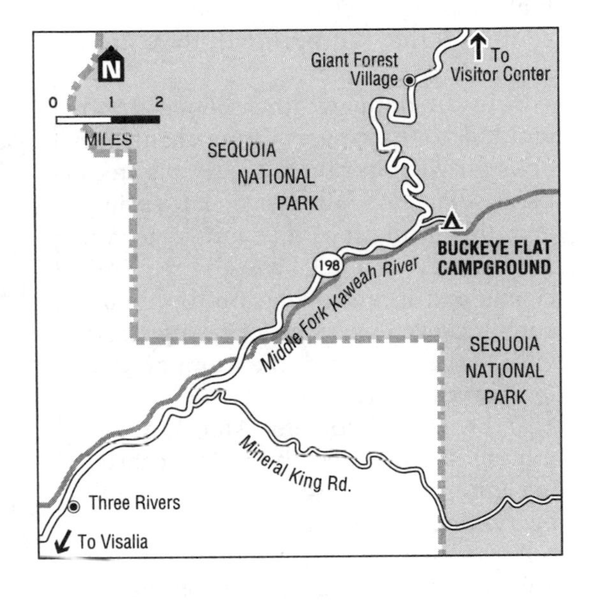

Don't expect to see any sequoias around Buckeye Campground. The big trees are up much higher—above 5,000 feet. The sequoia is the earth's largest living thing. (Termites compose the earth's largest biomass, however!) The tree reproduces by seed, and that seed is the size of a corn flake. Imagine.

Once growing all over the western United States—even as far south as the Santa Monica Mountains—the *Sequoiadendron giganteum* needed too much moisture. After the last ice age, the climate grew too dry for the big fellow, and he retreated to 75 groves on the western slope of the Sierra. Useless for anything but fence posts and shake shingles, the huge sequoias (named after a Native American, Sequoyah, who established an alphabet for the Cherokee language) were threatened by loggers in the jolly days of the West when anything that was big had to fall. "God has cared for these trees . . . but He cannot save them from fools. Only Uncle Sam can do that" (John Muir). And thank God, Uncle Sam did, in 1890, by establishing the Sequoia National Park.

Buckeye Flat offers good spring camping. Plan to visit when it opens in April and combine cross-country skiing on the mountain with camping and wildflowers lower down. (Buckeye has an elevation of 2,800 feet.) There are places to rent skis and groomed trails at Lodgepole. Buy the *Wildflowers* book at the Park Visitors Center and see how many you can identify. At the beginning of May, we saw yucca, buttercup, milkweed, sunflowers, purple lupine, and ceanothus (wild lilac), as well as the white flowers of the buckeye.

The first thing you'll notice about the campsites at Buckeye are the steel bear boxes. Use them! Keep your food in them at all times. Bring along a padlock and you can leave your valuables in there as well. There is water, but it's heavily chlorinated, so bring drinking water. The flush toilet bathrooms are spare and spotless. Considering the campground is on a mountainside, there are good flat places on each site to pitch tents. Don't forget to take the trail just south of the campground that goes along Paradise Creek.

Be aware of the weather. Phone ahead and talk to the rangers. Bring chains for your tires if you want to see the big trees because it snows here even in late spring, and they will stop you and turn you around if you don't have the required chains and it is snowing up top. Make sure Buckeye Flat is open. On August 10, 1995, rangers closed the campground temporarily because of a troublesome bear breaking into cars. And, buy last minute stuff at Three Rivers. This charming little mountain town has just about everything you could need.

A great drive on the way out is down Yokohl Drive through the Yokohl Valley to Springville. This is old California—a thin strip of asphalt running along the Yokohl through cattle country. This was the trail the mule teams followed coming from San Francisco to supply the Cerro Gordo mine over the Sierras in the Owens Valley. There was water and grass for the mules. And, the native grass in those days was green year-round. So much for the golden hills of California, which arrived only with the competing European seasonal grasses brought in by early ranchers.

KEY INFORMATION

Buckeye Flat Campground
Superintendent Michael J. Tollefson
Sequoia and Kings Canyon National Parks
Three Rivers, CA 93271

Operated by: Department of the Interior, National Parks Service

Information: (209) 565-3134; Weather (NPS), (209) 565-3351;

California Road Conditions (CALTRANS), (800) 427-7673

Open: April to October (depending on road and weather conditions)

Individual sites: 28 tent sites

Each site has: Picnic tables, fireplaces, bear boxes

Registration: At entrance

Facilities: Piped water, flush toilets

Parking: At site

Fee: $10

Elevation: 2,800 feet

Restrictions:

Pets—Allowed on leashes

Fires—In fireplaces

Vehicles—No RVs or trailers

Other—Don't leave food out; use bear boxes

To get there from L.A., take I-5 north over the Tejon Pass to CA 99. Drive north on CA 99 past Bakersfield. Take CA 65 north to Exeter. Go east (right) on CA 198 to Three Rivers. Continue to the CA 198 entrance to Sequoia National Park. Drive 6 miles into the park and take the signed mile-long side road on the right to the campground.

COLD SPRINGS CAMPGROUND

Mineral King, Sequoia National Park

Cold Springs Campground is the most beautiful campground in Southern California. Down by the gorgeous Kaweah River, this campground is situated in the shadows of Sawtooth and Mineral peaks, Needham and Rainbow mountains, and to the south, Miners Ridge. The sky is blue, and the air shines. Winter scours out the valley so it feels brand-new every summer. A cataract cuts through the walk-in camping area. The rush of the water is white noise; you'll sleep like a baby. I love this campground.

CAMPGROUND RATINGS

Beauty:	★★★★★
Site privacy:	★★★★★
Site spaciousness:	★★★★★
Quiet:	★★★★★
Security:	★★★★★
Cleanliness/upkeep:	★★★★★

This is the most beautiful campground in the Sequoia and Kings Canyon National Park. Check available space before driving up Mineral King Road—it's a bear!

Back in the 1870s the miners took one look at the rocks in Mineral King and rushed in. What excited them was metamorphosed rocks. This is the contact zone between reddish metamorphics and grayish granite. You can see it all over the mountainsides above the campgrounds.

So sure of silver was Thomas Fowler, a wealthy rancher from Tulare County, that he bet his entire fortune on the Empire Mine in Mineral King. He boasted that with his bonanza he would pay off the national debt of America and then buy Ireland and free it from the tyrannical British. First, Fowler built the road into Mineral King. Waiting for it to open in the last days were 150 wagons filled with merchandise. Fowler had the workmen carry his buckboard over the last quarter mile so he could be the first man to drive into Mineral King. A local reporter described

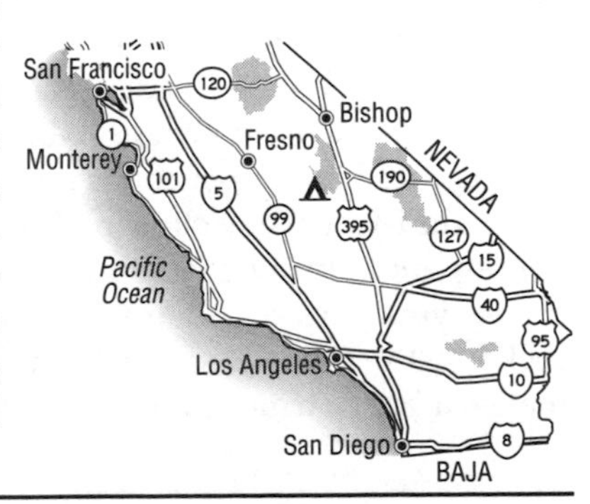

the moment. "I doubt that General Grant felt more proud when he rode into Richmond than did honest Tom Fowler when he rode into Mineral King . . . "

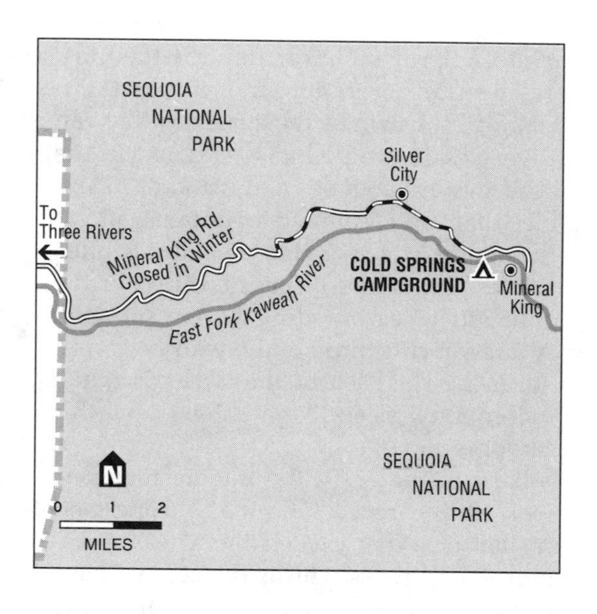

Of course, the mine went bust. Avalanches swept away his mine, the town, and the mile-long bucket tramway to the stamp mill in the valley. All that was left of Fowler's dream was the road, and folks used it to get away from the brutal heat down in the Central Valley below. In 1893, the federal government declared the area part of the Sierra Forest Preserve, and recreational cabin sites were leased to various people.

In the 1960s, the Forest Service entertained the idea of building a major ski resort at Mineral King. The Walt Disney Corporation proposed restaurants and hotels with a skiing capacity of 10,000 persons daily. (All this leverage coming from a cartoon mouse—the cattle rancher, Thomas Fowler, would have had trouble with that!) There was widespread opposition and law suits from environmental groups, and finally, in 1978, Congress made Mineral King part of Sequoia National Park.

Now, about the marmots. Mineral King is famous for its marmots. These little devils have a penchant for gnawing on auto parts from early spring to about mid-July. They chew on hoses, fan belts, and electrical wiring to get salt. Some people bring chicken wire to put around their cars. This is ineffective, unless you park on a hard surface and seal the edges of the wire with piled rocks, so the marmots can't dig their way in. Otherwise, your chicken wire just makes a big marmot playpen.

Why don't the rangers put out salt licks? Because this would attract deer, and deer attract mountain lions. The way to combat these pumped-up car-eating squirrels is not to park your car in marmot territory in early spring. Leave your car down in the hikers' parking lot in Atwell Mill Campground and get a lift up to the trailheads in Mineral King. As the summer progresses, marmot-safe parking territory reaches higher altitudes until it is safe to park at the trailheads in Mineral King. It's a good idea to phone the rangers for the latest marmot car-chewing activity. You don't want to have to get towed down to Three Rivers unless you have a loose $250.

Don't hate the humble marmot. He's a brave little rodent who will stand up and fight when cornered. With hair standing on end and long claws at the ready, the feisty marmot clatters his sharp teeth and hisses loudly at the enemy. Marmots are not to be trifled with.

Listen for their whistle and look for them in the early morning when they take a sunbath on the boulders above their burrow. They are short and stocky and hibernate during the winter. Car-chewing aside, they are God's creatures and are superbly created to survive in a harsh environment. Their bodies afford "clear and cogent arguments of the wisdom and design of the Author" (Robert Boyle, 1688). And, it's against federal

To get there from L.A., take I-5 north over the Tejon Pass to CA 99. Drive north on CA 99 past Bakersfield. Take CA 65 north to Exeter. Go east (right) on CA 198 to Three Rivers. Three miles past Three Rivers turn right onto Mineral King Road. It's about 25 miles to Cold Springs Campground. Plan on the 25-mile trip taking 1½ hours.

KEY INFORMATION

Cold Springs Campground, Sequoia National Park
Superintendent Michael J. Tollefson
Sequoia and Kings Canyon National Parks
Three Rivers, CA 93271

Operated by: Department of the Interior

Information: (209) 565-3341

Open: May to September (depending on road and weather conditions)

Individual sites: 40 tent sites

Each site has: Picnic table, fireplace

Registration: At entrance

Facilities: Piped water, pit toilets

Parking: At site

Fee: $5 (reservations not accepted)

Elevation: 7,500 feet

Restrictions:

Pets—Allowed on leash (no pets on trails)

Fires—Allowed in fireplaces

Vehicles—No RVs or trailers

Other—No marmot molesting

law to use poison or other substances to kill, deter, or otherwise foil marmots from car-gnawing.

Remember to get ice and beer in Three Rivers. The store in Silver City (near Cold Springs Campground) doesn't sell beer because of the perilous Mineral King Road. They don't sell ice either, since their ice machine ran amok. Buy block ice in Three Rivers because it lasts three times as long as cube ice. Bring a gunny sack or an orange bag and put your beer and soda in it. Tie a rope to it and leave it in the Kaweah River. That'll chill the cans.

Think about using the walk-in campsites at Cold Springs. They are quite spectacular nestled in a corner between the Kaweah River and a cataract that pours down to the river. To access the walk-ins, take the second right loop and follow it to the parking lot at the end. It's not a bad idea to bring rucksacks to carry your stuff the hundred yards or so into the sites. There is piped water and a pit toilet in among the sites.

A trail (round-trip 3 miles) heading east from the Cold Springs Campground (trailhead between sites #6 and #7) directs you along a signed Nature Trail. I found out that corn lilies are also called skunk cabbage and that juniper seeds need to be partially digested by birds in order to sprout, which means they grow far away from the parent tree. Stay on the trail, which hits a road to the right of Mineral King Village and arrives at the trailhead for Tufa Falls (another easy hike) and other destinations heading up Farewell Canyon.

Plan on spending more than a day or so in Mineral King. Atwell Mill is worth at least a day or two, and you could spend most of the summer hiking out of Cold Springs Campground. Give yourself a day or two to get used to the altitude. If you get a headache or nausea, stop hiking and head down to the campground to rest and get acclimated. Relax. Mineral King is a wonderful place.

DORST CAMPGROUND

Kings Canyon National Park

Dorst Campground is about family. What you'll notice first are the squads of juniors splashing in the nonthreatening Dorst Creek or racing up and down the grassy slopes, and, then, the pretty moms pushing their infants around in strollers. Most of the folks are tent campers laagered together in the tent-only loops, and their children become friends quickly. I saw lots of dads relaxing in aluminum lawn chairs, free, happy, on liberty at last.

On the Generals Highway, Dorst is a perfect base camp from which to explore Giant Forest, Grant Grove, and, farther afield, Cedar Grove. Not too far away is Hume Lake with big-time swimming prospects for the wee bairn. A quick run will get you groceries or restaurant grits at Lodgepole or Stony Creek Lodge.

Kings Canyon National Park is insanely beautiful. An early explorer, William Brewer, wrote of the area: "Such a landscape! A hundred peaks in sight over thirteen thousand feet—many very sharp, deep canyons, cliffs in every direction almost rivaling Yosemite, sharp ridges almost inaccessible to man, on which human foot has never trod—all combined to produce a view the subliminity of which is rarely equal, one which few are privileged to behold."

The Park Service has fought hard to keep it that way. In fact, one of their biggest fights was against sheep. The mountains

CAMPGROUND RATINGS

Beauty:	★★★★
Site privacy:	★★★
Site spaciousness:	★★★★
Quiet:	★★★★
Security:	★★★★
Cleanliness/upkeep:	★★★★★

Dorst Campground is a good summer family campground with wonderful side trips. Stay at least three days.

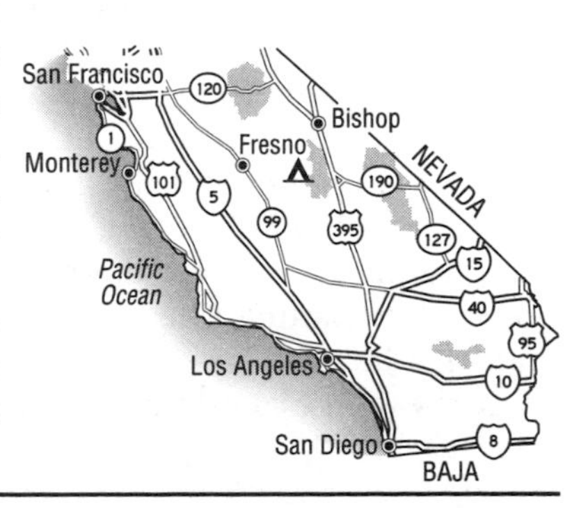

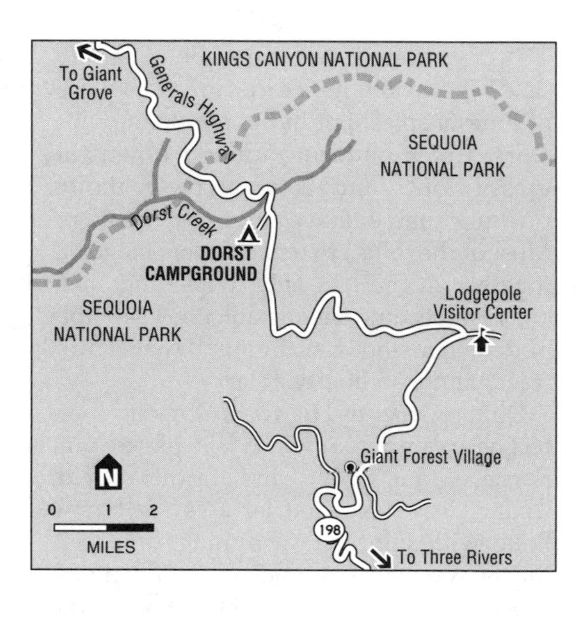

were perfect for sheepherding. The sheep ran amok through the forests eating everything in sight, ripping it all up by the roots. Kings Canyon was becoming a high-altitude desert. The park superintendent called out the U.S. Cavalry, and still the sheep and sheepherders kept coming. Only when the superintendent hit on the strategy of kicking the sheep off on one side of the Sierras and the sheepherders on the other side was the ovine feeding frenzy discouraged.

A great hike from Dorst Campground leads to the Muir Grove of giant sequoias. Even if you poke along, the round-trip shouldn't take more than four hours. Find the trailhead at the Dorst Campground amphitheater (follow the beehive symbol west). The trail is signed and leads you up through white firs and sugar pines, then over a ridge to the Muir Grove giants. The good news is that the return trip is mostly downhill.

Another nearby hike is up Little Baldy. The trailhead is 1.6 miles south of the Dorst Campground entrance on Generals Highway. Park in the pull-off area at the Little Baldy Saddle and head northeast. Two hard miles later you're on the bare granite Little Baldy summit. It's not a great place to be in a thunderstorm, but it's fine for lying in the noon sun.

If you get tired of Dorst Campground family fun, or if you arrive and the campground is full, an alternative place to camp is in the Sierra National Forest surrounding Kings Canyon National Park. Leave Dorst Campground and turn left up Generals Highway toward Grant Grove. Turn right on Big Meadow Road and drive about 5 miles to Big Meadows Campground

Number 3. Pass up Big Meadows Campground Number 1 and Number 2. These areas are more heavily used and not as pretty. Below Number 3, Boulder Creek spills down rocky chutes and gathers in pools. There is good dipping there, but be careful. The rock is slippery.

Or, pick up a fire permit as you pass the Hume Lake Forest Service Station on CA 180, and you can camp anywhere you want in the areas off Big Meadow Road. The last time I was in the area, I picked up a USGS map and drove up all the fire roads scouting good dispersed camping spots. There are literally thousands of wonderful sites where you can hunker down for the night.

Stay on Big Meadow Road until you get to Horse Corral Meadow. Drive carefully because the road is definitely white knuckle. In 1922, a cowpoke named Jessie Agnew killed the last grizzly bear in California there claiming it was after his cattle. Imagine, killing the last California grizzly, our state animal!

Back at Big Meadows Campground, look for a brown, Fiberglas post marking a trailhead. From here, you can hike up to Weaver Lake or Jennie Lake. Take the trail in for about 2 miles to Fox Meadow where there's a small wooden sign and a trail register. Weaver Lake is straight ahead. The trail to Jennie Lake heads south, to the right. Weaver is about 1.5 miles farther, while Jennie is about 5 miles.

The best way into Dorst Campground is up CA 180 from Fresno. The other

To get there from L.A., take I-5 north over the Tejon Pass to CA 99. Drive north on CA 99 to Fresno. Turn right on CA 198 and drive to Kings Canyon National Park. Turn right (south) on Generals Highway and drive 16 miles to Dorst Campground on the right.

KEY INFORMATION

Dorst Campground, Sequoia National Park
Superintendent Michael J. Tollefson
Sequoia and Kings Canyon National Parks
Three Rivers, CA 93271

Operated by: National Park Service, U.S. Department of the Interior

Information: (209) 565-3341

Open: June to September (depending on road and snow conditions)

Individual sites: 219

Each site has: Picnic table, fireplace, sometimes bear boxes

Registration: At entrance

Facilities: Piped water, flush toilets

Parking: At site

Fee: $10 (reservations not accepted)

Elevation: 6,700 feet

Restrictions:

Pets—Allowed on leash

Fires—In fireplace

Vehicles—No limits

Other—Don't leave food out—use bear boxes if on site

road in, through Three Rivers, is a bear. It's narrow, slow, and scary. When you arrive at Dorst Campground, check out all the loops. I camped in a loop allowing trailers and found the campsite much roomier and more private than the sites on the tent-only loops. Here at Dorst, the architect packed in the tent sites much tighter than the sites in the RV/trailer loops.

Try to camp at Dorst long enough to relax and get to know the area. I think three days is a minimum. One day just doesn't get it. By the time you unpack, do the camp chores, and pack again, there isn't time to do more than get familiar with your own campsite. Camping has its own clock, and it runs slow. Stay three days at Dorst Campground, and it will seem like home. Stay a day, and it will be a blur.

EAST FORK CAMPGROUND

Inyo National Forest

Driving from Los Angeles to East Fork, you'll go through Mojave, the desert, and then the Owens Valley, a *graben* according to geologists, which means it's a 100-mile-long, 5-mile-wide trench between the Sierras on the west and the White-Inyo Mountains on the east. It's a magical place, and the Native Americans coined the name *Inyo* meaning "dwelling place of the great spirit."

It is a land of dramatic contrast and incredible beauty, where mountain and desert meld into breathtaking scenery and glaciered peaks tower over shimmering alkali flats. Tumbling mountain streams become lost in the desert, and gem-like lakes shimmer against deep pine forests.

East Fork Campground on Rock Creek lies right in the heart of the beast. Rock Creek is in a glacial cirque (basin) and drops 6,000 feet and 20 miles to the Owens River. On the way to East Fork, you'll pass Bishop (the last good town for shopping); don't forget to stop at Mahogany Smoked Meats on U.S. 395 as you leave town. Buy some smoked pork chops for that night's dinner. Gnaw on some world-famous slab jerky as you drive up the infamous Sherwin Grade (or Vaporlock Grade as the old-timers called it). You'll climb 24 miles and about 3,000 feet up to Tom's Place where you will turn south on Rock Creek Road.

CAMPGROUND RATINGS

Beauty:	★★★★★
Site privacy:	★★★★★
Site spaciousness:	★★★
Quiet:	★★★
Security:	★★★★★
Cleanliness/upkeep:	★★★★★

Some say Rock Creek features the best camping in the Sierras. Don't forget the beef jerky in Bishop and the gut-plug pancakes at Tom's Place.

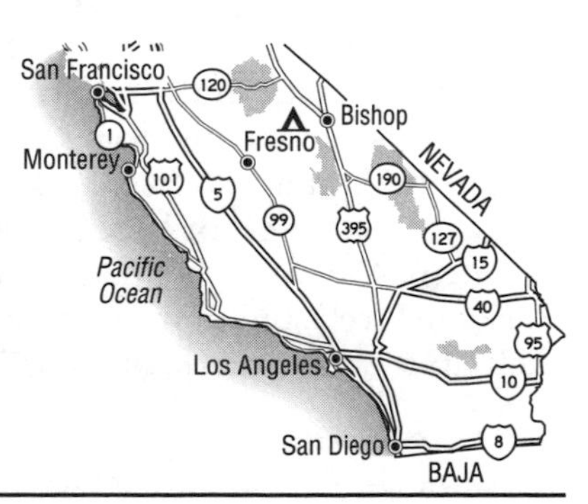

Stop at Tom's Place. It's a restaurant/store/bar/cabin complex where you can get fishing information and the bait the trout are hitting that day. You can buy last-minute camping supplies or eat some of the gut-plug pancakes for breakfast or chicken fried steak with gravy for dinner.

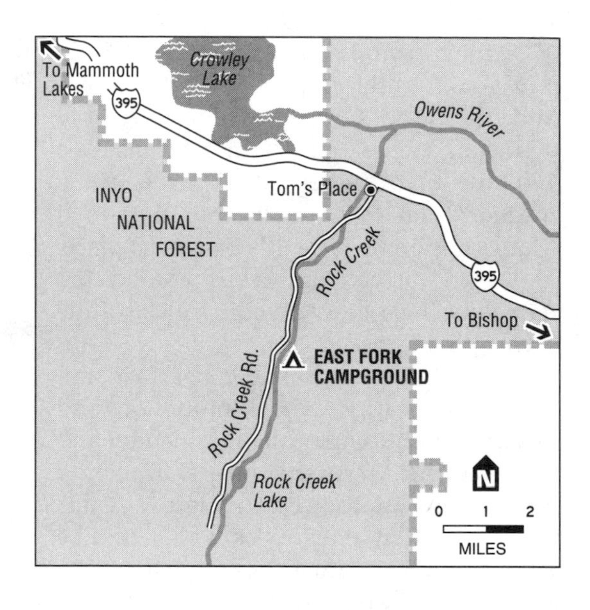

Head up Rock Creek Road. Pass French Camp Campground. It's a lovely campground by the creek. It's almost 1,500 feet lower than East Fork Campground, which makes it a good place to camp in the spring when the flowers are out down below and East Fork is still socked in with winter cold. At East Fork Campground the bloom arrives later in the summer.

As Owens Valley writer, Mary Austin, observed, "Well up from the valley, at the confluence of canyons, are delectable summer meadows. Fireweed flames about them against gray boulders; streams are open, go smoothly about the glacier slips and make deep bluish pools for trout. Pines raise statelier shafts and give themselves room to grow gentians, shinleaf, and little grass of Parnassus in their golden checkered shadows; the meadow is white with violets and all outdoors keeps the clock."

Find the entrance to East Fork Campground at about 9,000 feet (Pep Boys sells a car altimeter for less than $20, which is surprisingly accurate and fun to watch). The campground is down on Rock Creek. Most of the sites on the creek are lovely, but in the open, and have RV-size parking spots. Other sites, back up from the creek, are small and private. The parking spots are half a dozen yards from the campsites, which are mostly private and secluded in little copses of pine, brush, and aspen.

When I was there in late September, the aspen leaves were turning gold. When the wind blew they shimmered so prettily in the sunlight and made a soft, tinny clatter as they shook. The creek was well stocked. Happy fishermen tromped back to their campfires with strings of nice-sized trout for dinner. At night, the cold snapped, and, in the morning, our camping neighbors all exclaimed how nippy it was.

The hardy ridges above the riparian campground are covered with isolated foxtail pines. The creek goes north and south, so the sun is quick to set at night and slow to rise in the morning. At 9,000 feet, you really want the sun and will walk with your morning coffee to find it. A good evening walk is across the bridges to the other side of the creek. Go to site #108, the host's site, and across the access road, you'll find the first bridge. There is fine fishing here.

A good hike is up the creek to Rock Creek Lake. The trail leaves on the north side of the campground by site #82 and goes all the way to Rock Creek Lake, passing some small campgrounds and a resort before hitting the lake and trailheads to the high country.

Above Rock Creek Lake, you'll find Mosquito Flat. You can drive there and park at 10,250 feet. From there, it's an easy day hike into the John Muir Wilderness and Little Lakes Valley. The valley is a pretty glacial trough below 13,000-foot peaks. Bring your wildflower book because the meadows up there are loaded with them.

KEY INFORMATION

East Fork Campground, Inyo National Forest
873 North Main Street
Bishop, CA 93514

Operated by: U.S. Department of Agriculture, Forest Service

Information: (619) 873-2500

Open: June to November

Individual sites: 133

Each site has: Picnic table, fireplace

Registration: At entrance

Facilities: Piped water, flush toilets

Parking: At site

Fee: $11

Elevation: 9,000 feet

Restrictions:

Pets—Allowed

Fires—In fireplace

Vehicles—RVs up to 22 feet

To get there from L.A., take I-5 north to CA 14. Go north to U.S. 395 near Inyokern. Continue north on U.S. 395 to Bishop. From Bishop, drive 24 miles north on U.S. 395 and exit to the west at Tom's Place onto Rock Creek Road. Drive 5 miles up Rock Creek Road to the campground.

FAIRVIEW CAMPGROUND

Fairview, Sequoia National Forest

CAMPGROUND RATINGS

Beauty:	★★★★★
Site privacy:	★★★★
Site spaciousness:	★★★★
Quiet:	★★★★
Security:	★★★★
Cleanliness/upkeep:	★★★★

Fairview Campground offers the best tent camping in the Lake Isabella area. Be careful with children around the river. Don't miss McNally's "we-grind-our-own-meat" cheeseburgers.

About 60,000 years ago, a glacier flowing down an earthquake slip fault cut the U-shaped Upper Kern Canyon. Look southward along the Upper Kern Canyon and you can see how the glacier carved out the canyon, giving it rounded shoulders. In the Lower Kern Canyon, below Lake Isabella where the glacier didn't flow, the shoulders of the canyon are sharp and V-shaped.

Fairview Campground, near the head of the Upper Kern Valley, is the best camping spot in the area. It's set down by the river, well below the road and any traffic noise, with the mountains towering around. The sites are so well planned, it's hard to decide where to camp. The last time I was there it was spring, and the snow level was down to 5,000 feet, but it was warm and sunny down in the campground.

All the flowers were out—most ostentatiously the purple yerba santa. We made a tea out of its leaves, which the Native Americans thought was good for coughs, colds, asthma, and the like. Pretty bitter stuff. I've also heard that the leaves, when pounded into a poultice, cure sores. The Spanish used the leaves as tobacco, for chewing and smoking. Others claim that you can chew the leaves to quench thirst. After the first bitter taste subsides, you'll feel a sweet, cooling sensation. I tried it, and it wasn't too bad.

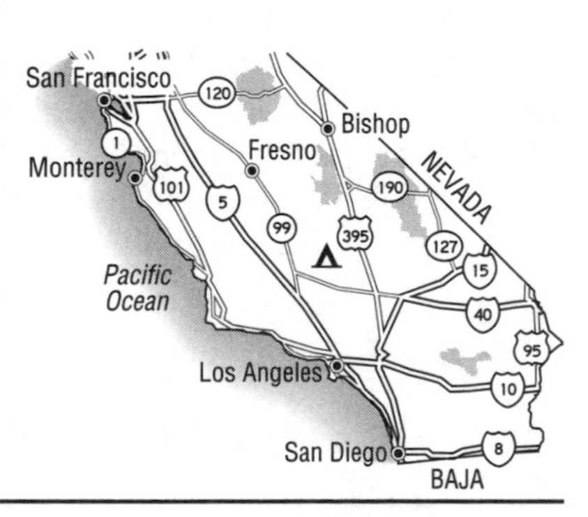

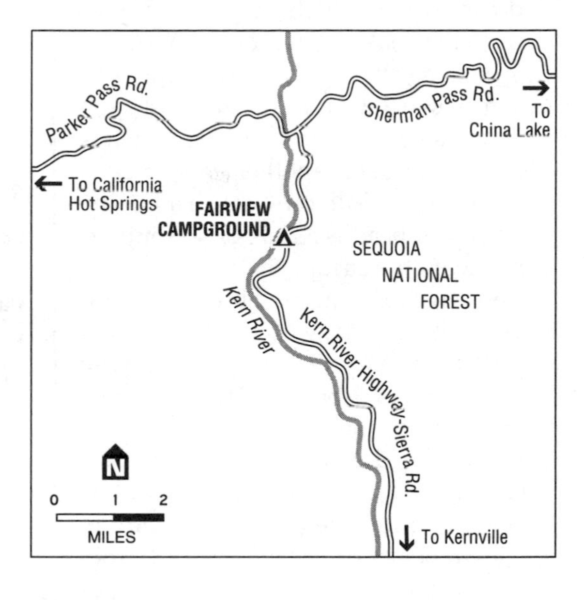

By our campsite, we found a flowering flannel bush (*Fremontia californica*) with brazen yellow flowers bright against the white water of the Kern. All night, the strong current rattled the rocks on the river bottom. In the morning, the ranger, who came by to collect our $12, admired our flannel bush and reported that the bark can be brewed and gargled to relieve a sore throat.

Fairview has always been blessed. The Native Americans used it as a fall and spring campground. In the late 1800s, Stony Rhymes and Lucien Barbeau had a cow camp on the bend of the river. In 1910, Matt and Lupie Burlando moved to Fairview and built the Fairview Lodge. They rented rooms to tourists who came for fishing and hunting. Matt built a swinging bridge (you can still see it today) across the river to the natural hot springs on the west side and ran packing trips into the backcountry. After Matt and Lupie's children reached school age, the entire family moved down to Kernville to be near the school. Fairview went back to being a cow camp for a while before Johnny McNally opened McNally's Steakhouse. Johnny was an amazing rodeo rider and a deputy sheriff, and his wife, Pauline, could shoot a running buck with a rifle from the back of a galloping horse.

To reach McNally's from the campground, walk south along the river 50 yards, and there's McNally's Steakhouse, the hamburger hut, and the gas station/grocery store. We loaded up on beer, hot dogs, and ice at the store and then hunkered down at the outside picnic tables for some rousing chili burgers before heading across the suspension bridge on a diet-redeeming hike along Flynn Trail. (See the map and handout sheet on the display by the parking lot near the hamburger stand.) You'll find access here for the Tobias Trail as well. Maybe the best short day hikes here are on the Whiskey Flat Trail, which runs from the bridge down to the north end of Burlando Road in Kernville. The trail parallels the west side of the river and runs through high chaparral, digger pines, and oak. There are wonderful places along the trail for picnicking. Put down a blanket and snooze while the river runs below you. I've heard there's good fishing here. Another good hike is up the trail to Salmon Creek Falls. The marked trailhead is a mile or so south of Fairview to the east.

One word of warning about the Kern River. It is very dangerous. When I was last there in May, it was running way above its natural banks. Camping there with children is only advisable if they are sternly warned and constantly watched. The water is cold, and the current is strong. If you're camping with children, go down below on Lake Isabella. I especially recommend Tillie Creek Campground, which is pretty, safe, and flat. Bring the children's bicycles. There is even a playground. In the spring, good fishing can be found in the lake as well.

To get there from L.A., take I-5 north over the Tejon Pass to CA 99. Drive north on CA 99 past Bakersfield. Take CA 178 east to Lake Isabella. Take CA 155 north to Wofford Heights. Bear right to Kernville. From Kernville, drive north 16 miles on Kern River Highway-Sierra Road to Fairview Campground on the left.

KEY INFORMATION

Fairview Campground, Sequoia National Forest
Cannell Meadow Ranger District
Kernville Ranger Station
P.O. Box 6, 105 Whitney Road
Kernville, CA 93238

Operated by: Department of Agriculture, Forest Service

Information: (619) 379-5646

Open: May to October

Individual sites: 37

Each site has: Fireplace, picnic table

Registration: At entrance

Facilities: Piped water, vault toilets

Parking: At site

Fee: $12

Elevation: 3,500 feet

Restrictions:

Pets—On leash

Fires—In fireplaces

Vehicles—RVs up to 22 feet

FOUR JEFFREY CAMPGROUND / SABRINA CAMPGROUND

Inyo National Forest

The princess of campgrounds on Bishop Creek above Bishop is tiny Sabrina Campground perched on the lip of Lake Sabrina. At 9,000 feet, the view of the picture-perfect lake, the glaciered mountain peaks marbled with rusty red metamorphic rock, and the deep blue sky is breathtaking. Sit on the sunny patio of the Lake Sabrina Boat Landing and eat an incredible old-fashioned hamburger grilled up by the pleasant hostess. That's how you know you're not in Switzerland after all, but in the Wild West.

You'll see lanky anglers swigging Bud, a big husky dog asleep atop an up-turned aluminum boat, and cowpokes in ten-gallon hats stepping out of canoes holding up six-pound trout, just caught, their bright colors catching the sun. Then, oddly, a pack train of laden llamas will file up the trail across the lake. Llamas? In the Wild West? Yes, apparently some of the local pack outfits use llamas. Indigenous to Peruvian high country, the llamas take to the Sierras like ducks to water.

Drive the vertiginous, short dirt road up to North Lake and check out the tiny North Lake Campground at the trailhead. No trailers, no RVs, only tents, but like Sabrina Campground and most of the campgrounds in the Bishop Creek area, it is tiny. The only campground around that has enough space to be a destination campground is Four Jeffrey, which is

CAMPGROUND RATINGS

Beauty:	★★★★
Site privacy:	★★★★
Site spaciousness:	★★★★★
Quiet:	★★★★★
Security:	★★★★★
Cleanliness/upkeep:	★★★★★

Four Jeffrey Campground is the best destination campground in the Bishop Creek Drainage area. Later, try to find a spot in Sabrina Campground or North Lake Campground.

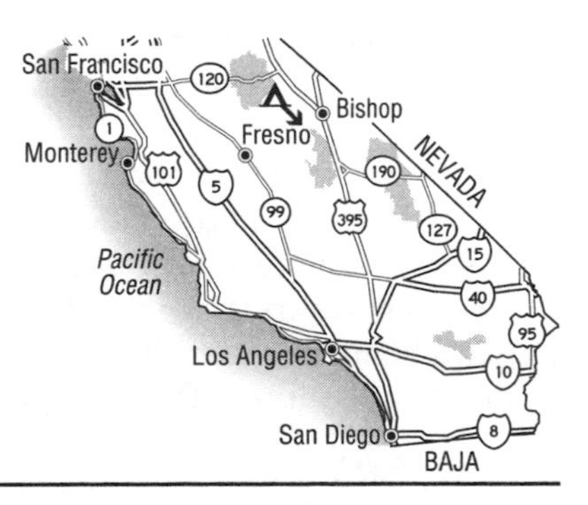

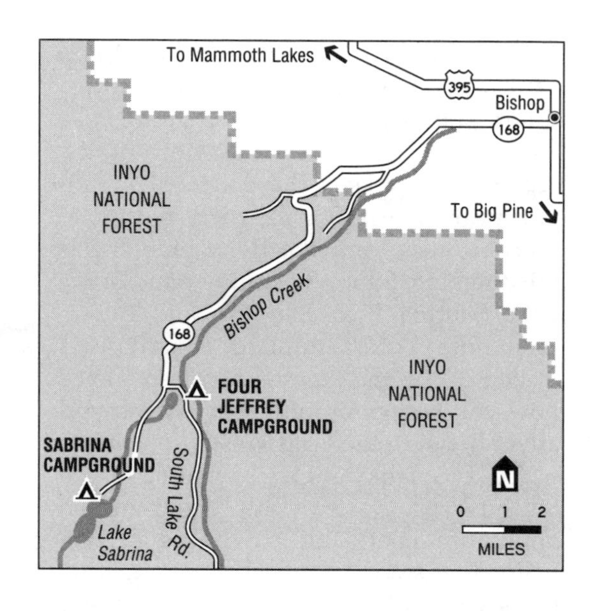

down the road from Sabrina Lake and to the right on the spur road to South Lake.

Four Jeffrey is an impressive campground. The surrounding mountains are spare and dry, and the view is incredible—although not eye-popping stunning like the views from Sabrina and North Lake. The South Fork of Bishop Creek runs through the campground. Many of the sites are down by the water, which is alive with trout. Others are up the hill in low brush. This area makes for good spring and early summer camping. By fall, the hillside is muted and austere. I like that look, but others want the green of the pines.

Make Four Jeffrey the first night destination campground in the Bishop Creek area. Chances of getting a site there are very good (the camping season at Four Jeffrey is two months longer than at Sabrina Campground). The next day, cruise around. Hit Sabrina Campground first, then North Lake Campground, then the other little campgrounds up and down the forks of Bishop Creek and see if you find something you like better.

It was at Four Jeffrey Campground that I thrilled to the efficacy of the cool, semi-new miner's lights sold in the camping stores. Ranging from cheap to pretty expensive, these babies are cinched around your head, so the light is on your forehead and the beam follows your eyes. My wife lost her contact lens somewhere around camp, and I went scouting for it. The light was better than ten camp lanterns. I found the lost lens with ease. Buy one of these lights. The more expensive ones are more comfortable, but the batteries and bulbs may be more difficult to purchase.

Part of my attraction to Four Jeffrey Campground is survival oriented. All the other campgrounds except little North Lake are by the streambed. And, the Bishop area is earthquake country. At 2:30 A.M. in March of 1872, a monster quake hit the Owens Valley. It was felt as far east as Salt Lake City, as far north as Canada, and as far south as Mexico. It shook old John Muir over in Yosemite Valley. He described the incident: "I was awakened by a tremendous earthquake, and though I had never enjoyed a storm of this sort, the strange thrilling motion could not be mistaken, and I ran out of cabin, both glad and frightened, shouting, 'A noble earthquake! A noble earthquake!' feeling sure I was going to learn something."

John Muir used to strap himself in the tops of pine trees during thunderstorms. He was lucky. Well, the 27 folks down in Lone Pine who died in the 1872 quake weren't so lucky. I figure a quake like that could happen again, and the dams up on Sabrina and South Lake would go pretty easily. I want to be sleeping on the high ground at Four Jeffrey Campground, so I can snooze right through the flood.

The best shopping is down the road in Bishop. The road in and out is good and fast. Bishop (named for Samuel A. Bishop, one of the original cattle ranchers) is a cow town recently encased in an ugly, fat pocket of fast food franchises. Fortunately, Schat's Dutch Bakery is there for sheepherder bread, Jack's Waffle Shop is open for breakfast with locals and cowpokes, The Firehouse Grill is still attracting tourists, and, thank God, the Meadow Farms Country Smokehouse (north on U.S. 395) still sells mahogany smoked slab jerky, sweet 'n' hot jerky, cheddar jerky, and other varieties, so you can gnaw your way through the High Sierras!

KEY INFORMATION

Four Jeffrey Campground, Inyo National Forest
873 North Main Street
Bishop, CA 93514

Operated by: U.S. Department of Agriculture, Forest Service

Information: (619) 873-2500

Open: April to November

Individual sites: 106

Each site has: Picnic tables, fireplace

Registration: At entrance

Facilities: Piped water, flush toilets

Parking: At site

Fee: $11

Elevation: 8,100 feet

Restrictions:

Pets—Allowed on leash

Fires—In fireplace

Vehicles—RVs up to 22 feet

To get there from L.A., take I-5 north to CA 14. Go north to U.S. 395 near Inyokern. Continue north on U.S. 395 for 123 miles to Bishop. From Bishop, drive 13 miles south on CA 168 to South Lake Road. Go left and drive a mile or so to Four Jeffrey Campground. Sabrina Campground is another 4 miles south on CA 168 from that turnoff.

HORSE MEADOW CAMPGROUND

Salmon Creek, Sequoia National Forest

Horse Meadow Campground is my favorite campground. I don't even know why. Maybe it's the long grind up the mountains or the the terrain, that dry, big-sky-country look with the pines, boulders, and open, green meadows. Maybe I watched too many westerns when I was a child, but the sky at Horse Meadow Campground just seems a little bit bluer than all the other beautiful skies at places where I've camped.

The campsites at Horse Meadow are roomy and offer a great view. Salmon Creek runs through the campground and gurgles just enough to lull you to sleep. Below the meadow, it gathers in pools deep enough to take a freezing dip. When you hop out, warm yourself on the hot granite slabs. Horse Meadow has that magical feeling that Laguna down in Cleveland National Forest has—only here we are at 7,600 feet, the water temperature is close to ice, and at night the temperature drops down near 40ºF.

Getting to Horse Meadow is part of the fun. Pass McNally's Hamburger Stand near Fairview Campground on your way north of Kernville. You're into the wilderness now, so stock up on ice and beer while you can. Here, the canyon narrows, and you see metamorphic rock cliffs colored by chartreuse lichen. Notice the tailings from Fairview Mine across the river. This is gold country. Pass Roads End (this

CAMPGROUND RATINGS

Beauty:	★★★★★
Site privacy:	★★
Site spaciousness:	★★★
Quiet:	★★★★
Security:	★★★
Cleanliness/upkeep:	★★★★

This is my favorite tent campground. It's difficult to get up here, but it's worth it for the beauty and solitude.

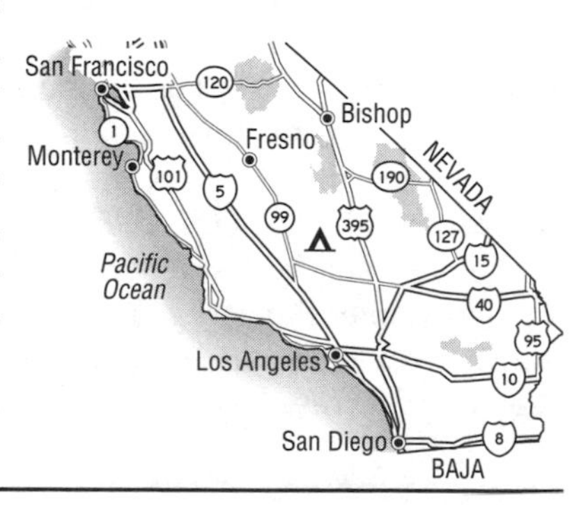

was the road's end until 1939) and soon enough you turn right on Sherman Pass Road. Look down at Brush Creek on the right and notice the good swimming and sunbathing for another trip.

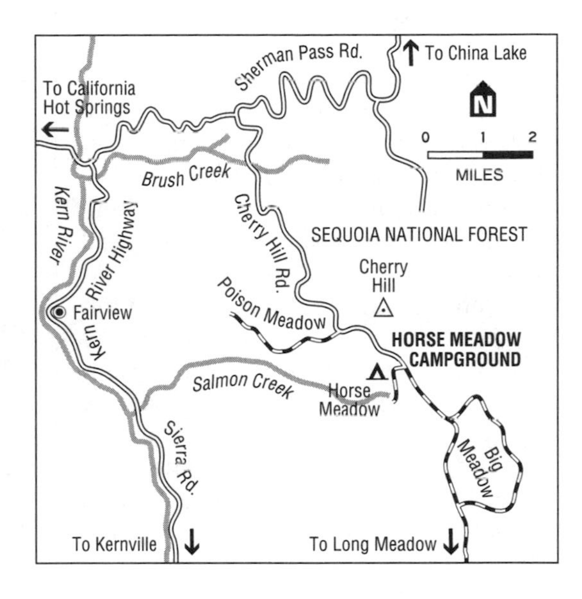

Sherman Pass Road grinds up past buck brush, mountain mahogany, and fremontia into chaparral with digger and pinyon pine, and finally, Jeffrey pine, black oak, cedar, and white fir as you turn off on Cherry Hill Road to the right.

It's about 10 miles up to Horse Meadow Campground past Alderand Brush creeks, then Poison Meadow (note the dispersed camping sites for another trip—get a fire permit), and, finally, the junction with Horse Meadow Road. Go right 1.3 miles and you are in tent camper's paradise.

The campground has two loops. The right loop is for tent camping only and runs along a hill above Salmon Creek and the meadow. The left loop is for tenters and small RVs. The last time I was there in July, most of the folks were tenters. The narrow ascents up Sherman Pass and Cherry Hill roads are a grind for RVs or cars pulling trailers. And, once you're up here, it's a long, long way down for supplies. There is good water (phone the Ranger Station before coming to make sure), but no trash bins. Haul out your garbage.

Horse Meadow is a good place to bring children. The campground loops are fine for biking, and Salmon Creek offers good trout fishing, but it's not wild and dangerous like the Kern. There are many easy hikes around the meadow, including several along Salmon Creek to some good dipping pools.

Horse Meadow is about contrasts. The campground area looks like the Cartwright's "Ponderosa" ranch country, but the meadow just below is alpine enough to imagine Heidi skipping through the grass and flowers yodeling in her milkmaid outfit. The creek to the south is classic high-country white water over rock and swirling, clear pools.

To find the upper bathing pools, go to the south side of the Horse Meadow Campground's main loop and find the trail that parallels the creek. Walk east along the left bank of the creek. Pass a Fire Safe Area to your left and cross a spur road over Salmon Creek. Keep climbing, follow the creek, and you'll come to the pools.

To visit the downstream pools, walk back past the camp entrance and go left down a road signed Salmon Falls Trail. Follow the signed trail from the parking lot and skirt the meadow. When the trail crosses Salmon Creek on a big log and goes left around a rocky butte, don't follow it. Instead, head west down the right side of the creek. The trail meanders along over rocky areas, bypassing clumps of willows, and leads you past some prime pools for dipping. The water is about as cold as it can get and still be liquid, but the sun is blazing hot. This is heaven!

For a major hike, go back to the big log crossing Salmon Creek. With a backpack filled with soda and sandwiches, head

To get there from L.A., take I-5 north over the Tejon Pass to CA 99. Drive north on CA 99 past Bakersfield. Take CA 178 east to Lake Isabella. Take CA 155 to Wofford Heights. Bear right to Kernville. From Kernville, drive north on Sierra Way 19.4 miles and turn right on Sherman Pass Road (signed "Highway 395-Black Rock Ranger District"). Drive 6 miles to Cherry Hill Road and turn right (signed "Horse Meadow-Big Meadow"). Drive up 9.1 miles on the surfaced (sometimes dirt) road to the signed campground entrance road on the right. The campground itself is 1.3 miles down the hill.

KEY INFORMATION

Horse Meadow Campground, Sequoia National Forest
Cannell Meadow Ranger District
105 Whitney Road, P.O. Box 6
Kernville, CA 93238

Operated by: U.S. Department of Agriculture, Forest Service, Sequoia National Forest

Information: (619) 376-3781

Open: June to November

Individual sites: 18 sites for tents only, 15 sites for tents or RVs up to 23 feet long

Each site has: Picnic table, fireplace, piped water (phone ahead to make sure)

Registration: At entrance

Facilities: Vault toilets

Parking: At site

Fee: $5

Elevation: 7,600 feet

Restrictions:

Pets—Allowed on leash

Fires—In fireplaces

Vehicles—Trailers not recommended

around the rocky butte toward the Salmon Creek Falls. The trail skirts the meadow and then heads into the woods. It goes up and down and crosses side canyons while following the south side of Salmon Creek. This is purple lupine country with monks hood, larkspur, and red bugler. Down by the creek, you'll see willows and dogwood. This is where we gave out, sat down, and picnicked.

I understand the trail continues down to the north side of Salmon Creek and ends with a view of the Greenhorn Mountains. Those more agile than I can rock hop down to the creek where there are more wonderful pools for bathing. Just beyond them, you'll find the top of Salmon Creek Falls. Rumor has it there used to be a trail down to the Kern and the base of Salmon Creek Falls. The trail far below up to the falls begins just south of Fairview Campground.

After a leisurely breakfast, some lazy packing, and a coast down the mountain, we arrived at McNally's just in time to see a proud child display a three-pound trout he caught in the Kern and for us to order the McNally "we-grind-our-own meat" cheeseburger. This is the last supper for reckless river rafters who cheerfully dice with death daily.

LOWER PEPPERMINT CAMPGROUND / CAMP 6 FIRE SAFE AREA

Sequoia National Forest

Lower Peppermint and Camp 6 are a few hundred yards apart and located smack dab in the middle of great Northern Sierra camping and the spectacular scenery of Dome Rock and The Needles. On your way up, obtain a fire permit because it increases your camping possibilities a hundredfold. You can get one from Greenhorn Ranger Station on CA 178, a few miles east of Bakersfield, or at Cannell Meadow Ranger Station in Kernville. The permit costs nothing and allows you to camp and build fires most anywhere in the Sequoia National Forest.

Sequoia National Forest calls this dispersed camping, which means you can camp wherever you want as long as it is not posted against camping. For example, when you explore the area around Lloyd Meadow Road, you'll see dozens of old logging roads or turnoffs where you can drive in a few hundred yards and camp in a private area of your own. Of course, you'll be expected to follow the fire regulations—cart out your garbage, dig cat holes for bodily waste, and burn your toilet paper. Try not to leave any traces of your visit.

Buy groceries at the big market in Lake Isabella or in Kernville at the market on the right when the road turns north up Sierra Way. This market features a good meat counter and carries just about anything you'll need at reasonable prices.

CAMPGROUND RATINGS

Beauty: ★★★★★
Site privacy: ★★
Site spaciousness: ★★★
Quiet: ★★★★
Security: ★★★
Cleanliness/upkeep: ★★★★

The Lower Peppermint/Camp 6 area is astonishingly beautiful with waterslides, waterfalls, and mountain peaks. Bring bikes for good cycling along the untrafficked Lloyd Meadows Road.

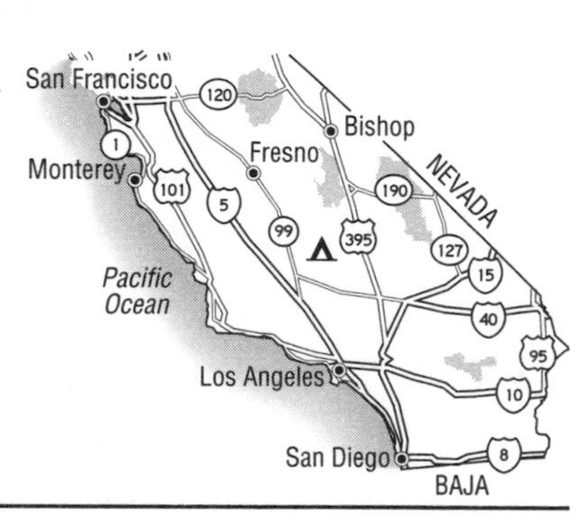

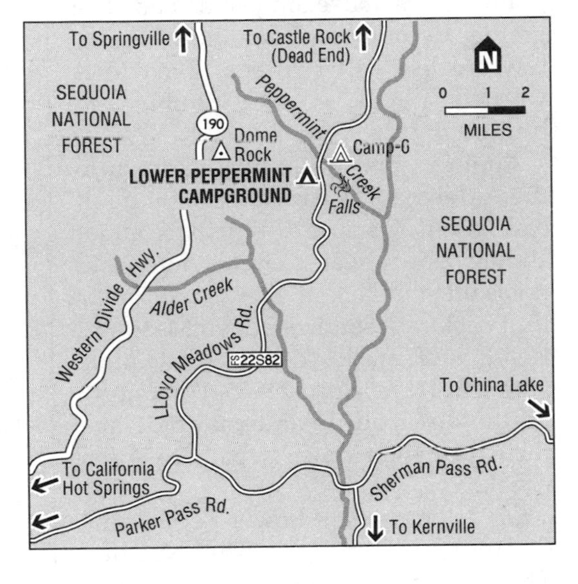

Once you get on Lloyd Meadows Road, there are no supplies available except beer, soda, and small bags of ice at the Johnsondale R-Ranch (0.6 mile east of the Lloyd Meadows Road turn off Parker Pass Drive). You'll pass a cowboy guard at the gate; tell him you want to shop at the store, and he'll wave you on. The R-Ranch is a private campground. The membership fee is $12,500 for life, which gives you access to cabins, horses, RVs, trails, etc. Look it over.

Lloyd Meadows Road heads up into pine, white fir, cedar, and oak where there is water nearby and manzanita, fremontia, and digger pine where it's dry. Note turnoffs to the numbered Fire Safe Area Camps, which offer good camping (a fire permit is required to camp in Fire Safe Areas as well as in other dispersed areas). I asked the ranger why they have Fire Safe Area Camps. She explained that in dry months or years dispersed camping is confined to these areas only.

Lower Peppermint Campground is a small, pretty campground mostly frequented by tent campers. When I was last up there in July, there was no potable water, so carry many jugs of drinking water or plan on purifying the water from Peppermint Creek. The campground is clean. I understand the nearby Camp Whitsett Boy Scouts maintain Lower Peppermint in return for the user fees on their own camp. The sites that back up to the creek are lovely. If these are taken, I recommend driving a few hundred yards north, then going down the dirt road signed for Camp 6. Here, you can camp down by the Peppermint Creek or up on the bluff overlooking piney meadows, a spectacular waterfall, and the Kern River below.

For a great hike and swim, scramble down the bluff to the foot of the falls. Stop and swim there. Or, bear left along the creek until you strike a trail that takes you east, then forks south to another area of rocky pools and cascades perfect for picnicking, swimming, and sunbathing.

Be careful. The water runs stronger than it seems. The wet rocks by the stream are like black ice, and the dry granite slabs above are just as bad. The granite decomposes, and the little dry bits are like ball bearings. Even forewarned, I took a quick tumble and bruised my leg.

Another good water hike is down to the Alder Slabs. Wear clothes you don't care about, because this trip is about sliding down water chutes into cold pools on your behind. *Raging waters!* It's fun! Backtrack south on Lloyd Meadows Road and park by gated Sequoia National Forest Road 22S83. Walk north on the dirt road up an easy grade and then turn right down a path to Alder Creek.

Or, drive north of Lower Peppermint Campground and see The Needles. These amazing rock formations are crystals formed under pressure from molten rock. Pushed up, The Needles cooled along vertical master joints. Ice and erosion have done the rest. Farther

To get there from L.A., take I-5 north over the Tejon Pass to CA 99. Drive north on CA 99 past Bakersfield. Take CA 178 east to Lake Isabella. Take CA 155 to Wofford Heights. Bear right to Kernville. From Kernville, drive north on Sierra Way 19.4 miles and turn left on Parker Pass Drive. It is 4.9 miles to the right-hand turn onto Lloyd Meadows Road (Forest Service Road 22S82). Drive north 13.4 miles to Lower Peppermint Campground. Camp 6 is a few hundred yards north on the right.

KEY INFORMATION

Lower Peppermint Campground/Camp 6 Fire Safe Area
Sequoia National Forest, Hot Springs Ranger District
Route 4, Box 548, California Hot Springs, CA 93207

Operated by: U.S. Department of Agriculture, Forest Service, Sequoia National Forest

Information: (805) 548-6503 or (209) 784-1500

Open: May to October

Individual sites: 17 family units

Each site has: Picnic table, fireplace, piped water (phone ahead)

Registration: At entrance

Facilities: Vault toilets

Parking: At site

Fee: $5

Elevation: 5,300 feet

Restrictions:

Pets—Allowed

Fires—In fireplaces

Vehicles—Trailers not recommended

Other—Fire permit required for Camp 6 Fire Safe Area

north, see the Freeman Creek Grove of sequoias. As you drive along, investigate all the little roads that turn off and look for good future camping sites. In the dead of summer, you might want to be near water, but in the late spring, this area is so beautiful it doesn't matter where you camp. You'll be blown away by the sight of all the flowers and the smell of the land.

Bring a saw for wood gathering, and don't forget a trowel for digging cat holes when hiking or camping in dispersed areas. I often bring a leaf rake with a sawed-off handle for clearing debris around the picnic table or the fire ring in a dispersed area. A shovel with a sawed-off handle is good for fire control and digging out if the car gets stuck. Remember to phone ahead to check about potable water at the established campgrounds. Otherwise, bring your own or be prepared to purify!

MINARET FALLS CAMPGROUND

Upper San Joaquin River, Inyo National Forest

Minaret Falls Campground is the prettiest in a string of beautiful and popular campgrounds on the Upper San Joaquin River west of Mammoth Mountain. When you drive down the dirt road into the campground, silvery Minaret Falls leaps out at you. Even by late September, on my last visit, the water was cascading down the mountainside like streams of crystal.

Right away, we drove into a campsite shrouded by trees. Through the willows we could see the riverbank and the falls. The tent pitch was clean and soft. A departing neighbor offered his stack of firewood. Fishermen waded up the river, and birds sang. It was the best of days.

We drove a few miles up the road to Red's Meadow store and cafe to buy worms and salmon eggs for trout fishing. A little bear was raiding the back room of the store, but the clerk and a tourist scared him away. A dog lunged at the end of his leash barking at the little bear as he scurried off.

We bought bait and postcards and learned that the original Red was a gold miner who turned to tourism when the depression and falling gold prices drove him out of business. His pack station at Red's Meadow was one of the first tourist draws in the Mammoth area.

We hiked down to Rainbow Falls along with a passel of other folks. The falls were exquisite. We took the rough stairs down

CAMPGROUND RATINGS

Beauty:	★★★★★
Site privacy:	★★★
Site spaciousness:	★★★★★
Quiet:	★★★★★
Security:	★★★★★
Cleanliness/upkeep:	★★★★

Minaret Falls Campground is the most beautiful campground in a string of popular campgrounds along the Upper San Joaquin River. Come in the fall for good fishing.

to the falls and stood in the spray. A rainbow did arc through the mist. The hike one way is 1.25 miles.

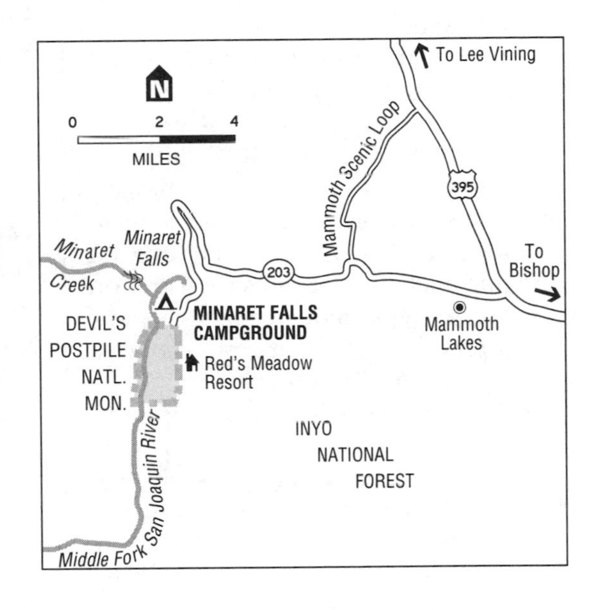

We hiked back through an area of burned firs, lodgepoles, and Jeffrey pines. This damage exists from the 1992 fire that burned most of Devil's Postpile National Monument. After the fire, the rangers walked through the burn to assess the damage, and charred trees came crashing down around them. It wasn't safe to walk there for months.

Back at the Minaret Campground we floated salmon eggs and earthworms down the river and caught six trout. My wife wrapped them in aluminum foil with herbs and cooked them over a campfire for dinner. It was a beautiful night. The Southern Sierra has hundreds of shooting stars.

Sleeping that night in our tent, I heard the rustle of a visitor. It was a bear. He ran away when I got up. I inspected the damage. My two treasured inflatable kitchen sinks from Basic Designs, which my wife and I use to wash the dishes, were ruined. The bear had bitten a big hole in each of them. To add insult to injury, he also bit into my plastic collapsible water jug. Were these acts of rancor, or did he think they were full of food?

A neighbor came over. The bear had tried to open the hatch of his Nissan Z; the telltale paw marks gave the intruder away. I told him about my sinks. He recommended wiping sinks, picnic tables, and cooler tops each night with Clorox. Bears like soap. Bears like lip ice. Bears like everything except Clorox. I went back to my sleeping bag and heard the bear slouch through the camp again.

The next morning we walked north along the river and crossed on a log at the end of the campground. There's a short trail to the foot of Minaret Falls. We bushwhacked up to the top of the falls and dipped in some nice pools there.

Later, we hiked up to Shadow Lake. It's no easy climb (round-trip is about 7 miles), but you'll agree it's worth it when you see how beautiful blue Shadow Lake banks against huge, craggy Mount Ritter. To find the trailhead, drive back toward Mammoth from the Minaret Falls Campground. Take the road to Agnew Meadows Campground. About .3 mile in, you'll find trailhead parking with toilets and drinking water. Follow the signs to Shadow Lake. Pass another parking lot and find another trailhead sign. Carry on across the creek under hemlocks, pine, and junipers. After about 1 mile notice a trail junction. To the left is Red's Meadow. To the right is Shadow Lake. With Mammoth Mountain at your back, climb up past Olaine Lake, cross the San Joaquin River on a wooden bridge, and hump it up the canyon wall to Shadow Lake. You'll find good fishing, so bring your fishing gear and bait.

Minaret Falls Campground is popular. Be sure to phone rangers ahead of time to make sure it's open and see how crowded it will be. Try to plan a trip before or after the prime summertime season and arrive on Thursday if you want to spend the weekend. The area is

To get there from L.A., take I-5 north to CA 14. Take CA 14 north to U.S. 395 near Inyokern. Continue north on U.S. 395 for 123 miles to Bishop. Continue another 37 miles on U.S. 395 to Mammoth Lakes. From Mammoth Lakes, drive 16 miles west on Highway 203 (Minaret Summit Road) to the campground.

KEY INFORMATION

Minaret Falls Campground, Inyo National Forest
873 North Main Street
Bishop, CA 93514

Operated by: U.S. Department of Agriculture, Forest Service

Information: (619) 924-5500

Open: June to October

Individual sites: 28

Each site has: Picnic table, fireplace

Registration: At entrance

Facilities: Piped water, chemical toilets

Parking: At site

Fee: $8

Elevation: 7,600 feet

Restrictions:

Pets—Allowed on leash

Fires—In fireplace

Vehicles—RVs up to 22 feet

Other—No dispersed camping in this area

so popular that during the summertime hikers (not campers) are required to park their cars at the Mammoth Ski Resort and take an intravalley shuttle down.

The other campgrounds in the valley—Devil's Postpile National Monument, Red's Meadow, Pumice Flat, Agnew Meadows, and Upper Soda Springs—are all small campgrounds. Try to arrive in the morning if the campgrounds are being heavily used, so you can grab choice campsites as previous campers leave.

You have 30 minutes from the time you occupy a campsite to pay. Put your car in the parking spot of the first empty campsite you find and use that 30 minutes to walk around and see if you like another site better. If you find one, leave something on the picnic table and go back and move your car.

MORAINE CAMPGROUND

Cedar Grove, Kings Canyon National Park

Everybody but Andrew Marvell, the 17th-century English poet, loves mountains. He called them "ill-designed excrescences" (abnormal growths). Of course, Andrew was a flatlander who never visited Kings Canyon National Park.

William Brewer did, however, and waxed eloquently about the Moraine Campground area in 1864: ". . . this is the grandest canyon I have ever seen. A pretty valley or flat half a mile wide lies along the river covered with trees. On both sides rise tremendous granite precipices, of every shape, often nearly perpendicular, rising from 2,500 feet to above 4,000 feet. They did not form a continuous wall, but rose in high points, with canyons coming down here and there, and with fissures, gashes, and gorges. The whole scene was sublime."

It is sublime. And it's the mountains, not the campground, that elicit this feeling. The campground is standard National Park issue; you wouldn't come to Moraine Campground if it weren't below Sentinel Ridge and Monarch Divide. However, just the drive is spectacular enough for a visit. You'll take the convict-built CA 180 all the way in from Fresno. It's wide and well banked, and when you come up over the rise and see the gorge and the mountains at the end of the gorge, it takes your breath away. Then, you circle down and follow the river all the way to Cedar Grove and Moraine Campground.

CAMPGROUND RATINGS

Beauty:	★★★★★
Site privacy:	★★★
Site spaciousness:	★★★★
Quiet:	★★★★★
Security:	★★★★
Cleanliness/upkeep:	★★★★★

Moraine Campground combines a grand canyon and a pretty valley for sublime scenery. Don't miss the sensational hiking.

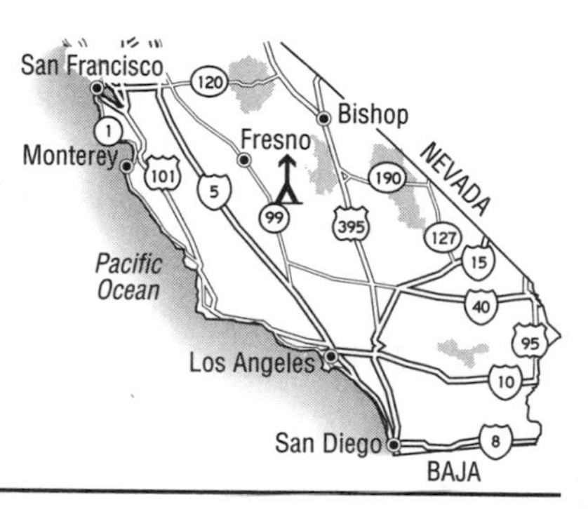

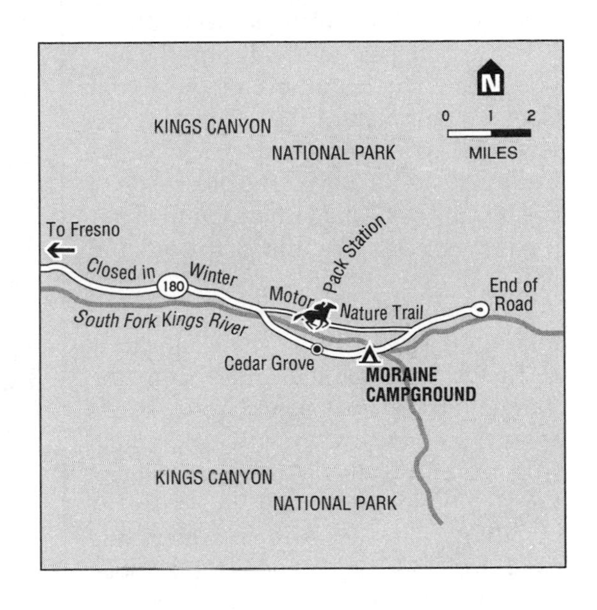

There is a store at Cedar Grove that sells ice, beverages, and some food. Gas is available, and there is a cafeteria for folks tired of camp cooking. There are hot showers and a laundromat. For an ice cream or a sandwich, stop at Kings Canyon Lodge on the way in or out. It's about halfway between Grants Grove and Cedar Grove. What a charming place! The lodge is rustic, but beautiful, with flower beds mixed in with old, rusted mining equipment. The little cabins were authentic dwellings of 20th-century miners from the area.

A little farther on is Boyden Cavern. I plunked down my $6 for the guided tour. Native Americans avoided the place feeling that bad spirits lived there. I can see why. I swallowed hard when the handsome guide turned off the lights and described the mile or so of solid granite over our heads. The children on the tour were thrilled to death.

Another fun activity at Cedar Grove for children is a horse ride at Cedar Grove Pack Station. Here, you can arrange anything from a one-hour ride to a week-long trip into the backcountry. They offer kiddy rides as well, although the resident pony had to have eye surgery and subsequently retired. Now they put the tiny pony saddle on a very gentle horse (minimum age is five). If you come to camp and want to arrange a more elaborate ride, it's best to phone ahead (209) 565-3464 and make reservations.

The river was running too fast for much fishing the last time I was at Cedar Grove in August. However, the cowboys at the stables told me you could do all right if you knew where to fish.

"Where's that?" I asked, but they laughed and wouldn't disclose any information. Clearly, the cowboys here don't tell the dudes where to go fishing.

Upriver from Moraine, there are several parking areas where you can pull over and walk down to the river. The second or third area accesses a part of the river where the current runs languidly even at flood tide. I wonder if this is the cowboy fishing hole? I got my lure wet, but there were no trout takers.

Farther on, past the bridge on the left, you'll find the beginning of the Cedar Grove Motor Nature Trail. Basically, this is a dirt road that heads back to the Cedar Grove Village on the other side of the North Fork Kings River. On the way, it passes several great places to park and hang out down by the water.

You can't leave Cedar Grove without hiking up to Mist Falls. The trailhead is at Roads End, about 6 miles from the Ranger Station in Cedar Grove. Right away, you'll cross Copper Creek, which was once a Native American village. Look carefully and you'll find flakes of obsidian that the Native Americans used for making weapons and tools. There was a store there at one time, and John Muir swore by the pies the owner's wife, Viola, made. About 2 miles in, head uphill following the river. This was as far as I got, but I found great dipping pools here and many tempting picnic spots. On your left is Buck Peak (8,776

To get there from L.A., take I-5 north over the Tejon Pass to CA 99. Drive north on CA 99 past Bakersfield 104 miles to Fresno. Go east on CA 180 to Kings Canyon National Park. Follow CA 180 for 29 miles to Cedar Grove Village. From Cedar Grove Village in Kings Canyon Park drive east on CA 180 for 1 mile to the campground.

KEY INFORMATION

Moraine Campground, Kings Canyon National Park
Superintendent Michael J. Tollelson
Three Rivers, CA 93271

Operated by: National Park Service, U.S. Department of the Interior

Information: (209) 565-3341

Open: June to October (depending on road and snow conditions)

Individual sites: 120

Each site has: Picnic table, fireplace

Registration: At entrance

Facilities: Piped water, flush toilets

Parking: At site

Fee: $10

Elevation: 4,600 feet

Restrictions:

Pets—Allowed on leash

Fires—In fireplace

Vehicles—No limits

feet), and The Sphinx (9,146 feet) is behind you. See if you can sort out the pines; you'll find ponderosas, Jeffreys, and sugars. To the east, don't miss the waterfall on Gardiner Creek. Soon enough, you'll reach Mist Falls, and the sight is worth the climb.

The best time to visit Moraine Campground at Cedar Grove is in the spring. It's cool enough then to hike comfortably all day long, and the campgrounds have been cleaned by the winter snow. Still, Kings Canyon National Park is beautiful any month of the year. Many folks think so too, so arrive by Thursday in August if you want a campsite for the weekend.

PRINCESS CAMPGROUND

Hume Lake, Sequoia National Forest

You'll love Princess Campground just like you love a golden retriever for being a basic, good dog. Princess is a campground's campground. Set under the shade of second growth sequoias and pines, Princess is covered on one flank by a shimmering alpine meadow. By the entrance, meet the campground hostess who is bluff and friendly. The campsites are private and level, and everything is well maintained and clean. There is a lot to do.

Hume Lake, 3 miles down the road, is a big draw for anybody from hundreds of miles around with a vinyl water toy or a fishing rod. A huge Christian campground is located at one end of the lake, and the healthy devotion shining on the faces of those campers lights up the sky. Dammed up by lumber folks, Hume Lake supplied the water for the flume that scooted timber down to Sanger in the San Joaquin Valley 54 miles away. Flumes work on the same principle as water slides at amusement parks; the water reduces friction, so you or whatever goes flying downhill.

Unlike the water in the mountain streams, Hume Lake warms up enough so you can actually swim without turning gelid. A path encircles the lake, and you can find your own grassy beach spot. Air mattresses or inexpensive blow-up boats are big hits. I actually saw people catching edible-sized fish as well.

CAMPGROUND RATINGS

Beauty:	★★★★
Site privacy:	★★★★
Site spaciousness:	★★★★
Quiet:	★★★
Security:	★★★
Cleanliness/upkeep:	★★★★

Princess Campground has everything—big trees, warm lakes, and fantastic gorge views. Come for a week with the family.

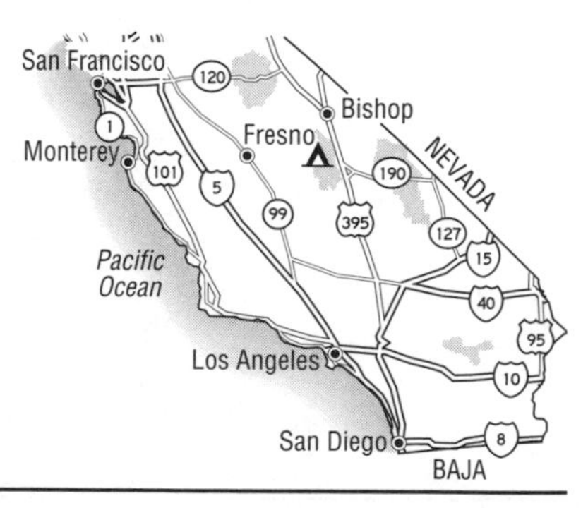

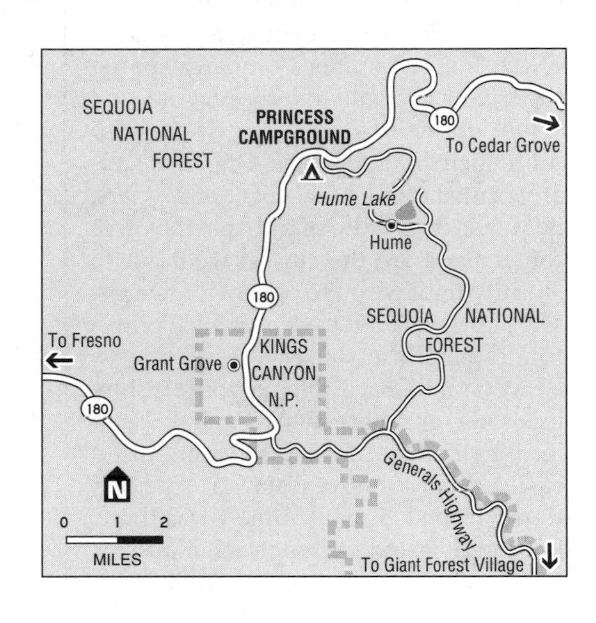

A choice spot is Sandy Cove Beach. Coming down from CA 180, pass Hume Lake Campground and follow the road around past the Powder Canyon Picnic Area, through the Hume Lake Christian Camp, and along Lakeshore Drive to Sandy Cove Beach where the trill of youthful swimmers' voices resounds. This is a fun and safe place to swim. Adults with more secluded sunbathing in mind can follow Landslide Creek up until they find a private spot. The road that heads south to Generals Highway follows the creek most of the way.

Princess is regarded as an overflow campground for Hume Lake, but I find it to offer much better camping. It's quieter and cleaner, and since you have to walk down to the lake from Hume Lake Campground, you might as well drive down from Princess. At least up there you won't suffer the incessant counselors' whistles wafting down the lake from the Christian camp as you try to cram in a few more zzzzs in the morning. And the added 700 feet of elevation at Princess cuts down on the bugs and the dust.

The Indian Basin Grove Trail is a good hike. It's an easy one-hour hike and starts about half a mile west of the entrance to Princess Campground. You can walk there from Princess or take a car and park in a turnout just west of the road. The trail follows Forest Service Road 13S50 north through ponderosas and cedars. Look for the sequoia stumps, then for the second-generation sequoias growing back. After a mile or so, you pass Forest Service Road 13S07, which could take you back to Princess Campground. But, persevere and follow the road north to a ridge. When the road turns east, find the trail in a patch of manzanita. The trail continues north to a point overlooking Kings Canyon.

Another good hike is into the Boole Tree. Drive west on CA 180 to Forest Service Road 13S55, then drive 2.7 miles to the trailhead parking lot. Follow the signed trail. It's an easy 2-mile trip in and out. Be sure to see the tree—it's an incredible sight. Why didn't loggers ever cut it down? Nobody knows, but some say Frank Boole, general manager of the Sanger Lumber Company, spared the tree as a tribute to himself.

Just up the road is Grant Grove with more incredible sequoias. One tree actually antedates Christ by 1,500 years. Sequoias do not die of old age; they live forever and are the closest we'll get to eternity until we go to our own rewards. The short walk out to Panoramic Point is fun, especially at sunset.

At Grant Grove Village you can buy ice, soda, and beer, which makes long-term camping at Princess Campground easier. Many families stay at Princess Campground. The last time I was there, I camped next to a schoolteacher and his herd of children. He was an erudite chap and taught his wee ones some of the games that the Monachi and Yokut Native Americans played. The children's favorite was the hand (guessing) game. They separated into two sides and covered their laps with blankets.

To get there from L.A., take I-5 north over the Tejon Pass to CA 99. Drive north on CA 99 past Bakersfield 104 miles to Fresno. Go east on CA 180 to Kings Canyon National Park. Follow CA 180 to Grant Grove. From Grant Grove in Kings Canyon National Park drive 6 miles north to Princess Campground on the right.

KEY INFORMATION

Princess Campground, Sequoia National Forest
Hume Lake Ranger District
36273 East Kings Canyon Road
Dunlop, CA 93621

Operated by: U.S. Department of Agriculture, Forest Service

Information: (209) 338-2251

Open: May to September

Individual sites: 50 tent sites, 40 RV sites

Each site has: Picnic table, fireplace

Registration: At entrance; for reservations, phone (800) 280-CAMP at least 10 days before desired dates ($7.50 fee)

Facilities: Piped water, vault toilets

Parking: At site

Fee: $12

Elevation: 5,900 feet

Restrictions:

Pets—Allowed on leash

Fires—In fireplace

Vehicles—RVs up to 22 feet

One side hid a stone in their blanket-covered hands, while the other side tried to guess whose hand held the rock. Raucous fun was had by all.

Remember the bears. There are no bear boxes at Princess Campground, but there are black bears. You must be careful with your food. As soon as you eat, take the trash to the bins. Leave your cooler in the car trunk; if you have a van or hatchback, disguise the cooler with a blanket or such. The bears recognize coolers and know food is kept in them. Don't leave anything in your tent that has a strong odor. This includes sun lotion, lipstick, skin cream, etc. Think about it. Rangers shoot bears when they become repeat food raiders, so be cool and save a bear!

QUAKING ASPEN CAMPGROUND / PEPPERMINT CAMPGROUND

Ponderosa, Sequoia National Forest

Quaking Aspen Campground and its nearby neighbor, Peppermint Campground, span the entire range of camping available in this part of the Sierras. Quaking Aspen is developed, clean, well maintained, and set in a stand of red fir, *not* quaking aspen as its name infers. Peppermint Campground is situated higher among pines, cedar, and black oak and is undeveloped (a fire permit is required). Quaking Aspen lies by meadows of willow, aspen, and yarrow. Peppermint is located by Peppermint Creek, offering trout fishing and bathing in chilly pools down from the campground.

Ponderosa Lodge, between the two campgrounds, is a fun place to grab a beer and chili or to pick up ice, but don't plan on shopping there. Springville is the last port of call for supplies. This pretty little town in Tule River country has just about everything you'll need. Before Jedediah Smith trapped beaver here in 1827, the Yaudanchis (a subtribe of the Yokut) lived in the foothills during the winter and trekked to the mountains to gather food in the summer. By 1857 the Yaudanchis were history.

Settlers poured into the area. John Nelson forged his way up the canyon of the Middle Fork of the Tule River (CA 190 east of Springville today) and filed a claim on property that is now Camp Nelson. Springville (named for the soda springs in

CAMPGROUND RATINGS

Beauty:	★★★★★
Site privacy:	★★★★
Site spaciousness:	★★★★
Quiet:	★★★★
Security:	★★★★★
Cleanliness/upkeep:	★★★★★

Come to Quaking Aspen Campground in the fall for autumn leaves and in the summer for hiking and mountain biking.

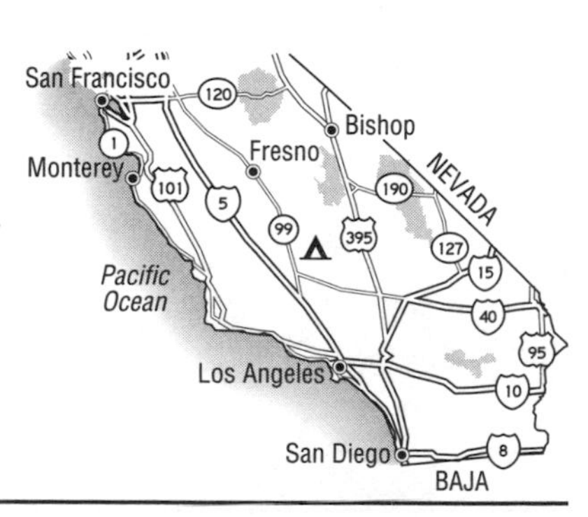

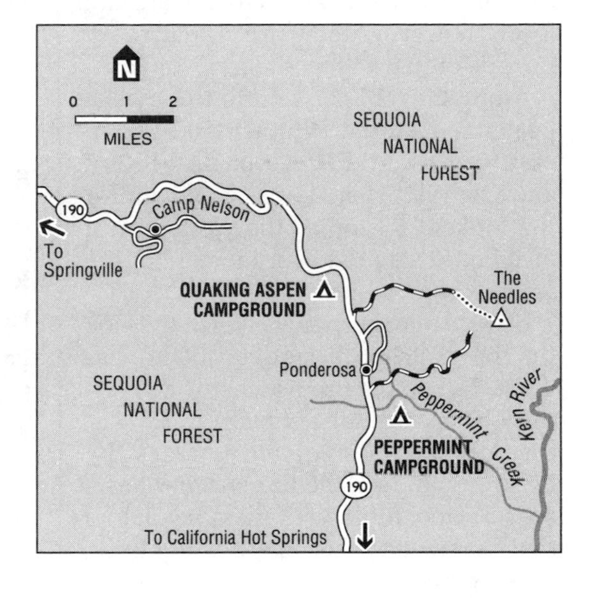

the area) was the site of a mill that processed the raw timber hauled down by horse- and mule-team wagons from the higher reaches of what is now Sequoia National Forest. Logging continued into the early 1900s when the Porterville Northeastern Railroad built a spur into Springville. Then, finished lumber, citrus fruits, and apples could be shipped to the valley below.

Now, citrus orchards dot the lower foothills leading into town along CA 190. Ranching operations spread across wide-open parcels of oak- and buckeye-studded hills. Apples are grown farther up on the cooler, protected slopes merging into the manzanita, black oak, cedar, and pine. Logging continues under the supervision of the Sequoia National Forest.

Between Quaking Aspen Campground and Ponderosa Lodge, note the actual quaking aspens that give the campground its name. These slender trees have light bark and roundish leaves. Vivid green in spring and bright gold in fall, the leaves quiver at the least breath of breeze. Hence the name "quaking aspen."

The good bathing holes on Peppermint Creek are downstream from the campground about a quarter of a mile. Stick to the south side of the creek, because it's hard to cross over from the other side. The wet rocks are extremely slippery. Don't even think of crossing on them. Find a place with a sandy bottom before you try getting in the water. Also, watch out for the granite slabs on the banks. Their surface decomposes, and the bits of rock are like ball bearings.

A great hike is out to the Needles Lookout. It's only a 4-mile round-trip of pretty easy walking, but plan on making a day of it. Take lunch. The dirt road to the trailhead takes off to the east about one-half mile south of Ponderosa Lodge. Drive 2.8 miles in and park. The trail begins at the east end of the parking lot. Note the small purple flowers along the trail. They are called pennyroyals (*Mentha pulegium*) and are used to make mint tea. Pennyroyals are not local, however; they are a native of Europe brought in by the forty-niners.

Along the trail, look north to Kaweah peaks and Mount Whitney and northeast to the Kern Plateau peaks of Kern and Olancha. Then, keep an eye out for the lookout on top of the westernmost Needle—it's a fire tower manned in fire season.

Believe me, the view is worth the slog up the switchback ladders to the catwalk. Talk to the fire watcher if he is on duty. This place can get hairy. In storms, the lookout is frequently struck by lightning. In fact, the fire watcher has a special stool fitted with glass insulators that he sits on when there is lightning striking nearby!

The camping at Quaking Aspen Campground is especially beautiful in the fall with the turning of the leaves. I enjoyed Quaking Aspen in the summer as well. It's a very gracious place and is the birthplace of my famous one-pot Hungarian potato/hot dog stew. Saute diced onions in a little oil in a pot. Add quartered potatoes and hot paprika. Stir and cover. Simmer until potatoes are almost done, then add hot dogs and simmer. Eat. Food good.

KEY INFORMATION

Quaking Aspen Campground/Peppermint Campground
Sequoia National Forest, Tule River Ranger District
32588 CA 190
Porterville, CA 93257

Operated by: U.S. Department of Agriculture, Forest Service

Information: (805) 539-2607 or (209) 784-1500

Open: May to October

Individual sites: 32 family units

Each site has: Picnic table, fireplace, piped water (phone ahead)

Registration: At entrance

Facilities: Vault toilets

Parking: At site

Fee: $10

Elevation: 7,000 feet

Restrictions:

Pets—Allowed on leash

Fires—In fireplaces

Vehicles—RVs up to 22 feet

Other—Permit required for Peppermint Campground

To get there from L.A., take I-5 north over the Tejon Pass to CA 99. Drive north on CA 99 past Bakersfield. Take CA 65 north to Porterville. Go east 17 miles on CA 190 to Springville. From Springville, drive 23.3 miles east on CA 190 to Quaking Aspen Camp-ground on the right. Peppermint Campground is 3 miles farther on the left.

RANCHERIA CAMPGROUND

Huntington Lake, Sierra National Forest

Rancheria Campground on Huntington Lake is big, handsome, and noisy. The acoustics around camp on the pine-shored lake are such that you can hear a mouse belch at dusk from the lake's south shore. You'll hear folks laughing on the boats at the nearby marina, outboards putting on fishing skiffs, chaps hammering siding on the cottages by the town of Lake Shore, and the occasional fly-by of a Fire Service helicopter. It feels like one big happy, beautiful neighborhood.

The campground has been around for a long time, and the sites are screened by pine and brush. Many sites are walk-ins along the lake, which allows you to pitch your tent right on the shore. Folks with boats can tie them to a root next to their campground. The beach slopes gently down into the water, which makes for good wading. There are sites back in the woods, too, for people who don't want all the aquatic activity.

Perched on the edge of the wilderness, Huntington Lake is a good first camp for anyone heading farther in to Thomas A. Edison Lake (a.k.a. Edison Lake) or Florence Lake. You'll find last-chance shopping at the country store in Lake Shore and the Ranger Station for information. There's a good chance that you just might want to settle in at Rancheria and forget the hairy drive up over Kaiser Pass.

CAMPGROUND RATINGS

Beauty:	★★★★★
Site privacy:	★★★★
Site spaciousness:	★★★★
Quiet:	★
Security:	★★★★★
Cleanliness/upkeep:	★★★★★

Rancheria Campground serves as a good base camp before camping at Vermilion or Trapper Springs campgrounds. Though crowded, Rancheria offers good, solid, safe tent camping.

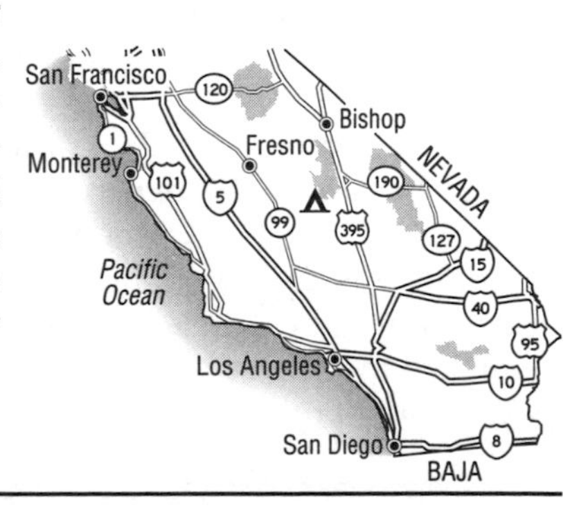

Huntington Lake is about hydroelectric power. Edison and Florence lakes run turbines. The water flows into Huntington Lake and runs more turbines, and in turn, flows into Shaver lake below to run more turbines. All this so we can watch television down in the flatlands.

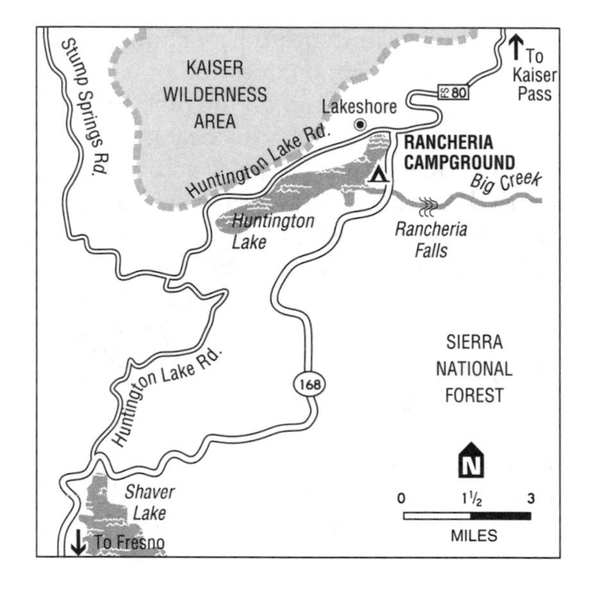

This system, owned by SCE (Southern California Edison), is called the Big Creek hydroelectric project. It all started near the site of present-day Shaver Lake when C.B. Shaver built a millpond to saw lumber to float down a 40-mile flume to Clovis in the flatland below. When the lumber gave out, the power company moved in, built dams, and impounded water in reservoirs.

For a power company, water in a reservoir is like money in the bank. It provides cheap, clean, reliable power that can be used almost immediately. As long as the power company can keep the lakes full, the vacationing public is happy. But, nothing is uglier than an empty lake, and nobody knows that better than the folks down at Shaver Lake who have had some dry years.

You can rent boats at the marina across from Rancheria Campground. Or, visit in the winter (Rancheria is open year-round) and ski at nearby Sierra Summit Ski Resort on Chinese Peak. I found the skiing spectacular, but heard some experts complaining that the best runs were too short. Hike up to Rancheria Falls from the trailhead across the road from Rancheria Campground. Or, hike in to the river pools. The trailhead is in the second parking lot of the ski resort.

Buy your meat down in the flatlands. There is decent shopping at Ken's Market in Shaver Lake, and you'll find beer, ice, and sundries at the friendly country store in Lake Shore. But, if you want a sirloin steak, you better bring it with you. While you're packing, it's not a bad idea to bring an old pair of running shoes or a pair of those aquatic slippers to wear while getting in and out of the lake.

And, don't accommodate the bears! Put all edibles in your car trunk. If you have a hatchback or van, disguise the cooler with a blanket. Bring a small bottle of Clorox and wipe down your cooking gear and picnic table before turning in. Bears don't like the smell; maybe they associate it with the nonfood-producing toilet facilities.

When I was there in September, the bears were especially active down at Lower Billy Campground on the other side of Lake Shore. I spoke to the lady at the Ranger Station, and she said that a bear broke into her storage shed a few nights before and ate everything but some frozen ears of corn. That was at 3:14 A.M. The next night, the bear came back at exactly 3:14 A.M. for the frozen ears of corn.

Be sure to read the memorial on the rock by the Ranger Station. It honors some airmen who died in 1944. Apparently, a B-24 bomber ran into trouble. The pilot gave the crew two options—

To get there from L.A., take I-5 north over the Tejon Pass to CA 99. Drive north on CA 99 past Bakersfield 104 miles to Fresno. Take CA 41 north to CA 168. Go northeast to Shaver Lake. From Shaver Lake, head 20 miles north on CA 168. Rancheria Campground is on the left as you come to the head of Huntington Lake.

KEY INFORMATION

Rancheria Campground, Sierra National Forest
Supervisor's Office
1600 Tollhouse Road
Clovis, CA 93611-0532
(209) 297-0706

Operated by: U.S. Department of Agriculture, Forest Service

Information: (209) 855-5355; California Road Conditions (CALTRANS), (800) 427-7673

Open: All year

Individual sites: 159 sites (some tents only)

Each site has: Picnic table, fireplace

Registration: At entrance; for reservations, phone (800) 280-CAMP at least 10 days before desired dates ($7.50 fee)

Facilities: Piped water, flush toilets

Parking: At or near site

Fee: $14

Elevation: 7,000 feet

Restrictions:

Pets—Allowed on leash

Fires—In fireplace

Vehicles—RVs up to 22 feet

Other—Camp in color-coded sites—yellow for tents, blue for RVs up to 20 feet, white for RVs up to 30 feet, red for RVs up to 40 feet bail out or stay with the ship and gut it out. Two men jumped and lived. The plane disappeared into the blue and was lost for a decade. Finally, in 1955, the power company lowered the Huntington Lake water level to do some repairs on the dam. The receding water revealed the wreckage of the missing B-24 and the bodies of the remaining men.

I thought of those young men as I swam in azure Huntington Lake and stood in the mist from the generator turbines by the Kaiser Pass Road. Maybe it would've been better if they hadn't been found. Then, you could always think of them out there somewhere, handsome and young in sheepskin flying jackets, their faces full of promise.

REDWOOD MEADOW CAMPGROUND

Sequoia National Forest

If campgrounds could have expressions, then Redwood Meadow would have a smiling face. This is an easy campground to like. The facilities are clean and well maintained. The sites are under well-spaced trees allowing shadow and sunlight with lots of room for tent pitches. Below is a big meadow with flowers that fills the world with light. All this, and the campground is not that crowded. There are so many free surrounding campgrounds, as well as a lot of dispersed camping, that Redwood Meadow doesn't get hit hard because it charges a fee. For me, it's worth the bucks to stay in this happy campground with the Trail of 100 Giants just across the road.

The Trail of 100 Giants is a great place to get acquainted with the "Big Trees." The largest tree in the grove has a diameter of 20 feet and is 220 feet in height. The trees' ages range between 500 to 1,500 years old. These old guys were babes when the Roman Empire fell.

Back in the glacial eras, the giant sequoias (*Sequoiadendron gigantuem*) grew all over what is now the western United States. When the climate dried out, the sequoias retreated to ecological islands with abundant rainfall and runoff where they grow mostly in granite basins or where bedrock is near the surface.

Try to burn a piece of redwood bark and you'll see how resistant it is to fire. The

CAMPGROUND RATINGS

Beauty:	★★★★★
Site privacy:	★★★
Site spaciousness:	★★★★
Quiet:	★★★★
Security:	★★★
Cleanliness/upkeep:	★★★★

A happy campground with the Trail of 100 Giants and a meadow full of flowers. You can't beat it.

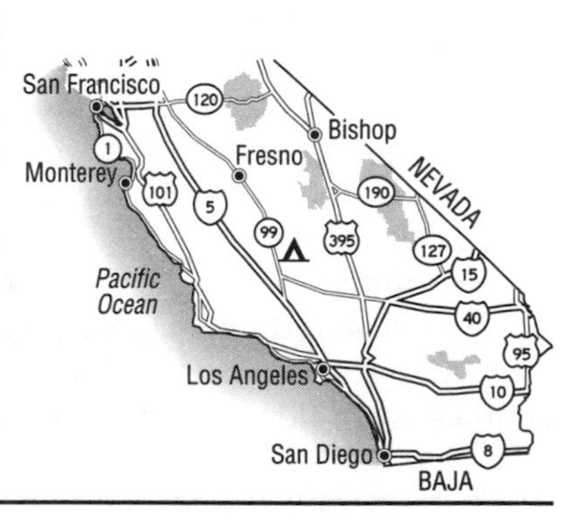

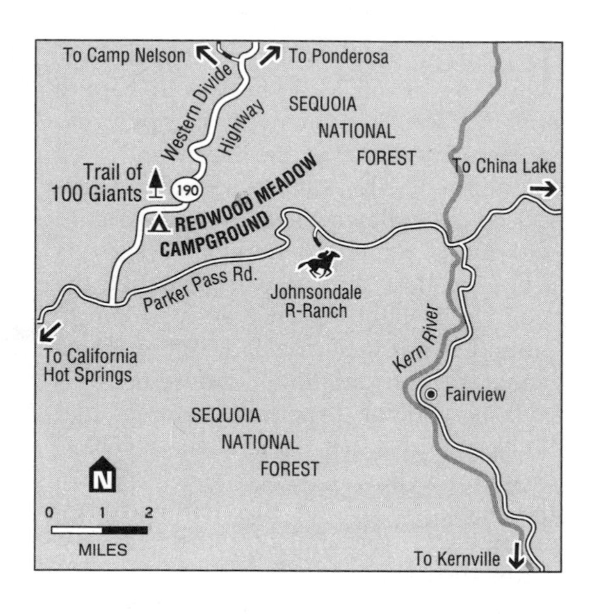

bark is impregnated with tannins that are resistant to both fire and insects. That allows the trees to grow very old. And, given abundant moisture, the trees are the fastest-growing tree in the United States. Age and growth rate—that's why the giant sequoias are so huge.

For years, foresters tried to protect the giant sequoia from fire. Only recently did they realize that the sequoias need fire to perpetuate. Ground fires do not burn through the bark, but the rising heat opens the cones, which remain on the trees for up to 20 years. When the cones open, the seeds fall on the soft, recently burned earth. When it rains, these seeds germinate in the sunlight that shines to the ground freely through the recently burned foliage.

An interesting friend of the giant sequoia is the giant carpenter ant who makes nests in the sequoias by hollowing them out. Try not to think about the ant when you're standing under a giant sequoia and pray for an occasional fire, since it reduces the population of the giant ants.

For bicycling, Western Divide Highway is a great option. The road is wide with no blind curves. On a weekday you'll hardly see a car. A good tour is from Redwood Meadow Campground to Ponderosa Lodge and back. The round-trip is about 24 miles. You'll bike from good clear water available at the campground to the Ponderosa Lodge's varied liquid refreshments and breakfast, lunch, and dinner choices, then back home again to the campground. On the way, a short section of dirt road takes you to Dome Rock—be sure to stop. A quick walk along an obvious path will lead you to a spectacular view. Look down and you'll see the slash of Kern Canyon. Spot The Needles, Peppermint Creek, and Lower Peppermint Campground below. What a wild, lovely vista!

Another great mountain bike trip is down the connector road that heads left from Western Divide Highway about 3 to 4 miles from Redwood Campground. It climbs Nobe Creek basin to Windy Gap, then passes Coy Flat Campground, and ends up at Camp Nelson (about 24 miles one-way). I found the trip out to be quite long, and was greatly relieved when someone in our party hitched a ride on a pickup truck back to Redwood Campground to get a relief vehicle.

Reserve a site at Redwood Meadow Campground on big weekends. I especially like sites #2 through #8 because they are off the highway and backed down to the little stream. If the campground is too busy, head north a half mile on Western Divide Highway. To the right is a dirt road leading down to Long Meadow Campground, a delightful place to pitch a tent. (Get a fire permit from the Ranger Station—it's good for the year!) Or, try Holey Meadow Campground. Or, head back to Parker Pass Road and go east. Almost immediately, you'll find turnoffs to good dispersed camping on the right by the stream. Armed with a fire permit, you can find great camping spots anytime in this area.

To get there from L.A., take I-5 north over the Tejon Pass to CA 99. Drive north on CA 99 past Bakersfield. Take CA 178 east to Lake Isabella. Take CA 155 to Wofford Heights. Bear right to Kernville. From Kernville, drive north on Sierra Way 19.4 miles and turn left on Parker Pass Road. Drive 10.4 miles to Western Divide Highway. Go right (north) and Redwood Meadow Campground is 3 miles up on the right.

KEY INFORMATION

Redwood Meadow Campground, Sequoia National Forest
Hot Springs Ranger District
Route 4, Box 548
California Hot Springs, CA 93207

Operated by: U.S. Department of Agriculture, Forest Service

Information: (805) 548-6503 or (209) 784-1500

Open: June to September

Individual sites: 15 family units

Each site has: Picnic table, fireplace, piped water (phone ahead)

Registration: At entrance

Facilities: Vault toilets

Parking: At site

Fee: $10

Elevation: 6,500 feet

Restrictions:

Pets—Allowed

Fires—In fireplaces

Vehicles—RVs up to 16 feet

SHAKE CAMP CAMPGROUND

Mountain Home State Forest

Shake Camp Campground will satisfy the buckaroo in you and your children. This place is about horses and the wild, open western sky. Perched on the edge of the Golden Trout Wilderness, Mountain Home State Forest is virtually unknown. When I was last there in August, I saw very few backpackers or campers. Most of the people there were fishing in the few stocked ponds, frolicking with their children in the Tule River at Hidden Falls, or getting ready to take horses back into the Sierra High Country for an incredible adventure.

A few hundred yards down the road is the Balch Park Pack Station run by Tim and Dianne Shew. I didn't meet Tim or Dianne on my last visit, but spoke instead with a young cowpoke who painted a glowing picture of wonderful high lakes full of golden trout and alpine meadows under rugged peaks. You can rent horses, pack animals, and a cowpoke packer to take you up to these incredible campsites where you can loll around for as many days as you desire. On the predetermined day, the whole circus comes back for you. By this time, your saddle sores will have mended enough to enjoy the return ride as well. We figured about $150 per person for four people; this includes one day in, one day out, and as many days as you want camping. A pretty good deal.

Balch Park Pack Station also arranges all-inclusive trips where they provide

CAMPGROUND RATINGS

Beauty:	★★★★
Site privacy:	★★★★
Site spaciousness:	★★★★★
Quiet:	★★★★★
Security:	★★★
Cleanliness/upkeep:	★★★★

Shake Camp Campground has horses, big trees, and the expansive western sky. Plan ahead—bring ice.

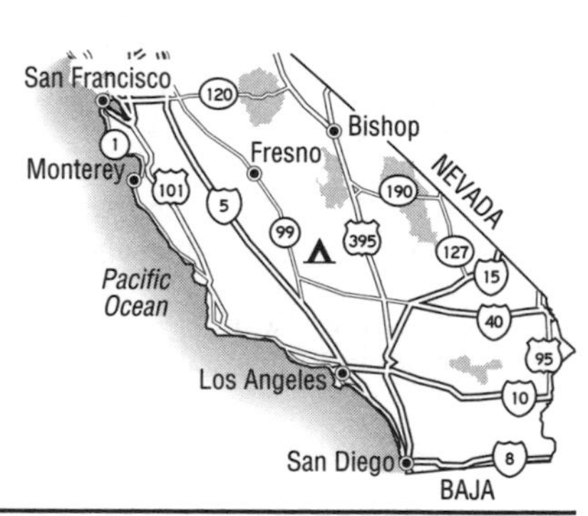

everything—packer, stock, cook, food, equipment, etc. Of course, the pack station also offers all-day rides from the stable with a guide and pack horse for $50 per day per person. Phone ahead for reservations at (209) 539-2227. This is very reasonable.

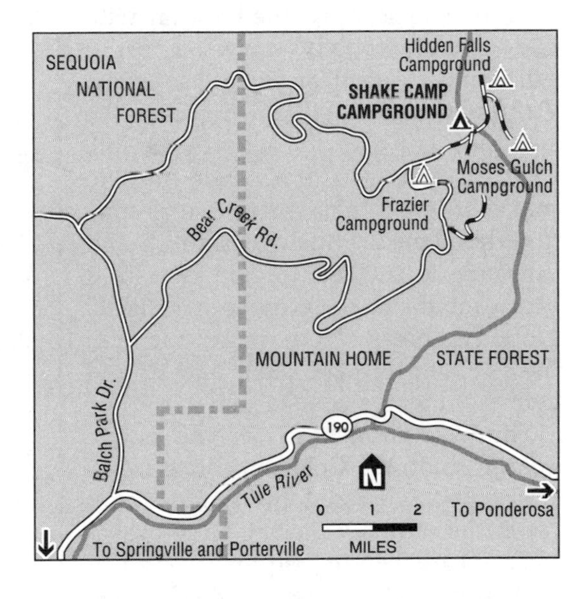

Between the pack station and the campground, there are all the public corrals for the privately owned horses and parking lots for their vans. Many of the horse owners and the folks renting from Balch Park Pack Station stay at the campground, so it's a horsy lot. I find horse people fun to camp with; most are fun loving, yet responsible people who live for their animals.

The campground itself is small, but well maintained. The campsites are roomy and fairly private down in a valley between Moses and Maggie mountains. There's an abundance of pine-needled pitches on which to set your tent. This is the best base camp for exploring Mountain Home State Forest.

If Shake Camp is full, try Frasier Mill Campground down the road. It offers good camping if you don't mind the darkness-at-noon aspect of the forest there. Forget Balch County Park; it's dusty as hell, and the campsites feel like parking places at a drive-in theater. Great springtime camping can be found at Hidden Falls on the Tule; however, when school is out, the place is overrun with roving packs of teenage campers wielding fishing rods.

A great hike from Shake Camp Campground is down the Moses Gulch Trail. Round-trip is around 7 miles. We took about five hours to do the loop, but this included lunch and a dip in the North Fork Middle Fork Tule River. Basically, the hike takes you down to Moses Gulch Campground, up to

Hidden Falls Campground, and farther up along the river trail. Ford the river at Redwood Crossing and head northwest, then south to Shake Camp Campground. Obtain the USGA 7.5 minute maps for Camp Wishon and Moses Mountain for this trip.

A shorter loop hike begins across from the public corrals and heads west up the hill to the giant sequoia, Adam Tree. Farther ahead is the Eve Tree, killed by loggers who stripped the bark off with axes. Why? Nobody knows. Cross a gulch and a stream, and you'll see some California hazelnuts growing near the sequoias. Look for the nuts in the fall. (Native Americans ground the nuts to make bread.) Carry on to the granite boulder signed "Indian Bathtubs" and scramble to the top to find oversized acorn mortar holes. Why so oversized? Nobody knows. From there, the trail heads south through cedar and fir and comes out where you started.

Think about fishing for the native golden trout, the California state freshwater fish. How did the golden trout reach the southern Sierra? They probably came up the San Joaquin River when high water in the Great Central Valley would push the Kern River via Tule Lake into the San Joaquin. All other trout in high-country lakes are stock trout. The only other native, the Kern River rainbow trout, is actually a golden trout with different markings.

Remember—Mountain Home State Forest is isolated. There is no store on the mountain. The nearest stores are in Springville, so bring everything you need. Use block ice, since it lasts three times longer than cube ice. It's not a bad idea to bring an extra sealed cooler of ice to replenish your regular cooler when it runs out. Fuel up before you head into the mountains.

KEY INFORMATION

Shake Camp Campground
Mountain Home State Forest
P.O. Box 517
Springfield, CA 93265

Operated by: California State Department of Forestry

Information: Summer: (209) 539-2321; Winter: (209) 539-2855

Open: June to October (phone ahead for weather and road conditions)

Individual sites: 11

Each site has: Picnic table, fireplace

Registration: Not required

Facilities: Piped water, vault toilets

Parking: At site

Fee: No fee

Elevation: 6,500 feet

Restrictions:

Pets—Allowed on leash

Fires—In fireplace

Vehicles—Small RVs

To get there from L.A., take I-5 north over the Tejon Pass to CA 99. Drive north on CA 99 past Bakersfield. Take Highway 65 north to Porterville. From Porterville, drive east on CA 190 through Springville. Then go left on Balch Park Drive for 3 miles. Turn right on Bear Creek Road and drive about 21 miles to the campground.

TILLIE CREEK CAMPGROUND

Lake Isabella, Sequoia National Forest

Tillie Creek is a campground for all seasons. I love Tillie in the fall when the leaves change, in the winter and spring when it's warm down on the plateau and there's snow up above in the mountains ringing the lake, and in the summer when it's hotter than Hades and all you have to do is sit in the water in an aluminum chair with a can of beer and fish for hungry bass.

I also love Tillie Creek when we go camping with my young niece, because Tillie Creek is very friendly to children. There's a beautiful stream that runs through the camp, and it's never fast or deep enough to carry off a child. The roads through the campground are just right for young cyclists. The lake is child-friendly with a gradually increasing bottom. There are real flushing toilets and real hot showers; thus, a newly toilet-trained child will not be intimidated, and adults have something hot to sluice the child with after a hard day of running around the campground.

This is not the forest primeval. Tillie Creek is what a scout camp or small town park used to be 30 years ago. There are many child-friendly things in the area for young ones to see and do, and Wofford Heights is just around the corner for a quick ice cream or fast food run.

Look out over Isabella Lake and see the watery grave of ancient Native American villages, historic towns, ranches, and

CAMPGROUND RATINGS

Beauty:	★★★★★
Site privacy:	★★★
Site spaciousness:	★★★★
Quiet:	★★★★
Security:	★★★
Cleanliness/upkeep:	★★★★

Tillie Creek is child-friendly and perfect for all seasons.

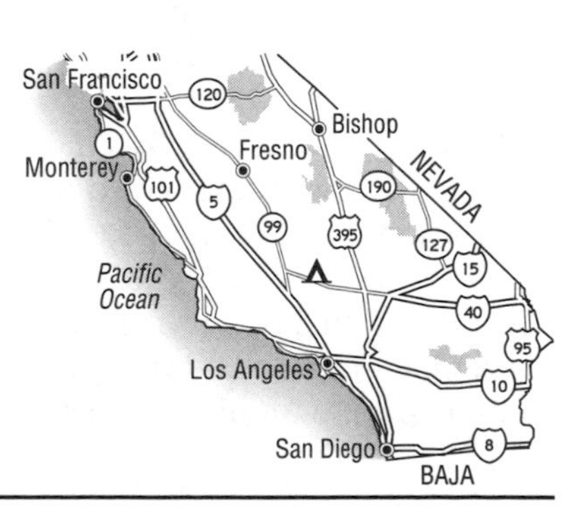

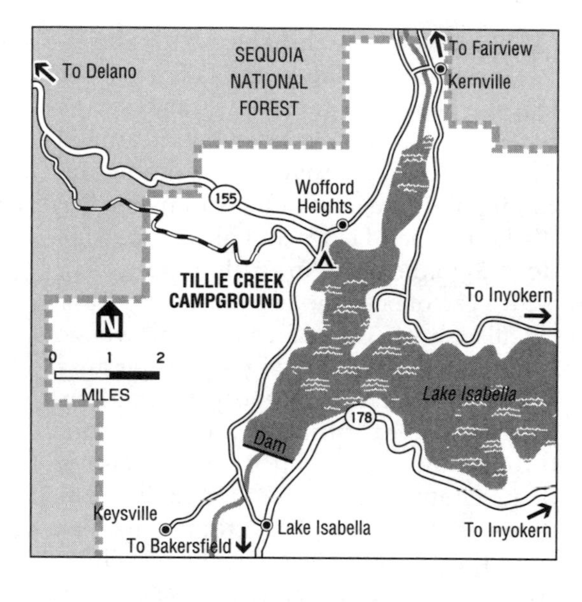

farms—all now submerged. When the dam was built in 1953, the Kern backed up and filled the hollow of the Kern River Valley. When the lake is low, search for a series of snags to see where the course of the north and south forks of the Kern once ran.

As you drive toward present-day Kernville, look to your right and see the old cemetery. Around the cemetery, you can find foundations of old Kernville. When Isabella Lake was created, the government helped move the town to its present site. Visit the Kern Valley Museum in Kernville and get a free map showing the streets and houses of old Kernville.

In Wofford, turn east on Evans Road and visit a site of infamy. Park near the El Segundo Rod and Gun Club and climb the hill just to the south called the Hill of Three Crosses. Look for the mortars in the rock where Tubatulabal Native Americans once ground acorns. It was here that Captain Moses McLaughlin and his men massacred a group of Native Americans in 1863. At the time, many in the community felt it was justified. This could be the basis for a good civics lesson.

Drive south on CA 155 to the Keyesville Road. Turn right (southwest) and drive to the end of the paved road. Turn right again and you'll find a historical landmark on Fort Hill. In 1850, Dickie Keyes, a Cherokee, hit gold-bearing quartz a few hundred yards northwest up Hogeye Gulch. To the south, the Mammoth Mine was found soon afterward. The wild town of Keyesville was born. One of the local hunters who supplied the miners with fresh meat was named Grizzly Adams because he had two pet grizzly bears. (Remember the

TV show of the same name?) Keyesville is long gone, but one house remains. Built in 1880, it was the scene of a big gunfight involving the "shootin' Walkers." Today, it is occupied and cared for by some local folks.

Another interesting trip is to the South Fork Wildlife Area. Go into Kernville and head south on Sierra Way to the Wildlife Area around South Fork Kern River. Take field glasses and look for the great blue heron who nests in the crowns of trees. Herons are open-minded and often share their tree with owls or hawks.

Just south of the Wildlife Area find cottonwood and willow stands that are managed by the Nature Conservancy. I searched an hour here without luck for the endangered yellow-billed cuckoo and the southwestern willow flycatcher who supposedly nest here. I found both in my *Birds of North America* guide and agree that they are both handsome birds in the illustration, but I failed to see either one in the flesh. Apparently, the cuckoos like to eat hairy caterpillars, and the flycatcher moves so fast through the air after insects it's hard to see.

All the marinas in the area rent boats. It's a good excursion, but remember to bring hats, sunscreen, food, and water, because everything becomes more intense out on the lake. Remember, too, that it can get rough. Shallow lakes are more prone to dangerous windblown waves than deep lakes. It has to do with

To get there from L.A., take I-5 north over the Tejon Pass to CA 99. Drive north on CA 99 past Bakersfield. Take CA 178 east to Lake Isabella. Take CA 155 toward Wofford Heights on the west shore of Isabella Lake. One mile before Wofford Heights on the right is the entrance to Tillie Creek Campground.

KEY INFORMATION

Tillie Creek Campground, Sequoia National Forest
Lake Isabella Office
P.O. Box 3810
Lake Isabella, CA 93240

Operated by: U.S. Department of Agriculture, Forest Service

Information: (619) 379-5646

Open: All year

Individual sites: 159 family units

Each site has: Picnic table, fireplace, piped water

Registration: At entrance

Facilities: Flush toilets, hot showers, sanitary disposal station, playground, fish-cleaning station

Parking: At site

Fee: $12

Elevation: 5,300 feet

Restrictions:

Pets—Allowed

Fires—In fireplaces

Vehicles—RVs up to 30 feet

the relationship between waves and the bottom (that's how you get surf when small ocean waves become huge and break as they approach the shallows near land).

How can you be in this area and not go river rafting? Depending on the age of your children, this can be a real experience. The trick is to marry the rafting experience with the age and daring of yourself and your companions. I've been on some sedate and bucolic rafting trips and others that turn your hair white. Ask around until you find an established rafting company with a solid reputation. It's better to pay a little more up front and have a good trip.

You'll have the most fun at Tillie, however, just hanging around the campground. The atmosphere encourages long coffee mornings. The playground attracts and engages the children. The changing sun and breeze off the lake combine for an incredible show. Tillie is a place to come with children for a weekend and actually relax.

TRAPPER SPRINGS CAMPGROUND

Courtright Reservoir, Sierra National Forest

Trapper Springs Campground is clean, uncrowded, and beautiful at a subalpine 8,200 feet. It's a granite land of peaks that fall away thousands of feet to thick pines below. But, up here it's twisted tamarack and juniper, pine growing out of rock, and lightning-blasted spars against a blue, blue sky. Courtright Reservoir is blue, too, like a sparkling gem against the gray granite, brown tree trunks, and green pine boughs.

What an incredibly beautiful place! John Muir, Scottish sheepherder turned naturalist wrote: ". . . the Sierra should be called not the Nevada or Snowy Range, but the range of light. And after ten years spent in the heart of it, rejoicing and wondering, bathing in the glorious floods of light, seeing the sunbursts of morning among the icy peaks, the noonday radiance on the trees and rocks and snow, the flush of the alpenglow, and a thousand dashing waterfalls with their marvelous abundance of irised spray, it still seems to me above all others the Range of Light, the most divinely beautiful of all the mountain chains I have ever seen."

Range of Light. That's all I could think about the two days my wife and I spent at Trapper Springs. We walked down the trail to Courtright Reservoir, hiked across the pined granite escarpments at dusk, and drank sundowners on a rock scoured clean by ice, sun, and wind.

CAMPGROUND RATINGS

Beauty:	★★★★★
Site privacy:	★★★★★
Site spaciousness:	★★★★★
Quiet:	★★★★★
Security:	★★★★★
Cleanliness/upkeep:	★★★★★

Trapper Springs Campground is an easy-to-access remote, beautiful campground. Since the campground is a half mile from the reservoir, it's not so heavily used.

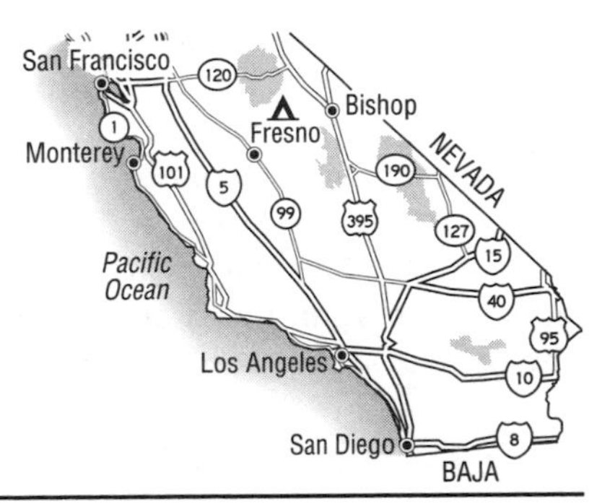

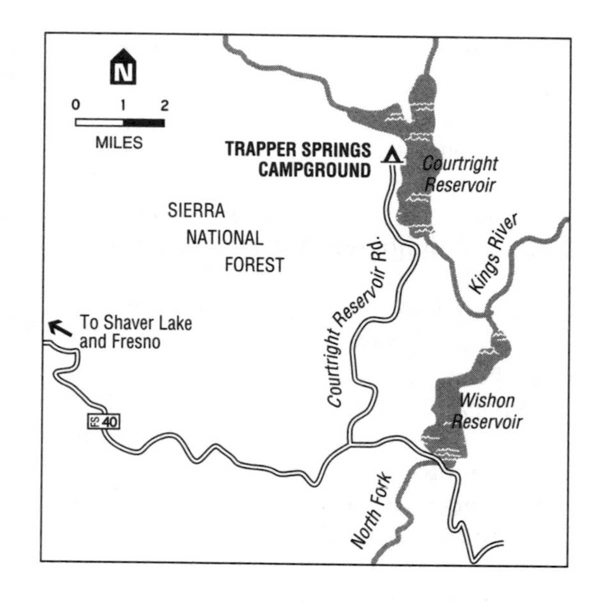

Then, the hunters came. September 15th is the beginning of hunting season in these parts. I expected campgrounds full of swaggering, gun-toting, beer-swigging NRA-ers; fusillades of rifle fire at dawn and screams of pain from Bambi's folks. Au contraire, the Trapper Springs Campground attracted a few polite gentlemen hunters, and there were a few far-off rifle pops, but otherwise nothing disturbed the sylvan peace of the reservoir and mountainside.

I'm not sure if this state of serenity had anything to do with Marv, our camp host, and his dog, but it's a possibility. The first night, the sweet campground hostess came around in her golf cart, and we asked her about the hunters. She said, "Well, if they get rowdy, I send my husband Marv down to talk to them, and he takes his dog." Well, we met Marv. He looked rawhide tough like an ex–rodeo rider, and his dog made your average pit bull look like a French poodle. Marv and his dog were quite a combo.

Granted, we did not take the trails up into the high lakes. We stayed around the campground and hiked around the reservoir where we wouldn't be mistaken for deer or other game. Still, Trapper Springs was the most pleasant experience of our trip.

The campground was built and is run by Pacific Gas and Electric. They do a fine job. All the facilities are well maintained and serviced by a friendly, energetic campground host and hostess. The sites are all secluded and clean, and the pitches are well off the service road. The pit toilets are clean, nice-smelling, and freshly painted. We paid for two sites—#9 and #10—sheltered under a huge granite tor.

The campground is located well off the reservoir shore, which keeps the place relatively uncrowded. A fact of life in Southern California camping is that wherever there's water, there are people. They come for fishing, boating, swimming, and the beauty and primitive peace of mind that a stream or lake gives a body. So, pick a campground like Trapper Springs that's a little off the water and you won't have too many neighbors.

The trail to the reservoir leaves from the bottom of the second campground loop. The shore is about a quarter of a mile downhill. Or, you can just head north up across the granite escarpments and work your way down. A fishing trail encircles the entire reservoir. There are great places to picnic, sunbathe, and fish.

A word on the fishing—find the nearest little grocery store and ask what bait the locals are using to catch trout. Some weeks they use worms, and other times it's salmon eggs. Be sure to obtain a license and to wear it visibly. Game wardens patrol the area, and the fine is considerable.

Considering how remote Trapper Springs Campground feels, the road in is pretty mild. Dinkey Creek Road is

To get there from L.A., take I-5 north over the Tejon Pass to CA 99. Drive north on CA 99 past Bakersfield 104 miles to Fresno. Take CA 41 north to CA 168 and go northeast to Shaver Lake. From the town of Shaver Lake, turn east on Dinkey Creek Road and drive 12 miles to McKinley Grove Road. Drive 14 miles to Courtright Reservoir Road. Go left and proceed 12 miles up Courtright Reservoir Road to Trapper Springs Campground.

KEY INFORMATION

Trapper Springs Campground, Sierra National Forest
Kings River Ranger Station
Trimmer Route
Sanger, CA 93657

Operated by: U.S. Department of Agriculture, Forest Service

Information: (209) 855-8321

Open: June to October

Individual sites: 45

Each site has: Picnic table, fireplace

Registration: At entrance

Facilities: Piped water, vault toilets

Parking: At site

Fee: $10

Elevation: 8,200 feet

Restrictions:

Pets—Allowed on leash

Fires—In fireplace

Vehicles—RVs up to 22 feet

wide and well graded; you'll thank God for this when you meet the heavily loaded lumber trucks. You'll pass the Ranger Station and small grocery store at Dinkey and head east on McKinley Grove (stop, picnic, and hike through the big trees). Past the turnoff to Courtright Reservoir road is the small Wishon Village store and private campground where you can buy last-minute ice, beer, soda, and campfire wood. I liked the sign on the door to their saloon, "Monday Night Football—Bring your own finger food." Then, head up the hill to Courtright Reservoir; the ascent is gradual, beautiful, and well graded. Before you know it, you're there.

TWIN LAKES CAMPGROUND

Mammoth Lakes Area, Inyo National Forest

The Twin Lakes around the Twin Lakes Campground look like blue beans joined at the hip. A little bridge connects the two lakes, and folks in rental rowboats and canoes scoot underneath it. Grandfathers teach their grandchildren how to fish as a waterfall cascades down the cliff above the lake.

The campground is friendly and accessible. There are rustic cabins, a lodge, and a store. A few miles away in the city of Mammoth Lakes, you'll find pizzerias, hardware stores, and a big wonderful Vons Supermarket on Old Mammoth Road. Twin Lakes Campground is a place to camp for a week; bring your family for the summer vacation.

The campsites sprawl around the two lakes and uphill across the road. If you find Twin Lakes Campground full, head a few hundred yards up the road to beautiful Coldwater Campground on Coldwater Creek. Or, head a mile or so up to Lake Mary Campground and Lake George Campground. All the sites are wonderful, but none is reservable. Phone the rangers to check on site availability and plan your trip so you arrive either in off-season or by Thursday for the weekend.

Head to the top of Coldwater Campground and walk a few hundred yards to the old Mammoth Consolidated Gold Mine on Mineral Hill. Here, you can see some of the old buildings from the mining

CAMPGROUND RATINGS

Beauty:	★★★★★
Site privacy:	★★★★
Site spaciousness:	★★★★★
Quiet:	★★★
Security:	★★★★★
Cleanliness/upkeep:	★★★★★

Twin Lakes Campground is a perfect place to spend summer vacation with the family.

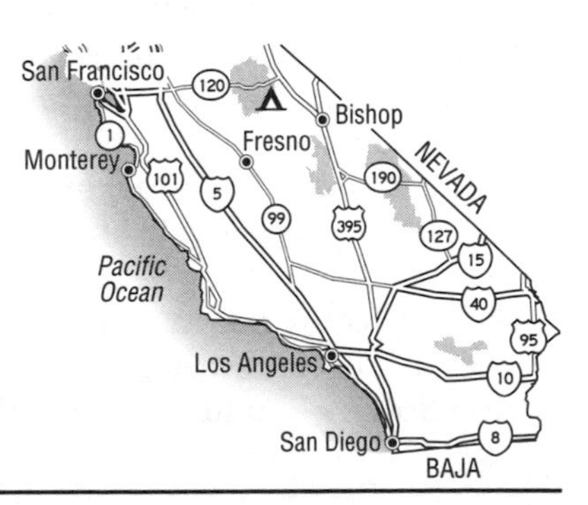

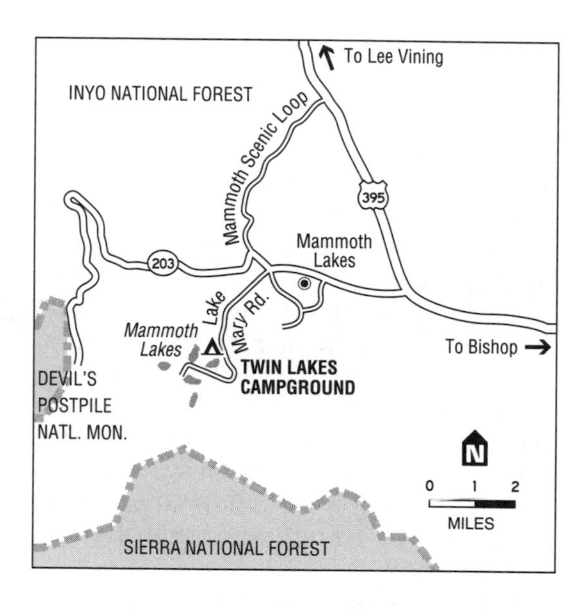

towns and locations of the many bawdy houses and a saloon named "The Temple of Folly"(long-since destroyed). Walk around the old buildings and rusted machinery and imagine the men that sweated in the summer sun and froze in the winter obsessed with gold fever. Climb up to the upper adit in the early morning for a view of Mount Banner and Mount Ritter.

Take the nice little hike to Emerald Lake. It's about a mile up the mountain. The trailhead and parking lot are next to the parking lot for the mine on Mineral Hill. Walk up by Coldwater Creek where there are lupine, monkeyflower, and fireweed. Bring a picnic and climb the rocks around the lake. Bring fishing gear as well. I watched one older woman reel in two decent trout while I ate my sandwich.

If you are ambitious, go around the left side of Emerald Lake. At the signed junction, go right to Gentian Meadow-Sky Meadows. Climb up by the inlet creek and reach tiny Gentian Meadow. Carry on up past a waterfall, and then, after a while you'll reach Sky Meadows. Look for paintbrush, corn lily, and elephant's heads among the grass. It's about 2.5 miles back down the hill.

Or, if you are truly ambitious, pick up the trail to Duck Pass (8.2 miles round-trip) back in the parking lot by the trailhead to Emerald Lake. Find the Duck Pass sign and start climbing. When you reach the entry sign for the John Muir Wilderness, bear right. Climb up through lodgepoles, pines, and hemlocks and carry on past the trail to Arrowhead Lake, Skelton Lake, and Barney Lake. Next, you'll see alpine Duck Pass ahead with all the high elevation flowers—columbine, gentian, and sorrel. Finally, traverse the pass and you'll see Duck Lake and pretty little Pika Lake on the left.

Back at Twin Lakes Campground, a nice stroll is around the shore to the falls. Access the trail behind campsite #24. You'll see a sign that says "Private/ Public Road." Bear left and follow the trail that heads through the trees to the waterfall. Or, walk over to Tamarack Lodge. This graceful establishment was built in 1923. The clerk from the grocery store averred that Tamarack Lodge has the best food in Mammoth Lakes.

However, my wife and I ate *chez* campsite the last time I was at Twin Lakes. I boiled some quartered potatoes and set them aside. Then I fried up some onions, garlic, jalapeno peppers, and strips of chicken breast in the pot. After a bit, I returned the potatoes to the pot and stirred it all about. *Très délicieux* for a one-pot meal!

About 3:15 A.M., I heard a visitor. I jumped out of my sleeping bag and poked my head out of the tent. A three-foot bear was rifling through my cooler of soft drinks. I shouted, and the midget bear looked at me insolently and pawed on. I threw a pebble, and he ran over to a tree and climbed up a few feet. I retrieved my cooler. He gave me the evil eye and ran into the underbrush. The next morning he was rooting around in the big trash container down by the bridge. He glared at me and sauntered off combing garbage out of his whiskers.

To get there from L.A., take I-5 north to CA 14. Go north to U.S. 395 near Inyokern. Go north on U.S. 395 for 123 miles to Bishop. Continue 37 miles north on U.S. 395 to Mammoth Lakes. From Mammoth Lakes, go west 3 miles on Lake Mary Road to the campground.

KEY INFORMATION

Twin Lakes Campground, Inyo National Forest
873 North Main Street
Bishop, CA 93514

Operated by: U.S. Department of Agriculture, Forest Service

Information: (619) 924-5500

Open: May to mid-October

Individual sites: 94

Each site has: Picnic table, fireplace

Registration: At entrance

Facilities: Piped water, flush toilets

Parking: At site

Fee: $11

Elevation: 8,700 feet

Restrictions:

Pets—Allowed on leash

Fires—In fireplaces

Vehicles—RVs up to 22 feet

VERMILION CAMPGROUND

Lake Thomas A. Edison, Sierra National Forest

Vermilion Campground is superb tent camping and worth every bit of the terrifying but sublimely beautiful drive in over Kaiser Pass. Plan on at least a one-and-a-half-hour drive from Huntington Lake. Bring all provisions—only ice, beer, and a few sundries are available at Vermilion Valley Resort. Expect your automobile engine to hiccup a bit while climbing the 8,800-foot Kaiser Pass. (Buy premium gasoline for the climb; your car will thank you.) Turn on your lights, since the road is narrow.

When you crest the pass, look out over the San Joaquin River Canyon and Kaiser Wilderness. John Muir wrote: "Westward, the general flank of the range is seen flowing sublimely away from the sharp summits, in smooth undulations; a sea of huge gray granite waves dotted with lakes and meadows, and fluted with stupendous canyons that grow steadily deeper as they recede into the distance."

Head down the narrow one-lane road. Remember, cars coming up have the right-of-way. Pass the seasonal Ranger Station at High Sierra and the turnoffs to Florence Lake and then Mono Hot Springs. You'll skirt the south side and dam of Edison Lake (the common name for Lake Thomas A. Edison). After a short dirt road, you'll see Vermilion Campground on the low ridge above the lake.

CAMPGROUND RATINGS

Beauty:	★★★★★
Site privacy:	★★★★★
Site spaciousness:	★★★★
Quiet:	★★★★
Security:	★★★★★
Cleanliness/upkeep:	★★★★★

Vermilion Campground proves that the best and most beautiful camping is usually the least accessible.

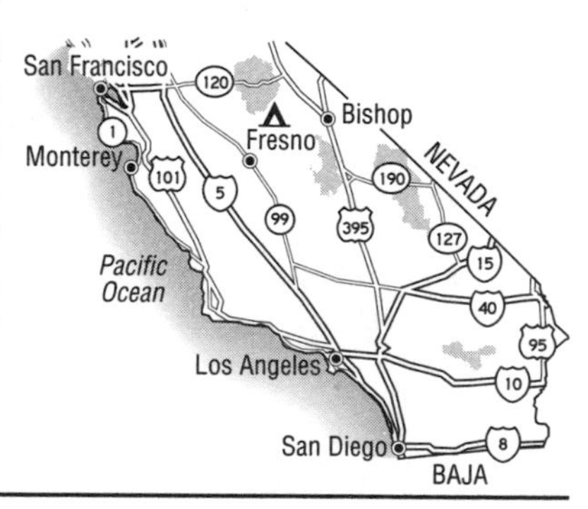

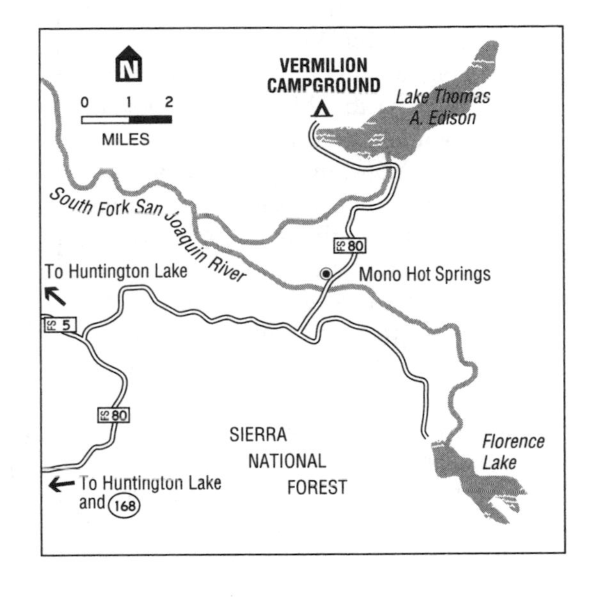

Most sites are for tents only. This is no easy access for RVs, and most of the parking places are too short for or at an uncomfortable parking angle for RVs. The pitches and picnic tables are a respectable distance away as well. Along the campground you'll find sandy beaches and granite, pined points creating private coves and bays.

The swimming was great. Granted, I was there in September, but you didn't have to be a polar bear to enjoy jumping in and splashing around. Bring little rubber shoes for the children, so they can race through the shallows.

A friendly couple camping near my wife and me invited us to use their kayaks. We paddled east about a half mile and beached on an island about 300 yards offshore. I swam and then lay on hot granite slabs and looked across at the snow fields on the mountains ringing the canyon. I saw a guy on a boat trolling by pull in at least a three-pound trout. What an incredible place!

The Vermilion Valley Resort runs a water ferry, which leaves the resort at 9:30 A.M. It drops you off to the east at the head of the lake. The fishing there is spectacular. Some folks hike up the trail toward Mono Pass, and some just lie around and wait for the ferry to come pick them up at 4 P.M. The round-trip costs $15, and you can bring your dog for free.

You can also hike east of the campground about a mile to a respectable brook. There is a bridge about 300 yards north, or you can wade across and freeze your feet off. This water comes off a glacier for sure. A little farther, the trail splits. The left fork heads up Silver Pass to the John Muir Trail/Pacific Crest Trail. The right fork takes you 15 miles up to Mono Pass and down the other side to Rock Creek below Mammoth (using the ferry cuts miles off this hike).

The resort rents boats for about $50 a day. This is reasonable, especially when you consider the alternative of trailering a boat up over Kaiser Pass. The resort also has a little cafe and rents some pretty basic rooms. For a hot bath, head down to nearby Mono Hot Springs where you can take a classy hot-spring soak in a deep tub. This is where most of the weary hikers wind up.

Try to pick a campsite at Vermilion well away from the resort, since they run a generator until about 10 P.M. Wood is at a premium, and bundles are expensive at the resort store. Instead, bring a saw. East of the camp, along the trail to the brook, there are quite a few deadfalls. Make sure the saw you bring is a good one. A cheap saw is no saw at all, but an instrument of torture. The sand around the pitches is fine and invasive. It's a good idea to bring along a bucket to dip your feet in before entering your tent. Of course, bring a small brush and tray to clean out the tent floor.

Be sure to check with rangers about the water before you arrive. The water at Vermilion is wonderful and spills out of a 400-foot artesian well, but, the day we

To get there from L.A., take I-5 north over the Tejon Pass to CA 99. Drive north on CA 99 past Bakersfield 104 miles to Fresno. Take CA 41 north to CA 168. Go northeast (right) to Shaver Lake. From Shaver Lake, head 20 miles north on CA 168 to Huntington Lake. From Lake Shore on Huntington Lake, take Kaiser Pass Road (FS 80) to Edison Lake Road at Mono Hot Springs. Continue 5 miles north to Vermilion Campground.

KEY INFORMATION

Vermilion Campground, Sierra National Forest
Pineridge Ranger Station
Shaver Lake, CA 93664

Operated by: U.S. Department of Agriculture, Forest Service

Information: (209) 855-5355 or (209) 297-0706

Open: June to October

Individual sites: 11 tent sites, 20 sites for tents or RVs

Each site has: Picnic table, fireplace

Registration: At entrance; for reservations, phone (800) 280-CAMP at least 10 days before desired dates ($7.50 fee)

Facilities: Piped water, pit toilets

Parking: At or near site

Fee: $12

Elevation: 7,000 feet

Restrictions:

Pets—Allowed on leash

Fires—In fireplace

Vehicles—RVs up to 16 feet

Other—15 mph limit for boats on Lake Edison

left, an inspector came through and posted the water spigots with "not safe to drink" signs. The few bottles of water at the resort store went like hotcakes. I wished I'd brought a filter to purify the lake water, because the only other alternative was boiling it. Luckily, an hour later, the water scare turned out to be a false alarm.

If Vermilion is full, head back down the road a few miles to Mono Creek Campground. It offers good camping, and the creek is only a hundred yards or so away from the sites. Or, try Mono Hot Springs, which has 26 sites. Since there is no dispersed camping in the area, the only other alternative is Jackass Meadow below the Florence Lake dam. I eliminated camping there when I heard a local character describe the noises the dam made during the last earthquake near Mammoth Lakes. After looking at the dam, my faith in modern engineering was quickly eroded by my fervent belief in Murphy's Law. Why chance it? Reserve at Vermilion.

WHITE WOLF CAMPGROUND

Yosemite National Park

Yosemite National Park is heaven on earth. With the Mariposa Battalion, the first English-speaking party to see Yosemite Valley, was Lafayette Bunnell. He wrote: "The grandeur of the scene was softened by the haze that hung over the valley—light as gossamer—and by the clouds which partially dimmed the higher cliffs and mountains. This obscurity of vision but increased the awe with which I beheld it, and as I looked, a peculiar exalted sensation seemed to fill my whole being, and I found my eyes in tears with emotion."

The Yosemite Native Americans, the original inhabitants, loved the valley too, but as soon as they came into contact with the forty-niners, it was all over for them. By 1852, Chief Tenaya of the Yosemites, his tribe decimated, was stoned to death by some raiding Mono Native Americans. Soon after, August T. Dowd, a miner hunting camp meat, saw a tree bigger than he'd ever seen before. He told his friends about it, and the tourists began flooding in. Yosemite Valley became a mecca to the world.

Now, four-hour traffic jams in Yosemite Valley are common, and all the campgrounds are constantly booked. You can see cars parked along the road for miles. Folks swarm across the road. Smog rises in the air. Run for your life!

CAMPGROUND RATINGS

Beauty:	★★★★★
Site privacy:	★★★★★
Site spaciousness:	★★★★★
Quiet:	★★★★★
Security:	★★★★★
Cleanliness/upkeep:	★★★★★

White Wolf Campground is the only campground in Yosemite National Park worth squeezing into.

Avoid Yosemite Valley, and explore the rest of the park instead. Come in from the east over the Tioga Pass off U.S. 395 or from the west on CA 120. Shun CA 41, and don't get stuck in the Wawona Tunnel. You don't need to see or camp in the Valley.

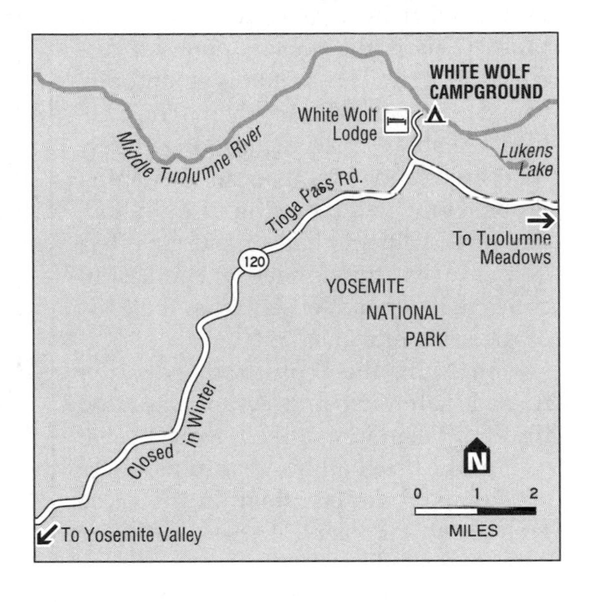

However, you should see Tuolumne Meadows and camp in White Wolf Campground. The Tioga Pass area is insanely beautiful. John Muir described it eloquently: "From garden to garden, ridge to ridge, I drifted enchanted, now on my knees gazing into the face of a daisy, now climbing again and again among the purple and azure flowers of the hemlocks, now down into the treasuries of the snow, or gazing far over domes and peaks, lakes and woods, and the billowy glaciated fields of the upper Tuolumne. In the midst of such beauty, pierced with its rays, one's body is all one tingling palate. Who wouldn't be a mountaineer! Up here all the world's prizes seem nothing."

White Wolf Campground is full of tiny meadows and stands of lodgepole pine, and the Middle Tuolumne River flows through the campground. The sites are set in the pines and around granite boulder gardens. The campground is constructed beautifully; each loop seems miles away from the others. The arrangement of the tables and sites create a sense of spaciousness. The facilities are clean and well tended. This is slow, elegant camping.

Only the little bear wandering around camp caused a little nervousness. Obviously he was a special bear because he had little colored tags in his ears.

Our neighbor shook a towel at the little bear, and he decamped, at least for that day. Following orders, of course, we were careful to put away our coolers even if we were only leaving camp for a moment. Bears get a record for raiding campers, and the rangers are forced to take steps. We didn't want that to happen to the little bear with tags in his ears.

We hiked up to Hardin Lake and sat under the pines reading John Muir. Here's what he wrote about the sugar pine. "This is the noblest pine yet discovered . . . The trunk is a smooth, round, delicately taped shaft. The needles are about three inches long, finely tempered and arranged in sweeping limbs. How well they sing in the wind, and how strikingly harmonious an effect is made by the immense cylindrical cones that depend loosely from the ends of the main branches!"

John Muir, the Scottish sheepherder turned naturalist and writer cavorted through the mountains. He wore a great coat and carried all his gear in its pockets. At night, he lay down in the same great coat and slept. These old-timers were real men!

Take John A. "Snowshoe" Thompson for example. Every winter from 1856 to 1876, Thompson carried the U.S. mail alone across the Sierra. Traveling on skis (called snowshoes in those days), Thompson carried a 100-pound pack and made the 180-mile round-trip in five

To get there from L.A., take I-5 north to CA 14. Head north to U.S. 395 near Inyokern. Go north on U.S. 395 for 123 miles to Bishop. Continue north on U.S. 395 for 57 miles to CA 120 (Tioga Pass Road). Go west 43 miles to White Wolf Road on the right. The White Wolf Campground is about a mile down that road.

KEY INFORMATION

White Wolf Campground
Yosemite National Park
P.O. Box 577
Yosemite, CA 95389

Operated by: U.S. National Park Service

Information: (209) 372-8502; for recorded information, call (209) 372-0200

Open: June to October

Individual sites: 87

Each site has: Picnic table, fireplace

Registration: At entrance

Facilities: Piped water, flush toilets

Parking: At site

Fee: $10

Elevation: 7,900 feet

Restrictions:

Pets—On leash

Fires—In fireplace

Vehicles—RVs up to 30 feet

days. His diet consisted of beef jerky and crackers, and he drank snow. He didn't carry a blanket or wear an overcoat.

At night, Thompson would find a tree stump. After setting fire to the stump, he'd cut some fir boughs for a bed. With his feet to the fire, he'd sleep through the worst blizzards. Thompson never bothered about storms.

If he was caught outside camp in a bad blizzard, he just stood on a rock and danced a jig to stay warm. Imagine this incredible man standing on a rock somewhere lost in the Sierras in a blizzard dancing his jig on a granite slab.

Today, camping life is a little easier. Still, remember to get supplies in the western flatlands or in Mammoth Lakes on your way in from the east. Only ice, beer, and soda are available in Tuolumne Meadows, Crane Flat, and White Wolf Lodge near White Wolf Campground (in the summer months only).

WISHON CAMPGROUND

Camp Wishon, Sequoia National Forest

As you leave the little town of Springdale and head east toward Camp Wishon, you feel as if you're leaving civilization behind. All the stores and gas stations have a last-chance look, and the road signs anticipate the high mountain passes ahead—"Chains may be required" or "No night plowing." The only vehicles on the road are big pickups with four-wheel-drive as CA 190 begins to climb, following the turns of the Middle Fork Tule River. The roadside scenery strips down to big rocks and chaparral. There are two picnic areas, then the huge flume carrying water down to the power plant below, and then the turnoff north up Wishon Drive along the North Fork of the Middle Fork Tule River.

Wishon Drive is steep and narrow and winds along a steep pitch down to the river. You'll find good fishing here. In the spring, the big pickups are parked at the turnouts, and their drivers are down below fishing for trout. Here, the snow level can come down to 3,000 feet. Think about chains for the ride down if you hit bad weather. Then, suddenly, you're out of the chaparral and into the Yellow Pine Belt with the pines, firs, big leaf maple, oaks, cedars, and lilac. The road dips into a beautiful, flat canyon where you'll see the campground—more of a forested glade—by the river with its alders and cottonwood.

CAMPGROUND RATINGS

Beauty:	★★★★★
Site privacy:	★★★★
Site spaciousness:	★★★★
Quiet:	★★★★
Security:	★★★★★
Cleanliness/upkeep:	★★★★

Wishon Campground offers good fishing, good hiking, and a long camping season.

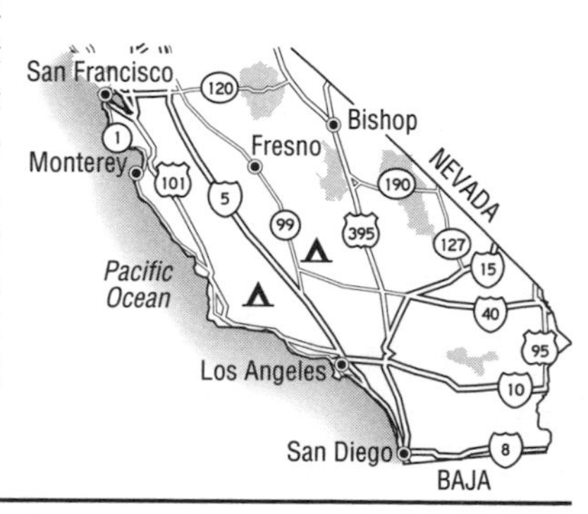

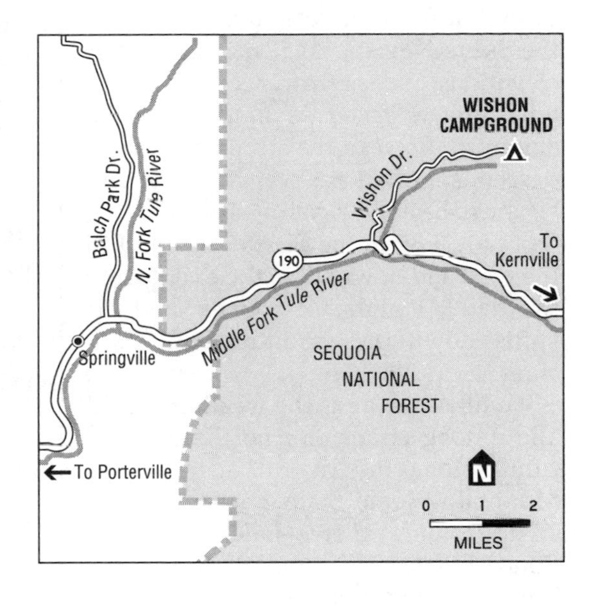

It was raining heavily the day we arrived at Wishon, and my wife fell in love with the place. The campsites are all spacious and private. There's a Ranger Station at the gate. We saw big, happy, wet men in rain gear stoking fires to keep warm, and you knew they'd spent the morning fishing. The way the campground is, where it is, and the feeling you get when you arrive make you want to pull up, relax, and stay for a couple days. At 4,000 feet, it will snow in late spring. We wanted it to, so we could stay longer. There was enough downed wood around our campsite to keep us warm around the fire that night. (Bring charcoal fire starter along to get wet wood going easily for your camp fire.)

I pitched the tent away from the stream to avoid the downward current of cold air that blows down the Sierras at night. It's always a good idea, too, if you're sleeping outside to point your feet into the wind; you'll stay a lot warmer.

The first thing we heard in the morning were the birds. It all began with the noisy black-headed grosbeak and its cheery rising and falling notes. It has a rust-colored body with a black head and black and white wings. With its very thick beak, you'd think it was a seed eater, but it also eats buds and insects in the upper canopy of trees. We saw the mountain chickadee and heard its sad song—three slow notes, two high tones, and one lower. It's a small bird with a gray body and black and white stripes on its head. Another was the dark-eyed junco, a small gray bird with a dark head.

We saw many western gray squirrels who survive the winter on buried cashes of acorns or pine seeds. They remember and dig down through the snow to dinner. If a squirrel dies, the acorns often germinate, which is why oak trees tend to grow in clumps. A botanist friend of mine also offered another explanation for clumped oaks—the regeneration of sprouts from a single clump after a fire.

During the day, the wind kicked up from west to east. I have read that this is caused by air heating up more rapidly in the desert, which makes it rise, which draws air from the coast over the top of the Sierra Nevada. As it reaches higher elevations and narrower canyons, the wind moves faster as it ascends (the chimney effect) to the summit where it descends into the Owens Valley and becomes heated by compression. So, the daily air flow in the Sierras is uphill in the west and downhill in the east during the day. At night, of course, cold air spills down the mountains on both sides.

We hiked as far as the weather would allow along a trail going northeast out of camp along the river that heads to Mountain Home State Forest and the campgrounds there—Balch, Hedrick Pond, Frazier Mill, and Shake Camp. This is lovely country.

To get there from L.A., take I-5 north over the Tejon Pass to CA 99. Drive north on CA 99 past Bakersfield. Take CA 65 north to Porterville. From Porterville drive 25 miles east on CA 190. Turn north (left) on Wishon Drive and go 3.5 miles. There's a Ranger Station on the right and a few campsites. The main campground is farther to the right over a bridge and then left.

KEY INFORMATION

Wishon Campground, Sequoia National Forest
Tule River Ranger District
900 West Grand Avenue
Porterville, CA 93257

Operated by: U.S. Department of Agriculture, Forest Service

Information: (209) 784-1500 or (209) 539-2607

Open: April to October

Individual sites: 10 sites for tents only, 26 sites for tents or RVs

Each site has: Picnic table, fireplace

Registration: At entrance

Facilities: Piped water, vault toilets

Parking: At site

Fee: $12

Elevation: 4,000 feet

Restrictions:

Pets—On leash

Fires—In fireplaces

Vehicles—RVs up to 22 feet

SOUTHERN CALIFORNIA

THE SOUTHERN SIERRAS

DARK CANYON CAMPGROUND

San Bernardino National Forest

I drove through Idyllwild in a mist so thick the neon lights of the cute little mountain town could only blush through the fog. I found a place to park and drifted along a sidewalk until I ran right into a Mt. San Jacinto state park ranger who said this fog never happens this time of year. It was June 15th; it was supposed to be sunny and at least 80ºF.

Back on CA 243, I leaned out the window and navigated by the stripes down the middle of the highway until Forest Service Road 4S02 split off to the right, and I could reckon the road by aiming for the gap in the pines. After traveling down the narrowing road and across a stream, I was at Dark Canyon Campground, one of the most charming campgrounds in the very charming Idyllwild area of the San Bernardinos.

The campground hosts popped out of their trailer by the entrance and helped me find the perfect campsite down by the stream that runs through the canyon. The water is cold and runs clear around granite boulders through pools with clean sand bottoms. In this area, and most parts of the San Bernardino National Forest, water is at a premium, and here it's at its most attractive.

The 22 campsites in Dark Canyon are perfect for tent camping. The fireplaces and picnic tables for most of the sites are a 15-yard walk away from the parking lot

CAMPGROUND RATINGS

Beauty:	★★★★★
Site privacy:	★★★★
Site spaciousness:	★★★★
Quiet:	★★★★★
Security:	★★★★★
Cleanliness/upkeep:	★★★★★

Dark Canyon Campground is a heartbreaker—so beautiful and so near Los Angeles. Reserve!

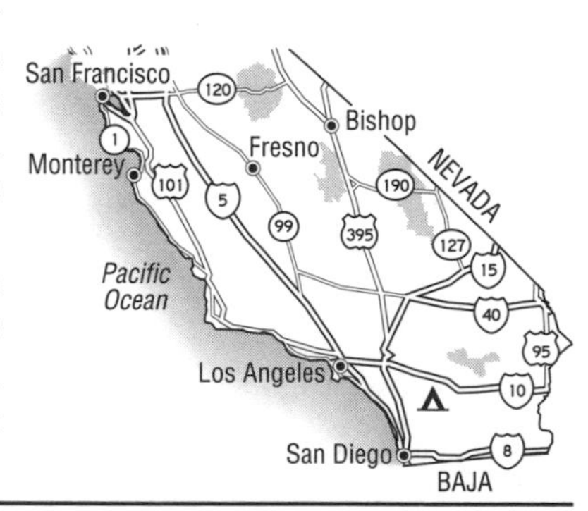

(ample enough for an RV, however). A good quarter of the camping sites are down by the stream, and another half are up in the pines above the campground.

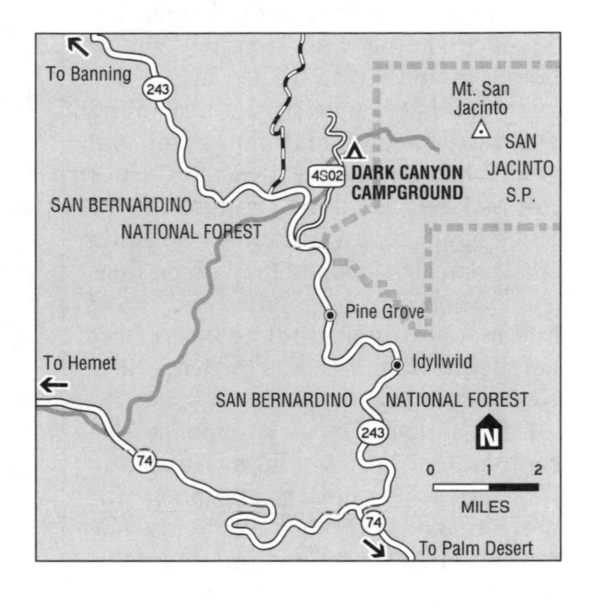

Shortly after I arrived, it started snowing, and my hikes around the canyon were screened through hard-driving sleet and wet snow. What I saw were pines; Dark Canyon is right on the line between north-facing Upper Chaparral and the higher Yellow Pine Forest. Both of these areas are packed with pines—Douglas fir, Coulter pine, white fir, incense cedar, sugar and yellow pine. Down by the stream, you'll see riparian trees like alder, willow, and black cottonwood.

I saw no birds. Where were they all? Hiding from the bitter weather, I'm sure. How do they survive? Birds have a very high rate of metabolism. The smaller the bird, the higher the metabolic rate. For example, a resting hummingbird has a metabolic rate 50 times faster than man. They eat a lot. Robins eat 14 feet of earthworms in one day—good Lord! The down side of all those earthworms and high metabolic rates is a shorter life span (less than two years for most songbirds).

Birds also fluff up and take cover when it's cold. By fluffing they can treble their bulk for insulation. By the same token, when it's a normal, 85ºF June day in Dark Canyon, the birds hold their feathers close to their bodies—keeping cool, pressing out the insulating air, and letting their body heat go.

I hiked a mile or so up the dirt road to the trailhead that heads east into Mt. San Jacinto State Park to Deer Springs. By this time, it was sleeting harder, so

I double-timed back to buy a generous bunch of firewood for $4 from the sweet campground hostess and endeavored to light a fire in my fireplace.

Fortunately, I had a can of charcoal lighter fluid, which, when combined with a little dry paper and a modest amount of kindling, will start up just about any campground wood, whether it be flammable pine or reluctant, but long-burning oak. I know lighter fluid doesn't sound kosher to the former Boy Scout planning the camping trip at home in the living room, but, when everyone is blowing hard and fanning wet pine needles and chunks of wet wood, this petroleum distillate cheater can make you look like a hero. On the other hand, hardware stores also sell a small hatchet-sized splitter, which does a good job chopping purchased wood into more easily lit kindling if you can't handle the humiliation of the tenderfoot charcoal fluid.

Dark Canyon is very popular. The campground hostess told me it usually fills up early Friday afternoon for the weekends. On big weekends, she recommended arriving on Thursday. Otherwise, it's a great idea to make a reservation.

If you decide not to reserve, on FS 4S02 you will see a sign informing you if Dark Canyon Campground and its two sister campgrounds, Fern Basin and Marion Mountain, are full. If so, drive to Idyllwild and go to the Ranger Station on the left as you enter town. They will direct you to dispersed camping areas. Some of these are "yellow post" areas,

To get there from L.A., drive east on I-10 to Banning. Take CA 243 south 22 miles toward Idyllwild. Turn left on FS 4S02 and go another 3 miles to the campground.

KEY INFORMATION

Dark Canyon Campground
San Bernardino National Forest/San Jacinto Ranger District
P.O. Box 518, 54270 Pinecrest
Idyllwild, CA 92349

Operated by: Department of Agriculture, Forest Service

Information: (909) 659-2117

Open: May to mid-October

Individual sites: 22

Each site has: Fireplace, picnic table

Registration: At entrance

Facilities: Piped water, vault toilets

Parking: Within 20 yards of sites

Fee: $9; for reservations, phone (800) 280-CAMP at least 10 days in advance ($7.50 fee)

Elevation: 5,800 feet

Restrictions:

Pets—On leash

Fires—In fireplace

Vehicles—No RVs over 22 feet

Other—Road in is very narrow

which means you can have a fire in the fire ring. Other areas require a fire permit, which will be issued at the station if fire conditions allow it. In any event, you'll find a great place to tent camp all by yourself out in the wilderness.

Other alternatives include the two Mt. San Jacinto State Park campgrounds. Idyllwild Campground is right smack in town by the Mt. San Jacinto State Park Ranger Station. It is clean (flush toilets and showers), safe, and especially wonderful on Sunday morning when you feel like walking 100 yards to Idyllwild for brunch and the Sunday paper. Many of Idyllwild's sites are for tents only, which makes it especially friendly. Stone Creek, also a Mt. San Jacinto State Park Campground, is out of town and a little more primitive.

The last time I was there, Stone Creek Campground was closed. I asked a particularly crusty ranger why. "Plague," he said. "My God, I guess I don't want to camp there!" I whined. "Oh, hell!" he said. "We're just going to dust all the squirrels down for fleas, and that's that." He'd be damned if he ever heard of anybody getting the plague from squirrels and allowed that it was not a reason to give up camping anywhere. "Just don't feed the little beggars corn chips and you'll be all right," he assured me.

DOANE VALLEY CAMPGROUND

Palomar Mountain State Park

Palomar means "place of the pigeons," and Palomar Mountain feels so Mediterranean, you'll think you're in Italy. There's a sense of tradition and civilization on the mountain. Maybe it drifts down from the incredible hand-crafted observatory on the summit, or comes from the gentle Native Americans who gathered acorns here, or maybe it stems from the sense of awe observatory visitors get when they realize what a tiny part of the universe we live in and how insignificant we really are. Anyway, Palomar Mountain State Park Campground offers good tent camping and great family camping.

Built in the 1930s by the Civilian Conservation Corps, the campsites are styled in stone and set under huge trees. That was back in the days when folks tent camped, and cars were tiny Fords, so the campground is geared toward tent campers. The toilets are clean, and the hot showers cost a few quarters. The park headquarters is back up the road on the way in and, when I was there, was staffed by a helpful lady ranger who looked like a young Elke Sommer. Included in the park area is a Christian Conference Center and a School Camp, both infested with boisterous junior high schoolers having the time of their lives. If you tire of camp grub, at the intersection of County Road S6 and S7, you'll find Mother's Kitchen Restaurant, which serves good feed.

CAMPGROUND RATINGS

Beauty:	★★★
Site privacy:	★★★★
Site spaciousness:	★★★
Quiet:	★★★
Security:	★★★★★
Cleanliness/upkeep:	★★★★

Camp at Doane Valley Campground to see the stars at Palomar Observatory, eat at Mother's Kitchen Restaurant, and bring home 10 pounds of gems.

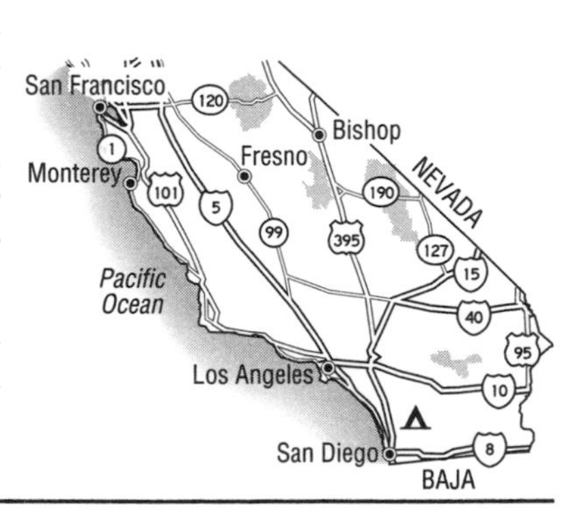

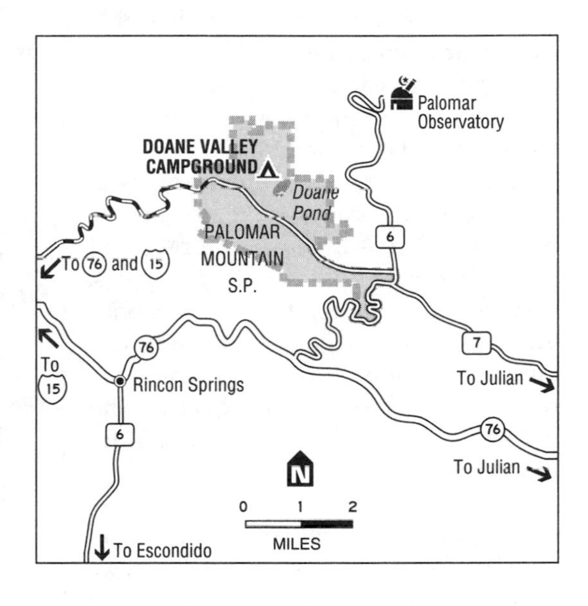

Near the campground is Doane's Pond, inhabited by the world's largest bullfrog who sounds like Nick Nolte with laryngitis. It's a cute pond with picnic tables set around it under ramadas, since it gets hot here in the summer. On the road in, you'll see a sign threatening a $500 fine for miscreants throwing snowballs at cars or inhabitants of cars, so you know snow drifts up a bit here in the winter. I think the best time to visit is in the spring or in the fall when the leaves change. But, the Palomar Observatory qualifies the mountain as a wonderful place to visit year-round, regardless of the weather. I think seeing ourselves as creatures of the universe is easier if we are camping rather than home flipping on a light switch or a television set. Buy the star map in the observatory gift shop and go out in the meadow by Doane's Pond at night. Imagine how the ancients must have felt in a world lit only by starlight and fire.

I followed a group of junior high schoolers and heard their teacher try to pique the loutish pupils' interest in the observatory. It really is amazing. The dome weighs 1,000 tons and is so well engineered that it may be moved by hand. The telescope, which weighs 750 tons, can also be moved by the touch of a finger. The glass disk at the heart of the telescope was ground and polished to the two-millionth part of an inch. Incredible! Craftsmen capable of this work are all gone now. If the telescope broke down, it would be prohibitively expensive in this day and age to repair it.

It wasn't hard to spot the band-tailed pigeon which gives Palomar Mountain its name. The band-tail is not your ordinary "rat with wings" pigeon cadging food at the local patio restaurant, but a lovely bird with a yellow bill, green nape, and white neck band. It's call is a low-pitched, owl-like "coo-coo." The band-tail likes acorns, as does the acorn woodpecker.

The acorn woodpecker goes around storing acorns by the thousands in small, specially drilled holes—each containing a single acorn—in dead trees, telephone poles, fence posts, and even the sides of buildings. Its diligence is equaled only by the gray squirrel who hides acorns in underground caches and later smells them out when hungry. Acorns are a big industry on the mountain.

The Luiseno Native Americans, who also collected acorns on Palomar, ate manzanita berries, choke cherries, and toyon berries. For salad and veggies, they ate lily bulbs, tree mushrooms, yucca blossoms, sage shoots, wild mustard, clover, and celery. In season, they relished watercress, lamb's quarter, and Indian lettuce. Palomar is a bountiful mountain.

If you strike out at Doane Valley Campground (reserve ahead for weekends!), there are two Forest Service Camps up the road to the observatory. I stayed at Observatory Campground once during off-season in the middle of the week and loved it. The oaks there are huge, and it's wide open with views of the ridges. The trail up to the observatory is fun. However, it does get crowded on weekends. Just a quarter-mile up is Fry Creek Campground. This is a nice campground in the woods that favors

To get there from L.A., drive east on I-10. Take I-15 south to the intersection with CA 76. Drive east 21 miles to County Road S-6. Go north (left) 6.8 miles, then left on County Road S-7 3 miles to the campground.

KEY INFORMATION

Doane Valley Campground, Palomar Mountain State Park
19952 State Park Road
Palomar Mountain, CA 92060

Operated by: Department of Parks and Recreation, State of California—The Resources Agency, P.O. Box 942896, Sacramento, CA 94296-0001

Information: (619) 742-3462 or (619) 765-0755

Open: All year

Individual sites: 21 for tents only, 10 for RVs

Each site has: Fireplace, picnic table

Registration: At entrance, reserve through MISTEX at (800) 444-PARK (fee charged)

Facilities: Flush toilets; piped water; coin-operated, hot showers

Parking: Near site

Fee: $12

Elevation: 4,700 feet

Restrictions:

Pets—Allowed on leash ($1 fee), not allowed on trails

Fires—In fireplace

Vehicles—RVs up to 21 feet

tent campers because the road in is too narrow for RVs or trailers. (For more information on these campgrounds, phone Palomar Mountain District Office, Goose Valley Ranger Station at (619) 788-0250.)

A good side trip from Palomar is Gems of Pala, just down the road toward I-15. It's open Thursday through Sunday 10 A.M.–4 P.M. For a fee, you get to dig in one of the world's foremost tourmaline locations. Bring a garden shovel, a spray bottle, and an eighth-of-an-inch mesh screen about one foot by two feet. You get to take home up to ten pounds of pink, blue, green, black, and watermelon tourmaline. It's fun. Call Gems of Pala at (619) 742-1356 for more information.

HANNA FLAT CAMPGROUND

Fawnskin, San Bernardino National Forest

"Abandon hope all ye who enter here" is a good motto for campers coming to Big Bear Lake on holiday weekends, but during mid-week or off-season, the north shore is downright civilized. It's a beautiful place, and the rangers and civilians are genuinely friendly. Most of the land is National Forest.

Hanna Flat Campground features good tent camping. The sites are set in stands of Jeffrey pine (smell the vanilla of the bark) and spaced nicely to allow vistas of pine-covered and rocky hills with the blue sky big country look. Manzanita grows under the pines, and there's a mild riparian community by the cut along the campground. Best of all is how the sites are engineered to give the camper maximum privacy and space. There is an abundance of flat room for tents at each site, and the ground is spongy and pine-needled.

Hanna Flat Campground is run by Alpine Camping Services, a private organization, and they do a good job. They are represented at Hanna Flat by a Grizzly Adams–type fellow wearing rawhide boots and his dad back at the Camp Host trailer. The pit toilets are clean, and there are some flush toilets as well.

The few miles of dirt road coming in discourages most RVers who prefer a site down by the lake in parks with hookups. In the nearby ville of Fawnskin, you'll find a little grocery store and two homespun

CAMPGROUND RATINGS

Beauty:	★★★★
Site privacy:	★★★★★
Site spaciousness:	★★★★★
Quiet:	★★★★★
Security:	★★★★★
Cleanliness/upkeep:	★★★★★

Hanna Flat Campground is "Big Sky" country camping with fishing, biking, and hiking. Don't get caught alive here on big holidays.

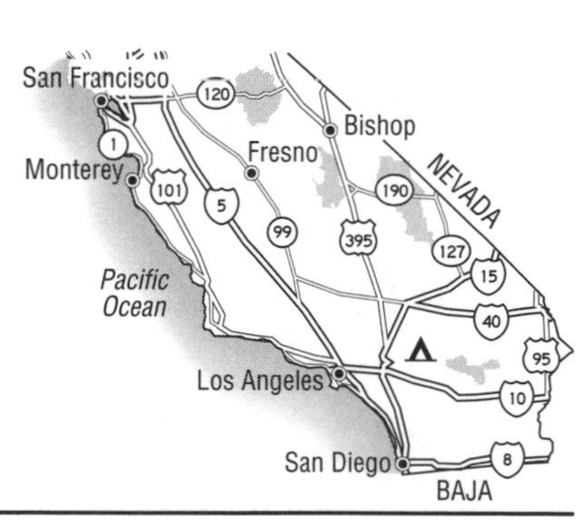

eateries for breakfast, lunch, and beer. For serious shopping go around the lake to Big Bear City. There's a Thrifty as big as an aircraft carrier and more banks than you can shake a stick at. Big Bear City has everything a body could conceivably desire.

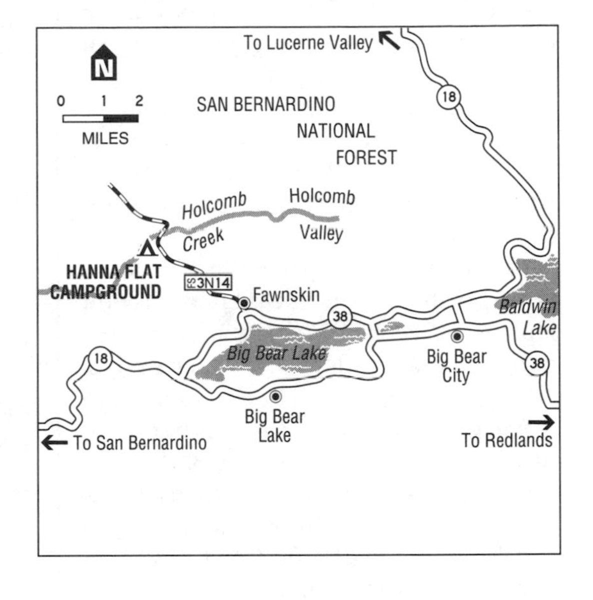

Lake access from Hanna Flat Campground begins in Fawnskin's Dana Point Marina, which is open to the public and has a bait shop, picnic tables, a lake beach, and toilets. A sign announced roosting bald eagles from November to March. On my visit, the main attraction was a machine working on the lake flora trying to keep the channel clear. Apparently, this variety of lake flora escaped from somebody's aquarium. To add to the excitement, an elderly fisherman calmly caught a good-sized bass. I could see a little snow on the peaks south of the lake. I loved all the rustic wood cottages. Fawnskin is charming.

More lake access is below Serrano Campground a few miles east of Fawnskin. There's a marina renting boats and bicycles, an observatory, a paved hiking/biking path, and Meadow's Edge Picnic Ground with all the amenities and a nice lake beach. The observatory is unique for its study of the sun. The dome is out on the water at the end of a dock, since water cuts down on image distortion. The observatory is open to visitors on Saturday, from 4–6 P.M., between July 4th and Labor Day.

Just past Serrano Campground is the Big Bear Ranger Station where you can get maps of all the hiking trails. Big Bear offers good hiking and is a world-renowned mountain biking center. Snow Summit, a snow ski resort, utilizes its chair-lifts in the summer for taking mountain bikers to the top of the mountain at 8,200 feet. From there on, it's your fancy. There are 60 miles of trails accessible from there. Of course, the real fanatics go down Snow Summit's single-track downhills about 90 mph.

Back at the Hanna Flat Campground, you'll find two fun hikes; one heads out from site #51 to Grout Bay, and the other goes from site #25 north and back along the road. The trail to Grout Bay is an 8-mile round-trip with lovely views of the lake from the plateau. Look for eagles on the tops of dead trees in the area. From this trail, you can also access the trail to Gray's Peak. I understand the trail is a bit rough as you near the summit of Gray's Peak.

The second hike, from site #25, takes you north to the beaver dams on Holcomb Creek. Here, the beavers live in dens in caves along the water's edge. An easier access to the beaver dams is to drive your car out of the campground, turn left on the dirt road (FS 3N14) you came in on, and go a mile or so to a parking lot on the right before Holcomb Creek. Find the Pacific Crest Trail just north across the creek and to the left of FS 3N14. Follow the trail west for about a mile, and you will see the beaver dams. Look for wildflowers along the way. I was able to identify wild rose, lupine, Indian paintbrush, and scarlet bugler.

Look at the mountains around Big Bear Lake and imagine—this was once

To get there from L.A., go east on I-10 to near San Bernardino. Then take CA 30 north to CA 330. About 35 miles later, you will arrive at the Big Bear Lake dam. Go left on CA 38 for 4 miles to Fawnskin. Turn left on Rim of the World Road. It becomes FS 3N14. Follow this dirt road a couple miles to Hanna Flat Campground on the left.

KEY INFORMATION

Hanna Flat Campground, San Bernardino National Forest
Big Bear Ranger District
P.O. Box 290
North Shore Drive, CA 38
Fawnskin, CA 92333

Operated by: Department of Agriculture, Forest Service

Information: (909) 866-3437

Open: May to September (phone ahead)

Individual sites: 88

Each site has: Picnic table, fireplace

Registration: At entrance (or with host); for reservations, phone 10 days ahead (800) 280-CAMP ($7.50 fee)

Facilities: Piped water, some flush toilets

Parking: At site

Fee: $12

Elevation: 7,000 feet

Restrictions:

Pets—Allowed on leash

Fires—In fireplaces

Vehicles—RVs up to 15 feet long

the bottom of the ocean! Of course, that was about 600 million years ago. Then, 60 million years ago, the earth's plates ground together and pushed the ocean floor up to make the San Bernardino Mountains. The bodies of the sea creatures became the limestone so apparent around Big Bear. The cataclysmic conditions produced the gold and silver that prospectors would find in the area.

The Big Bear Lake area is near greater Los Angeles, so it's easy to access. It can get crowded, so time your visits for maximum enjoyment. As you drive your air-conditioned car up the mountains to Big Bear, remember the first tourists who came to the Bear Valley Hotel by stage from the desert to Mill Creek Canyon. From there, they rode two days on burros up to the lake. I'm sure it was worth it; this place is beautiful.

On the way home, drive the Rim of the World Highway (CA 38) to Redlands. This road was built in 1915 and was the first automobile access to Big Bear (no more burros!). The scenery is sensational. This is an experience. There is incredible dispersed camping along the way (talk to the rangers at the Big Bear Station) and good camping at the Heart Bar Campground.

HEART BAR CAMPGROUND

San Bernardino National Forest

Drive up to Big Bear on CA 330 and you feel like a rat in a maze. The road zips up through carnival-ride corners shouldered with impenetrable chaparral. Oncoming traffic appears out of nowhere. Suddenly, behind you, there's a string of impatient cars. You pull over, and they fly by in a flash of waxed paint and chrome.

You'll find a different scene on old CA 38, Rim of the World Scenic Highway. Drive out of Big Bear into a sea of granite and lodgepole pine and feast your eyes on "Greyback" himself, San Gorgonio Mountain at 11,502 feet (named for a very, very obscure Christian martyr). Come up from the bottom, from Redlands down in the desert, and suddenly you are in subalpine (boreal) forests of lodgepole pine twisted by the storms. The chaparral is high-altitude chaparral. There's manzanita, bush chinquapin, snowbrush, and all the alpine wildflowers. It's incredible! One moment you're driving through the mess of the city of San Bernardino, and the next you're in the splendor of the San Gorgonio Wilderness.

Heart Bar Campground is right in the belly of the beast. Why Heart Bar? It's a beautiful name. Here, in an area settled by pioneer Mormans, cattle herds were summered up in the meadows by the headwaters of the Santa Ana River. One of the local brands was the Heart Bar, a heart with a bar beneath it.

CAMPGROUND RATINGS

Beauty:	★★★★
Site privacy:	★★★
Site spaciousness:	★★★★★
Quiet:	★★★
Security:	★★★★★
Cleanliness/upkeep:	★★★★★

Heart Bar Campground is in the heart of San Gorgonio Wilderness. This is real mountain camping right near Los Angeles. Reserve for big holidays.

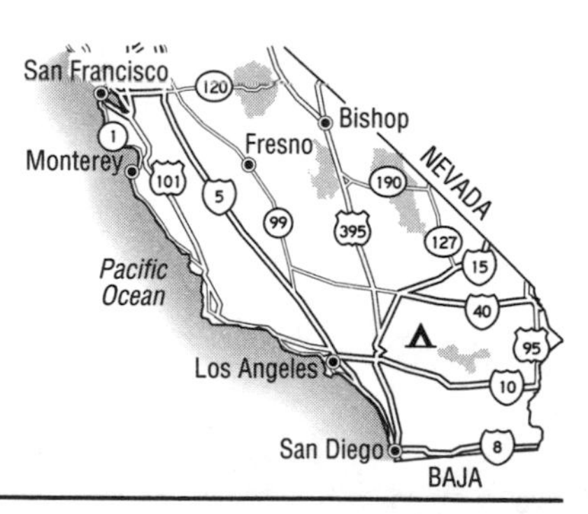

I love this campground. It's big and shaded, but it feels wide open. The meadow is green and bright in the sunlight. The pitches are clean and softened by pine needles. The sites are spaced out nicely. And, the campground is not nearly as heavily used as nearby South Fork Campground, bunched along Lost Creek, or Barton Flats down below.

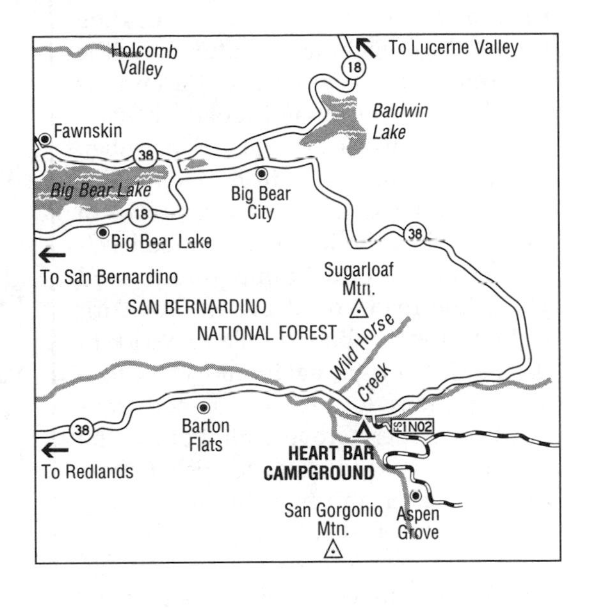

There is great hiking from the campground, stream fishing down by the South Fork Campground, and great lake fishing a short shot up at Big Bear Lake. At Big Bear, you can buy anything a body could need from big chain stores and little antique joints. Or, the other way, in Angelus Oaks, there's a general store as well as the Oaks Restaurant and El Mexicano Restaurant. You can also go farther and then left along Mill Creek to Forest Falls where there is another general store.

For an easily accessed hike, head south a few hundred yards from Heart Bar Campground and connect with a trail that goes east to the headwaters of the Santa Ana River or west along its banks to South Fork Campground. Up here, the Santa Ana is a beautiful little stream flowing through meadows and forests of black oak, fir, and Jeffrey and ponderosa pine. Formed from natural springs and snowmelt, the Santa Ana River looks incredibly beautiful up here, yet hideously ugly down in Orange County in its concrete channel.

Or, hike up Wildhorse Creek. Walk out to the main road and go left. About 300 yards along you'll see a signed turnoff to the Wildhorse Trail on the right. Follow the dirt road up to a parking lot. The trail leaves from here. At first, it is an old road up through pines and juniper. Then it winds up a series of chaparral-covered ridges before going down into Wildhorse Creek Canyon. Walk about a mile and find Wildhorse Creek Trail Camp. Right now, you are about three-and-a-half miles out.

An ambitious hiker could continue on and climb Sugar Loaf Mountain. Sugar Loaf has an elevation of about 9,952 feet and is a big lump on the divide between Big Bear country and the Santa Ana River Canyon. The best way is to hike up the saddle east of Sugar Loaf, then follow the trail along the ridgetop to the summit. I kept hearing about a famous rare black butterfly and looked in vain for it when I was last there in September.

Another fun hike from Heart Bar Campground is to Aspen Grove. Go in the fall when the leaves are golden yellow. Head out of the campground to FS 1N02 (the road you drove in on). Turn right and walk about a mile to a fork in the road. Go right again and walk to a small parking lot near the signed trailhead for Aspen Grove Trail. Follow the old dirt road southeast to Fish Creek. Cross the creek and enjoy the aspens—or what's left of them. Apparently, the California golden beaver enjoys them, too. A fellow hiker said that this particular beaver is not a San Bernardino native, but was introduced by Forest Service wildlife experts who had not counted on the beaver's sudden passion for eating aspen.

Check out the dispersed camping in the area for future trips. Stop at the Mill Creek Ranger Station on CA 38 near the burg of Mentone. You'll need a wilderness permit for ambitious hiking anyway. Ask the ranger to show you where dispersed camping is allowed and where the the yellow post sites are. There is spectacular tent camping in the San Gorgonio area, and much of it is outside the organized campgrounds.

KEY INFORMATION

Heart Bar Campground, San Bernardino National Forest
San Gorgonio Ranger District
34701 Mill Creek Road
Mentone, CA 92359

Operated by: Forest Service, Department of Agriculture

Information: (909) 794-1123

Open: May to mid-October (phone ahead)

Individual sites: 94

Each site has: Picnic table, fireplace

Registration: At entrance (or with host); for reservations, phone 10 days ahead (800) 280-CAMP ($7.50 fee)

Facilities: Piped water, vault toilets

Parking: At site

Fee: $7

Elevation: 7,000 feet

Restrictions:

Pets—Allowed on leash

Fires—In fireplaces

Vehicles—RVs up to 50 feet long

Other—Get a wilderness permit from Mill Creek Ranger Station

To get there from L.A., go east on I-10 to Redlands past San Bernardino. Then take CA 38 east 33 miles to FS 1N02 and go right. The campground entrance is immediately on your right.

LAGUNA CAMPGROUND

Mount Laguna

Laguna Campground offers some of the best camping in Southern California and the cheekiest ground squirrels and jays in the West. Hardly had my wife and I arrived at an incredible campsite on the edge of a yellow-flowered meadow stretching away to islands of pine against a cerulean blue sky, when a larcenous stellar's jay swooped down on the picnic table and tried to make off with a particularly shiny spoon.

Then, the California ground squirrels moved in boldly making for the package of corn chips on top of the cooler. I stomped my feet and threw gravel. They scurried a few feet away, rolled defiantly in the dust, and rose to attack the corn chips again. Then, I saw what I thought was a golden eagle (it would've been my first) wheel through the sky. There was a shrill squeak, and all the varmints ducked for cover. Upon closer examination, the golden eagle turned out to be a red-tailed hawk (*Buteo jamaicensis*), the nemesis of the California ground squirrel.

Run by the Laguna Mountain Volunteer Association, Laguna Campground is clean and well run. There's a feeling of serenity and order. The ladies in the electric golf carts who came by to check the clean vault toilets were clearly retired from a life of gentility. I like it. The little community of Laguna with its stores, churches, fire department, restaurants, and cabins for

CAMPGROUND RATINGS

Beauty:	★★★★★
Site privacy:	★★★★
Site spaciousness:	★★★★
Quiet:	★★★★★
Security:	★★★★★
Cleanliness/upkeep:	★★★★★

Laguna Campground is clean, well run, and near the proud community of Laguna. Come for alpine meadows all year.

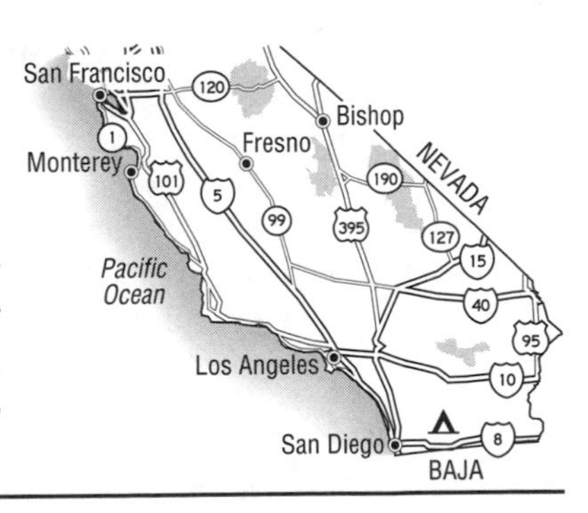

rent reflects the pride of the people who live there. This is a very special place.

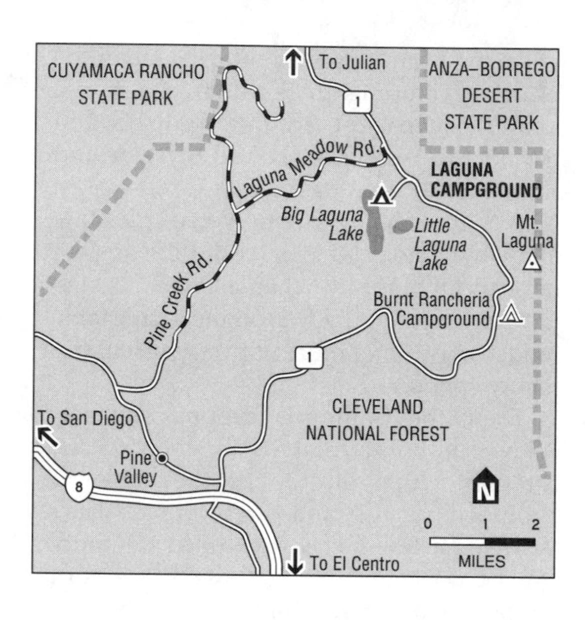

The campground is set in a meadow in a stand of Jeffrey pines, which are almost indistinguishable from ponderosa pines. The giveaway, however, is the vanilla scent of the Jeffrey pine's bark. Put your nose right up to the tree and take a whiff. That's the Jeffrey pine. Also, the bark on the Jeffrey tends toward narrow ridges while the ponderosa bark is in large, flat plates. Roll the cones from a Jeffrey between your hands, and the spines won't prick—they are turned under. The ponderosa spines stick out and will get you.

Native Americans used the roots of the Jeffrey Pine to make baskets. They waited until the tree flowered and the roots became tough enough to be used. Then, the roots were dug up, cleaned, and slow cooked in a fire pit. After that they were split and scraped until soft and pliable enough to be woven into baskets.

I met a German naturalist camping a few sites over who gave me the rundown on the cheeky squirrels. They are supposed to eat seeds, herbaceous vegetation, and acorns, but they prefer to hang around campgrounds and eat corn chips. They hibernate in the winter in Laguna where it's cold and snows; when spring comes, they have some catch-up eating to do. According to the naturalist, the shrill squeak I heard when the hawk cruised overhead comes from the oldest squirrel in the colony. Apparently, the squirrel who sounds the alarm has the greatest chance of being picked off by the hawk. So, for the good of the squirrel band, the oldest squirrel protects his own offspring, and the band, by sounding the alarm and offering himself as the victim if need be. Pretty brave stuff for the little guy.

In the meadow by the campground is Little Laguna Lake. Little more than a wallow, it is still home to many ducks, birds, and loudly croaking frogs. By the lake is a kopje (stand of rocks in a meadow) conveniently placed for sitting while watching wildlife through binoculars. The meadow was carpeted with tiny sunflowers, tidy tips, Achilles's fern, and the edible miner's lettuce when I was there in June.

We picked up a trail to Big Laguna Lake to the south of the campground. The trail meanders across meadows and along the edge of the pined hummocks that beg for picnickers. About a mile down the trail is Big Laguna Lake, which is only a lake indeed in the spring and summer of wet years. When I was there, it was big and beautiful. From the lake, the trail turns north and connects with Noble Canyon Trail and Pine Creek Road. This is not power hiking. The trail is pretty flat the whole way and about as pleasant a walk as I've ever had.

If you get tired of camping Laguna Campground, try Burnt Rancheria Campground a few miles south. Also run by the Laguna Mountain Volunteer Society, this campground is as clean and pleasant as Laguna Campground. Trade the pines in for oaks and Little Laguna Lake and meadows for a stunning

To get there from San Diego, drive 50 miles east on I-8 to the Laguna Junction exit. Drive 11 miles north on Sunrise Highway to Mt. Laguna, then 2.5 miles farther north to the signed entrance on the left marked "Laguna/El Prado." Laguna is the campground you want. El Prado is the nearby group campground.

KEY INFORMATION

Laguna Campground, Cleveland National Forest
Laguna Mountain Recreation Area
Descanso Ranger District Office/Laguna Mountain Volunteer Association
3348 Alpine Boulevard
Alpine, CA 91901-9630

Operated by: U.S. Department of Agriculture, U.S. Forest Service

Information: Ranger Office, (619) 445-6235 or (619) 473-8824 (Monday–Friday, 8 A.M.–4:30 P.M.); Visitors Center, (619) 473-8547 (Friday–Sunday, May through September)

Open: All year

Individual sites: 75 for tents only, 30 for RVs

Each site has: Picnic table, fireplace

Registration: At entrance; for reservations, phone (800) 280-CAMP—keep trying! Phone at least 10 days in advance ($7.50 fee)

Facilities: Vault toilets, piped water

Parking: Near site

Fee: $10

Elevation: 5,800 feet

Restrictions:

Pets—On leash; at night must be kept in tent, car, or RV

Fires—In fireplace

Vehicles—RVs, trailers

view of the Anza-Borrego Desert, and you have an equally nice camping experience.

Laguna Campground is open all year (Burnt Rancheria is open May to October), but I think spring is the best time to visit. In winter, there's snow and snow sports, but half of San Diego flocks there on wintry weekends. Summers get a bit hot and dusty, but if you can't get up into the High Sierras, then go for Laguna. Both Laguna and Burnt Rancheria Campgrounds are popular, so plan on getting there Friday by noon if you don't have a reservation.

Available activities include a run down to Tecate, Mexico (a half hour to the south). Or, take I-8 down into the desert and drive into the Anza-Borrego Desert State Park. Or, take the Sunrise Highway north to Julian. Fish in Lake Cuyamaca. There is a lot to do around here. Go horseback riding or mountain biking. Stargaze from the night sky observatories at the south end of the Recreation Area. This is a wonderful part of Southern California, and I just hope it stays that way.

MARION MOUNTAIN CAMPGROUND

San Jacinto, San Bernardino National Forest

From L.A., the ride to Marion Mountain Campground on I-10 through "The Inland Empire" (a.k.a. "Land of Swirling Gases") is, at best, horrifying. Persevere, though, and head up CA 243 to Banning, and, in a few short minutes, you'll be in a different world. You'll come up out of the chaparral into the pines and peaks. What a contrast!

Marion Mountain Campground is as sunny and airy as nearby Dark Canyon Campground is dark and safe down under the sheltering trees. Between the two, you'll see the entire spectrum of good San Jacinto tent camping.

The access road to Marion Mountain Campground from CA 243 is narrow and winding. This cuts down on the trailers and RVs. The site parking spaces are short—about 15 feet tops. The picnic tables and fireplaces are down in the trees away from the parking area. All this discourages RVers and gives an edge to tent campers.

The water from a spring above the campground is good. Let the tap run for a moment to clear any sediment if the campground has been lightly used. All the facilities are well maintained. The pit toilet bathrooms are surprisingly clean and tiled on the floors and walls. The campground host is obliging and friendly. I wanted to stay for a week.

When you first arrive at Marion Mountain Campground, it's difficult to locate

CAMPGROUND RATINGS

Beauty:	★★★
Site privacy:	★★★★★
Site spaciousness:	★★★★★
Quiet:	★★★★★
Security:	★★★★★
Cleanliness/upkeep:	★★★★★

Marion Mountain, nestled in the clouds, is a great break from nearby Los Angeles. Come for fun hiking and stay for good tent camping.

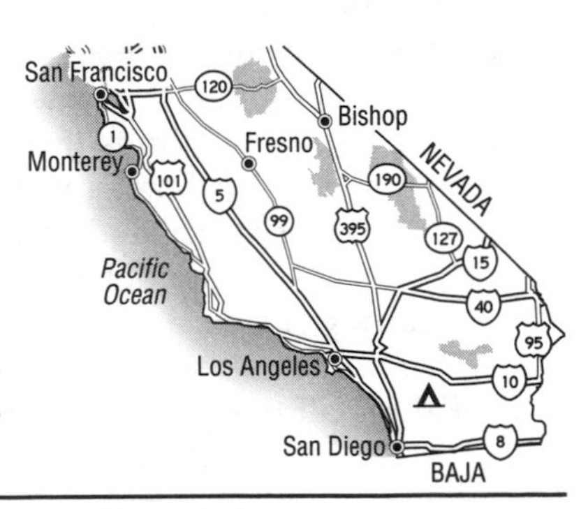

the sites. This is because most of them are isolated from each other down in the pines. The pitches are nicely spongy and on pine needles. Through the pine boughs, you'll see the steep slopes of the mountains across the canyon all covered with pines, oaks, and rocky tors.

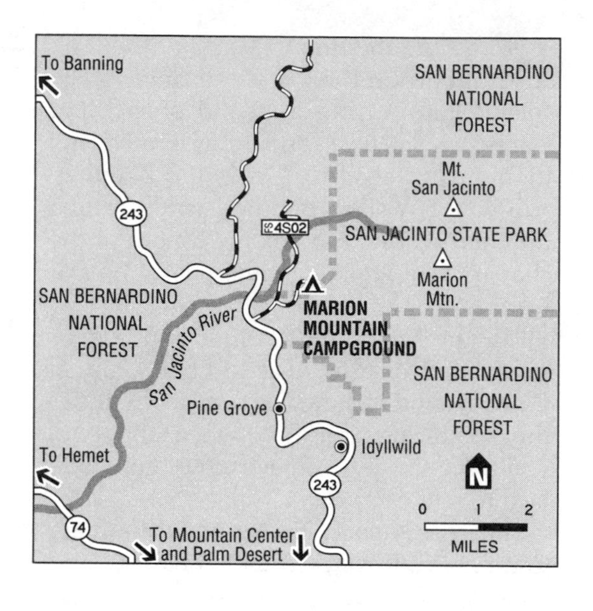

I brought along a portable radio/cassette player with a few classical music tapes. What a wonderful experience! Camping in the mountains goes with classical music. A music professor once told me that music began when primitive man, imbued with the "like produces like" principle, endeavored to wake the sleeping earth from its winter nap by beating it with a stick in the spring. From this came the percussion drums and then the more sophisticated woodwinds that imitated the birds.

To hike from the campground, go to site #23. Across from that site's picnic table, there is a dirt road that heads up the slope. Follow it for 20 yards and notice the trail arrows pointing right and left. The right arrows lead you down the hill to the trailhead. The left ones indicate the Marion Mountain Trail that goes up into the State Park and joins the Pacific Crest Trail (PCT) near Deer Spring. It climbs the heavily forested northwest flank of Marion Mountain and is the shortest way to climb San Jacinto Peak.

Take plenty of water and inform the campground host of your whereabouts. Be aware of thunderstorms. When there is lightning, avoid open areas like meadows, ridges, and mountaintops. Stay away from isolated trees and take cover under dense, small trees in lower areas, in a boulder field, or in a cave. Failing all this, lie flat on the ground. And, in all cases, remove metal frame backpacks and metal tent poles. Really, lightning is no joke. I suffered a near miss in the Mojave Desert a few summers ago that burned my calves and scared me half to death.

In early September, when I last visited Marion Mountain, there were thunderstorm clouds over the mountains. The dry air carried a hint of rain. As we were hiking up the slopes around the campground, there was a roll of thunder, and a splatter of rain hit the dusty rocks. What drama! The campground host told me they'd had a hard storm hit in the middle of August. It rained like hell for a couple of hours, and then the sun came out. This is typical of the Southern Sierras in late August and September and something to watch for.

A good place for a sundowner is up the dirt road across from site #23. Go past the arrows for the Marion Mountain Trail. About 20 yards up, climb the ridge to the right, and there are some nice big boulders to sit on and watch the sun set. Back on the dirt road, walk to the end of it. There's a short trail that switchbacks up the slope to some cabins where there is an incredible view of the southwest side of the range.

For supplies, head south to Pine Cove where you'll find gas and ice. For a town with everything, go a few miles farther to Idyllwild, a lovely little mountain town. Idyllwild even has a shopping center with a supermarket and a hardware store. They have butchers, restaurants, artists, writers, and, of course, the San Jacinto Ranger Station on the left as you enter town. If Marion Mountain and the other campgrounds nearby are full, and/or you want to disperse camp or yellow-post camp, that's where you need to go. The rangers will fix you up with a fire permit and show you where to go.

KEY INFORMATION

Marion Mountain Campground, San Bernardino National Forest
San Jacinto Ranger District
P.O. Box 518, 54270 Pinecrest
Idyllwild, CA 92549

Operated by: Forest Service, Department of Agriculture

Information: (909) 659-2117

Open: May to mid-October

Individual sites: 24

Each site has: Picnic table, fireplace

Registration: At entrance; for reservations, phone (800) 280-CAMP 10 days in advance ($7.50 fee)

Facilities: Piped water, pit toilets

Parking: Near site

Fee: $12

Elevation: 6,400 feet

Restrictions:

Pets—Allowed on leash

Fires—In fireplace

Vehicles—No RVs longer than 15 feet

Other—No dogs on trails

To get there from L.A., drive east to Banning. Go south on CA 243 for 22 miles. Turn left at FS 4S02 and drive 1.7 miles to the campground.

PASO PICACHO CAMPGROUND

Cuyamaca Rancho State Park

This campground will keep you coming back season after season. Even in the dead of winter, under a blanket of snow, the days have a warm promise about them reflected in the wonderful patchwork of pines, oak, and open meadows. The atmosphere is drowsy. Even the apple trees seem to find it easygoing.

It's the rain and its geographical location between coast and desert that make the Cuyamacas a unique ecosystem. I spent a year working on a private nature preserve on North Peak and never saw a day in Cuyamaca that didn't have some calm majesty. Even the rattlesnakes are forgiving. I've stepped on several of them, and they just eyed me with mild rebuke and slithered away.

Although it's true there was a recent mountain lion attack on a jogger here, I maintain it was a pilot error. Mountain lions have notoriously bad eyesight and make regrettable misjudgments. If I'm ever lucky enough to see one (the Native Americans called them the ghosts), I shall stand dead still, then rise up and try to look like a grizzly bear.

Paso Picacho means "mountain pass," and *Cuyamaca* in Native American means "rain above." Most of Cuyamaca State Park was in the Cuyamaca Rancho, about 35,501 acres of meadow and mountain timberland granted to Agustin Olvera by

CAMPGROUND RATINGS

Beauty:	★★★★
Site privacy:	★★★
Site spaciousness:	★★★★
Quiet:	★★★
Security:	★★★★★
Cleanliness/upkeep:	★★★★

Paso Picacho Campground, blessed with meadows and mountains, is good for any time of year. Reserve ahead for peak times.

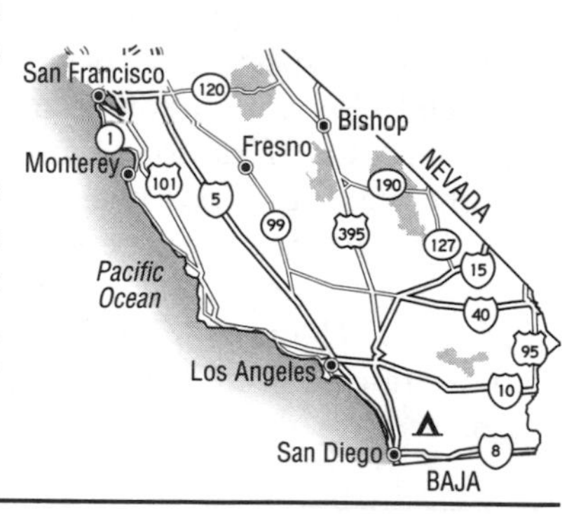

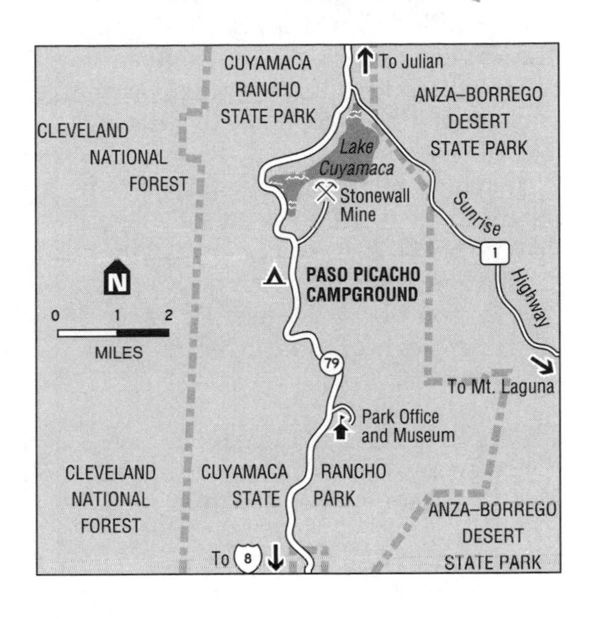

Governor Pio Pico in 1845. There's no record of how the resident Native Americans felt about it—unless random acts of mayhem and vandalism are translated as disapproval. Olvera didn't care much for his Rancho and sold it in 1869 just before William Skidmore chased his stray mule around Cuyamaca Lake and spotted gold not far from the Paso Picacho Campground. Skidmore filed a claim and opened a mine calling it Stonewall Jackson after the Civil War General. Local GAR (Grand Army of the Republic) veterans protested, and the mine became Stonewall Mine, befitting the rocky mountain behind it. Before the mine closed in 1893, more than $2 million of gold were taken from it ($2 million in 1893 dollars).

Most of the Rancho was sold to the state for the park. The lake is leased to the Cuyamaca Recreation and Park District. The ore cars and other relics from the old Stonewall Mine were rolled down the mine's open, 630-foot shaft with its 2,700 feet of drifts. The buildings were sold for scrap to a Los Angeles wrecking company.

The Paso Picacho Campground is roomy and well planned with flat, drained tent sites and clean rest rooms featuring flush toilets and showers. It is clean and well patrolled. It feels like a campground from the 1950s. The campers who come to Paso Picacho tend to be hikers, fishing people, or bird watchers (almost 300 species of birds have been observed in the park) who tend to come back year after year. They appreciate the four seasons of Cuyamaca and the more than 100 miles of hiking and equestrian trails.

Don't forget nearby Julian, which has blossomed into a relentlessly pleasing tourist attraction in the last 25 years. But don't come if you don't like apple pie. The cafe on Cuyamaca Lake with its very friendly staff and sunny outside deck is perfect for breakfast, lunch, or an afternoon beer. Wally's Waterwagon across the road and down a little is perfect for a less sedate happy hour or country western band later on. Climb the 3.5-mile Cuyamaca Peak Trail from the campground to the summit for a spectacular view of the Pacific Ocean, the desert, Mexico, and the distant Salton Sea.

Watch for raptors (birds of prey). You might see golden eagles, red-shouldered hawks, bald eagles, and turkey vultures. Think like a mouse; you'll find raptors where their prey is located. Fields with good perches nearby are excellent places to see raptors.

To get there from L.A., take I-10 east to I-15. Go south to Temecula. Take CA 79 southeast 11 miles past Julian to the campground entrance on the right.

KEY INFORMATION

Paso Picacho Campground
Cuyamaca Rancho State Park
Route 1, Box 2700
Descanso, CA 92016

Operated by: Department of Parks and Recreation, P.O. Box 942896, Sacramento, CA 94296-0001

Information: (619) 765-0755, H.Q.; (619) 765-3023, Campground. Reserve through DESTINET, (800) 444-7275 ($6.75 fee)

Open: All year

Individual sites: 81

Each site has: Picnic table, fireplace

Registration: By entrance

Facilities: Piped water, flush toilets, showers, wood for sale

Parking: At individual site

Fee: $14, May 1–September 30; $12, rest of year

Elevation: 4,900 feet

Restrictions:

Pets—Allowed on leash; must be under control at all times ($1 per pet)

Fires—In fireplace

Vehicles—RVs up to 30 feet and trailers up to 24 feet allowed

Other—Reservations on holidays and summer weekends recommended

WILLIAM HEISE COUNTY PARK

Near Julian

Among the many reasons to tent camp in William Heise County Park are the incredible drives in from L.A. via Warner Springs or from San Diego via Ramona or Cuyamaca Rancho State Park. All three show Southern California at its most charming and very best—the rolling, forested hills, the green meadows, the tiny western towns. This was the real gold the forty-niners found when they arrived in California—this beautiful land. On all three drives, near Julian, you climb 2 miles south on Pine Hills Road, then left on Frisius Drive. Those final 2 miles carry you through farmland that echoes of bucolic Vermont or New Hampshire. The resemblance is eerie. You can only imagine the argonauts; after walking 3,000 miles across the continent they must have looked around Frisius Drive and thought, "My God! I'm home."

With 900 acres of oak, pine, and cedar, William Heise County Park is Upper Chaparral; this area is also known as Cold Chaparral because most ofthe precipitation comes from snow and fog drip. As you hike on the trails around and in the park, watch the slope orientation to see the effect. On south-facing slopes there are evergreen shrubs with thick oval leaves like the manzanita. Note how the manzanita leaves are mealy and waxy and are often oriented vertically to reduce the amount of light that directly strikes the

CAMPGROUND RATINGS

Beauty:	★★★★
Site privacy:	★★
Site spaciousness:	★★★
Quiet:	★★★
Security:	★★★
Cleanliness/upkeep:	★★★

Visit California high country and feel like you're in Vermont all at once. This campground near historic Julian offers solid enjoyment.

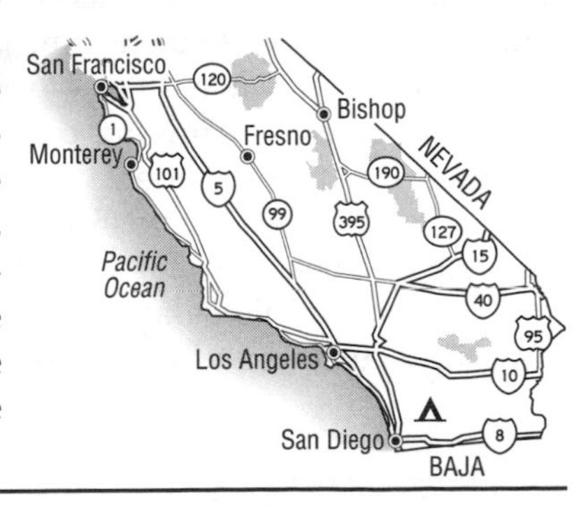

leaf surface. Manzanita are drought-tolerant, fire-adapted, and able to withstand cold and snow. On north-facing slopes look for California live oak; Jeffrey, Coulter, sugar, and ponderosa pines; incense cedar; and white fir.

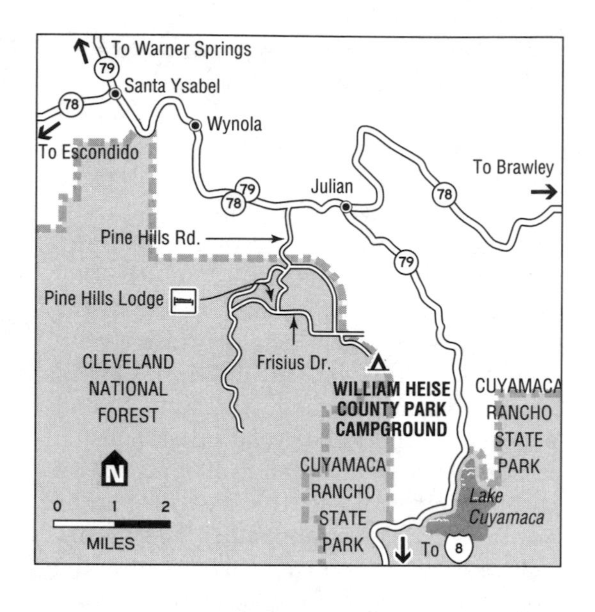

Like Cuyamaca Rancho State Park, William Heise is birder's paradise. Look for various hawks, eagles, owls, woodpeckers, vireos, warblers, sparrows, sapsuckers, and the like. Also, look for the full complement of Southern California reptiles and various rodents eating the plethora of acorns. Acorns, a Cahuilla Native American staple, were made into a meal and then bread.

Once, camping at William Heise, we experimented with acorn bread. First, we ground the acorns into a coarse meal, then following local Cahuilla recipe, we filled a colander with fine sand, patted the coarsely ground acorn meal down into a bowl-like depression in the sand, and poured water slowly over the meal to leach out the bitterness. Then we pounded the meal down finer in a mortar until it resembled a fine powder. Finally, the meal was sifted, mixed with water, and baked on a hot rock—not bad, but a little bitter.

Encouraged, my camping companion resolved to fatten up a pig on the acorns in his yard at home. He found a candidate piglet and penned it up under his oak trees. For weeks, it ate acorns heartily. Then, a carelessly guarded plate of chicken enchiladas and refried beans was left out. The pig got it, and that was it; his palate was ruined. No more acorns. He rejected Native American cuisine, and he, himself, became Thanksgiving dinner.

Heise is a friendly place to camp. Half of the sites are for tents only, which separates you from the RVs that feel like city blocks on wheels when you're lying there in a little tent. The park is roomy, and the rest rooms are very clean. Once, we rented one of the two rental cabins at Heise. It had six wooden bunks and a maximum capacity of eight ($25 per night plus reservation fee). Bring your own bedding and a padlock for the door. Cooking is done outside on a barbecue. It was as jolly as a good school trip. For reservations, call (619) 565-3600.

Heise is a fine base camp from which to explore Julian, Wynola, and Santa Ysabel. Do an apple pie comparison test. Stop for a drink or breakfast at the much-fabled Pine Hills Lodge right by the junction of Pine Hills Road and Frisius Drive. Visit the Santa Ysabel Mission 2 miles north of Santa Ysabel on CA 79. See the museum in Julian. Take the Eagle Mine tour. Ask the ranger/ campground host at Heise about trips to Boulder Creek and Boulder Creek Falls. Don't miss a killer hike (11 miles round-trip) down Kelly Ditch Trail to Cuyamaca Rancho State Park.

To get there from L.A., take I-10 east to I-15. Go south to Temecula. Take CA 79 southeast to Santa Ysabel. Go left toward Julian 5.8 miles to Pine Hills Road. Go right and drive 2 miles to Frisius Drive and make a left. Go 2 miles, and you are at the park.

KEY INFORMATION

William Heise County Park
Department of Parks and Recreation
5201 Ruffin Road, Suite P
San Diego, CA 92123-1699

Operated by: San Diego County Department of Parks and Recreation

Information: (619) 565-3049; reservations, (619) 694-3049

Open: Weekend of Palm Sunday until week after Thanksgiving

Individual sites: 43 tents only; 40 tents or RVs

Each site has: Picnic table, fire ring, tent pad, water nearby

Registration: By entrance

Facilities: Piped water, flush toilets, showers, playground

Parking: At individual site

Fee: $11, $3 reservation fee per site

Elevation: 4,200 feet

Restrictions:

Pets—Permitted on leashes; not allowed on hiking trails

Fires—In fire ring

Vehicles—Motor homes, small trailers

Other—No generators; check-out time is 2 P.M.

APPENDICES

APPENDIX A
Camping Equipment Checklist

Except for the large and bulky items on this list, I keep a plastic storage container full of the essentials of car camping so that they're ready to go when I am. I make a last-minute check of the inventory, resupply anything that's low or missing, and away I go!

Cooking Utensils
Bottle opener
Bottles of salt, pepper, spices, sugar, cooking oil, and maple syrup in waterproof, spill-proof containers
Can opener
Corkscrew
Cups, plastic or tin
Dish soap (biodegradable), sponge, and towel
Flatware
Food of your choice
Frying pan
Fuel for stove
Matches in waterproof container
Plates
Pocketknife
Pot with lid
Spatula
Stove
Tin foil
Wooden spoon

First Aid Kit
Band-Aids
First aid cream
Gauze pads
Ibuprofen or aspirin
Insect repellent
Moleskin
Snakebite kit (if you're heading for desert conditions)
Sunscreen / chapstick
Tape, waterproof adhesive

Sleeping Gear
Pillow
Sleeping bag
Sleeping pad, inflatable or insulated
Tent with ground tarp and rainfly

Miscellaneous
Bath soap (biodegradable), washcloth, and towel
Camp chair
Candles
Cooler
Deck of cards
Fire starter
Flashlight with fresh batteries
Foul weather clothing (useful year-round in the Northwest)
Paper towels
Plastic zip-top bags
Sunglasses
Toilet paper
Water bottle
Wool blanket

Optional
Barbecue grill
Binoculars
Books on bird, plant, and wildlife identification
Fishing rod and tackle
Hatchet
Lantern
Maps (road, topographic, trails, etc.)

APPENDIX B
Suggested Reading and Reference

The Anza-Borrego Desert Region. Lindsay, Lowell and Diana. Wilderness Press, 1991.

Best Short Hikes in California's Northern Sierra. Whitehill, Karen and Terry. The Mountaineers, 1990.

Best Short Hikes in California's Southern Sierra. Whitehill, Karen and Terry. The Mountaineers, 1991.

California Camping. Stienstra, Tom. Foghorn Press, 1994.

California's Desert Trails. Chase, J. Smeaton. Tioga Publishing Company, 1987.

California's Eastern Sierra. Irwin, Sue. Cachuma Press, 1991.

Day Hiking Kings Canyon. Sorensen, Steve. Manzanita Press, 1992.

Day Hiking Sequoia. Sorensen, Steve. Manzanita Press, 1992.

Exploring the Southern Sierra: East Side. Jenkins, J.C. and Ruby Johnson. Jenkins and Jenkins, 1995.

Exploring the Southern Sierra: West Side. Jenkins, J.C. and Ruby Johnson. Jenkins and Jenkins, 1992.

Gem Trails of California. Mitchel, James R. Gem Guides Book Co., 1986.

Gold! Gold! Petralia, Joseph F. Sierra Outdoor Products Co., 1992.

History of the Sierra Nevada. Farquhar, Francis P. University of California Press, 1965.

A Natural History of California. Schoenherr, Allan A. University of California Press, 1992.

Roadside Plants of Southern California. Belzer, Thomas J. Mountain Press Publishing Company, 1984.

San Bernardino Mountain Trails. Robinson, John W. Wilderness Press, 1986.

A Treasury of the Sierra Nevada. Reid, Robert Leonard. Wilderness Press, 1983.

Walking California's State Parks. McKinney, John. HarperCollins West, 1994.

Walking Southern California. McKinney, John. HarperCollins West, 1992.